Provincial Democracy

Situated within the context of seismic global transformations of the early twentieth century—namely the two World Wars and the crisis of the imperial order—*Provincial Democracy* delves into the period between the decline of empire and the rise of the nation. This period, the book contends, is defined by not only the dominance of the nation state and debates over a new global order, but also the expansion of democratic participation in defining and negotiating political futures and an increased use of the language of liberalism, political rights, and self-government in colonial India. Moreover, it shifts the focus from the dominant narrative of linguistic nationalism as defining regionalism on to debates over questions of representation, rights, political reforms, and federalism. Thus, it uncovers a broad perspective on political imaginaries that anticipated democracy in independent India.

Rama Sundari Mantena is Associate Professor in the Department of History at the University of Illinois Chicago. She is the author of *The Origins of Modern Historiography in India: Antiquarianism and Philology, 1780–1880* (2012), which examines the emergence of modern practices of history writing in colonial India.

Provincial Democracy

Political Imaginaries at the End of Empire in Twentieth-Century South India

Rama Sundari Mantena

CAMBRIDGE
UNIVERSITY PRESS

Shaftesbury Road, Cambridge CB2 8EA, United Kingdom

One Liberty Plaza, 20th Floor, New York, NY 10006, USA

477 Williamstown Road, Port Melbourne, VIC 3207, Australia

314–321, 3rd Floor, Plot 3, Splendor Forum, Jasola District Centre, New Delhi – 110025, India

103 Penang Road, #05–06/07, Visioncrest Commercial, Singapore 238467

Cambridge University Press is part of Cambridge University Press & Assessment, a department of the University of Cambridge.

We share the University's mission to contribute to society through the pursuit of education, learning and research at the highest international levels of excellence.

www.cambridge.org
Information on this title: www.cambridge.org/9781009339544

© Rama Sundari Mantena 2023

This publication is in copyright. Subject to statutory exception and to the provisions of relevant collective licensing agreements, no reproduction of any part may take place without the written permission of Cambridge University Press & Assessment.

First published 2023

Printed in India by Avantika Printers Pvt. Ltd.

A catalogue record for this publication is available from the British Library

ISBN 978-1-009-33954-4 Hardback

Cambridge University Press & Assessment has no responsibility for the persistence or accuracy of URLs for external or third-party internet websites referred to in this publication and does not guarantee that any content on such websites is, or will remain, accurate or appropriate.

Contents

List of Figures — vii

Acknowledgements — ix

List of Abbreviations — xiii

Introduction: Self-Determination, Federation, and Civil Liberties in Twentieth-Century South India — 1

1. Liberalism and Anti-Colonialism in South India — 30

Part I Federation

2. Self-Determination, Federation, and the Provinces — 67
3. Princely Hyderabad, Anti-Colonialism, and Federation — 104

Part II Civil Liberties

4. Publicity, Civil Liberties, and Political Life in Princely Hyderabad — 137
5. The Break-Up of Hyderabad — 170

Conclusion: After Empire—Language and Regionalism — 204

Bibliography — 220

Index — 233

Figures

Map of British India		xv
Map of northern Madras Presidency, 1909		xvi
Map of southern Madras Presidency, 1909		xvii
Map of Hyderabad and Berar, 1894		xviii
1.1	Cover page of the Andhra Conferences Committee's publication *The Andhra Movement*, 1913	47
1.2	Map of the Telugu country from the Andhra Conferences Committee's publication *The Andhra Movement*, 1913	48
2.1	Map of Andhra, 1937	88
2.2	The Andhra national flag from the *Madras Mail*, 1939	89
5.1	Map of 'Greater Andhra', 1945	196

Acknowledgements

The book is dedicated to Kavita S. Datla (1975–2017) whose life and work were cut short by a terribly aggressive cancer in the summer of 2017. The idea for the book took shape during many conversations with Kavita over the years, prodded on by her unwavering passion for archival research on princely Hyderabad and south India more broadly. It was from 2013, at the height of the Telangana movement to bifurcate Andhra Pradesh into two states, that I began to rethink questions of language and region in relation to the colonial history of Andhra, Telangana, and princely Hyderabad. Thankfully the research and scholarship on the Hyderabad state is extensive, which proved critical in charting out an idea bringing together questions of regionalism and the Andhra movement with debates over federation in the Hyderabad state. The scholars who worked on Hyderabad were generous, providing me support by leading me to critical archival material and inviting me to workshops and talks to test out my ideas. In particular, I must single out and thank John Roosa for his incredible generosity in scanning and sharing with me his copies of the Nizam Andhra Mahasabha proceedings that he collected when he was conducting his own doctoral research. And many thanks to A. Suneetha at Anveshi Research Centre for Women's Studies in Hyderabad, who invited me to present to a very engaged audience discussing Hyderabad's history in the 1930s and the 1940s. There I met Sangishetty Srinivas who offered to share with me a rare copy of Suravaram Pratapa Reddy's pamphlet, *Prajaadhikaaramulu* (People's Rights).

I began to seriously conceive this project as a book after participating in an American Institute for Indian Studies (AIIS) workshop organized by Benjamin Cohen and Sumit Ganguly in New Delhi in the summer of 2013, which led to an article published in a special issue of *India Review* (2014). The AIIS conference in New Delhi on regionalism encouraged me to think through the question of language and regionalism and to consider how the Andhra movement impacted Hyderabad politics. In addition to the AIIS workshop, at the University of Illinois Chicago (UIC), I was fortunate to not only have Marina Mogilner as my colleague but also be able to collaborate with her on a workshop titled 'After Empire and Nation: Rethinking

Anti-Colonial Pasts and the Future of Democracy', sponsored by the UIC Institute for the Humanities in October 2016, which brought together scholars working on Russia, India, and Africa, discussing decolonization, anti-colonial nationalism, and federation proposals at the end of empire. The workshop led to the publication of a thematic cluster of articles on anti-colonialism and federation in the journal *Ab Imperio* (2018), thanks to the encouragement and support of Marina and her colleagues at the journal.

While working on this book project, I was fortunate to have opportunities to present and receive valuable feedback from diverse audiences at the University of Texas at Austin; Indiana University Bloomington; Yale University (conference on 'The Long Indian Century: Historical Transitions and Social Transformations'); the Newberry Library British History Seminar; the National Research University Higher School of Economics, St Petersburg, Russian Federation (international conference on 'Nationalism, Empire, and State'); Northwestern University (workshop on 'Globalization, Global, and World'); the University of Pennsylvania; the University of Hyderabad; Anveshi Research Center for Women's Studies, Hyderabad; the University of Michigan (the Kavita Datla Memorial Lecture); a workshop organized by the Max Planck Institute for Legal History and Legal Theory; and, finally, Heidelberg University (workshop on 'From Empire to Federation'). In addition to these forums, I benefitted enormously from presenting versions of the book's chapters at UIC's History Department's Brown Bag series where our faculty and graduate students meet on a weekly basis to share each other's work. I want to also especially thank Manamee Guha who worked as my research assistant during the last leg of my research for this book project and was critical in helping me wade through the Madras legislative debates at the Center for Research Libraries, Chicago.

Special thanks are due to my many interlocutors over the years: Karuna Mantena, Bhavani Raman, Mrinalini Sinha, Sunil Purushotham, A. Suneetha, M. Moid, Neilesh Bose, Farina Mir, William Glover, Rohit De, Atiya Khan, Bhukya Bhangya, Chinnaiah Jangam, Gautham Reddy, Sravanthi Kollu, Chris Chekuri, Himadeep Muppiddi, Benjamin Cohen, Afsar Mohammad, Syed Akbar Hyder, and Lisa Mitchell. My discussions with the late Bernard Bate (1961–2016) ever since graduate school have shaped my thinking about language in south India, and it was with his encouragement that I pursued the research that eventually led to this book. Much gratitude to Atiya Khan (University of Chicago) for directing me to the amazing Kim Greenwell for help on the editing of my manuscript before submitting it to potential presses. Kim was a meticulous reader of the entire manuscript, and even though the research is not in her field of expertise, she provided me with critical comments and suggestions on improving the manuscript. Sohini Ghosh from Cambridge University Press & Assessment India (CUPAI) helped shepherd my manuscript through the long process of reviews and revisions to bring it to the stage of publication.

Acknowledgements

Many thanks to the anonymous reviewers at CUPAI, who gave valuable feedback to bring much-needed clarity to the main arguments framing the book. UIC provided a supportive community to complete my book project. In particular, I am grateful to be surrounded by wonderful colleagues at UIC who work on South Asia in the departments of History, Global Asian Studies, Anthropology, Gender and Women's Studies, and Art History: Mark Liechty, Gayatri Reddy, Catherine Becker, and Tarini Bedi. I am fortunate to have incredible graduate students at UIC who challenged me to think beyond my own research interests in the broad interdisciplinary field of South Asian studies: Maria Ritzema, Manamee Guha, Deepthi Murali, Karen Greenwalt, Javairia Shahid, Aviral Pathak, Sohini Majumdar, Hashim Ali, Avash Bhandari, Ajapa Sharma, Lakshita Malik, Sravanthi Dasari, Anindita Ghosh, and Sohini Mukhopadhyay. My home department of History at UIC proved to be collegial and encouraging towards my book project from start to finish.

My father, M. Suryanarayana Raju, has been the most enthusiastic supporter of my research into the history of Andhra, Telangana, and Telugu literature and history. While I was immersed in archival research for this book, he embarked on translating nineteenth-century Telugu texts—partly to keep himself busy in retirement but also to feed his deep love of Telugu history and literature. My father's passion was instrumental in making available numerous Telugu publications from this period as potential sources for my research. I have only begun to tap the surface of this treasure trove of translations my father embarked on, and I hope I can do justice to all the effort he put into the translations beyond this single book project. My sister, Karuna Mantena, has always been a strong advocate of my projects and incredibly generous with her time. She read the entire manuscript just before the final submission by putting aside her own work and deadlines in order to provide me with valuable advice. And finally, I owe much gratitude to my family—Sunil, Anish, and Maya—who have not only tolerated but also championed this project as it grew from an idea during our family and research trips to London, New Delhi, and Hyderabad to a concrete book manuscript.

Abbreviations

ACC	Andhra Congress Circle
ACLU	American Civil Liberties Union
ADL	Andhra Defence League
AIML	All-India Muslim League
AISPC	All-India States Peoples' Conference
AMS	Andhra Mahasabha
APCC	Andhra Provincial Congress Committee
ASP	Andhra Swarajya Party
BJP	Bharatiya Janata Party
CPI	Communist Party of India
CSP	Congress Socialist Party
FSC	Federal Structure Committee
HPC	Hyderabad Political Conference
HRA	Hindustan Republican Association
HSC	Hyderabad State Congress
INC	Indian National Congress
ICLU	Indian Civil Liberties Union
MLA	Madras legislative assembly
NCCL	National Council for Civil Liberties
NMML	Nehru Museum and Memorial Library
NSL	Nizam's Subjects League
RSS	Rashtriya Swayamsevak Sangh
TSA	Telangana State Archives

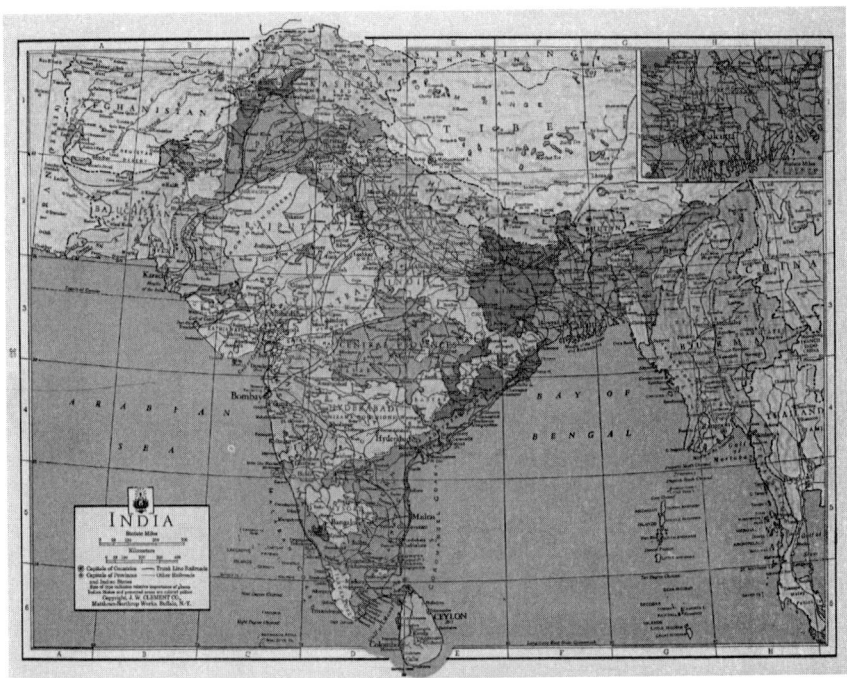

Map of British India

Source: J. W. Clement Co., *The New Matthews-Northrup Global Atlas of the World at War* (Buffalo, NY: Matthews-Northrup Works, 1943).

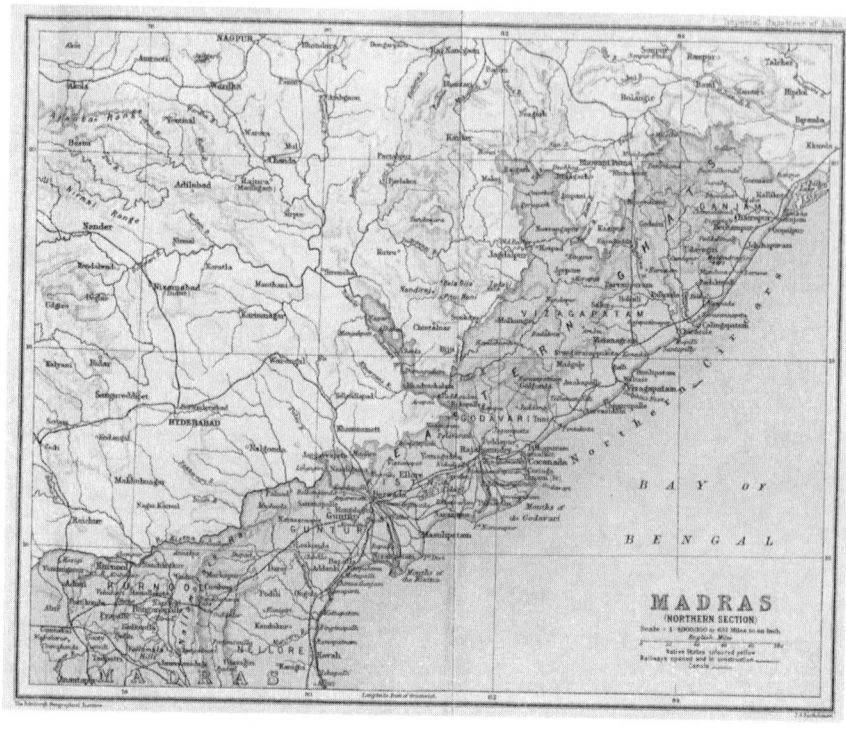

Map of northern Madras Presidency, 1909

Source: John George Bartholomew, 'Madras (Northern Section)', in *The Imperial Gazetteer of India*, vol. 18 (Oxford: Clarendon Press, 1909) (public domain via Wikimedia Commons).

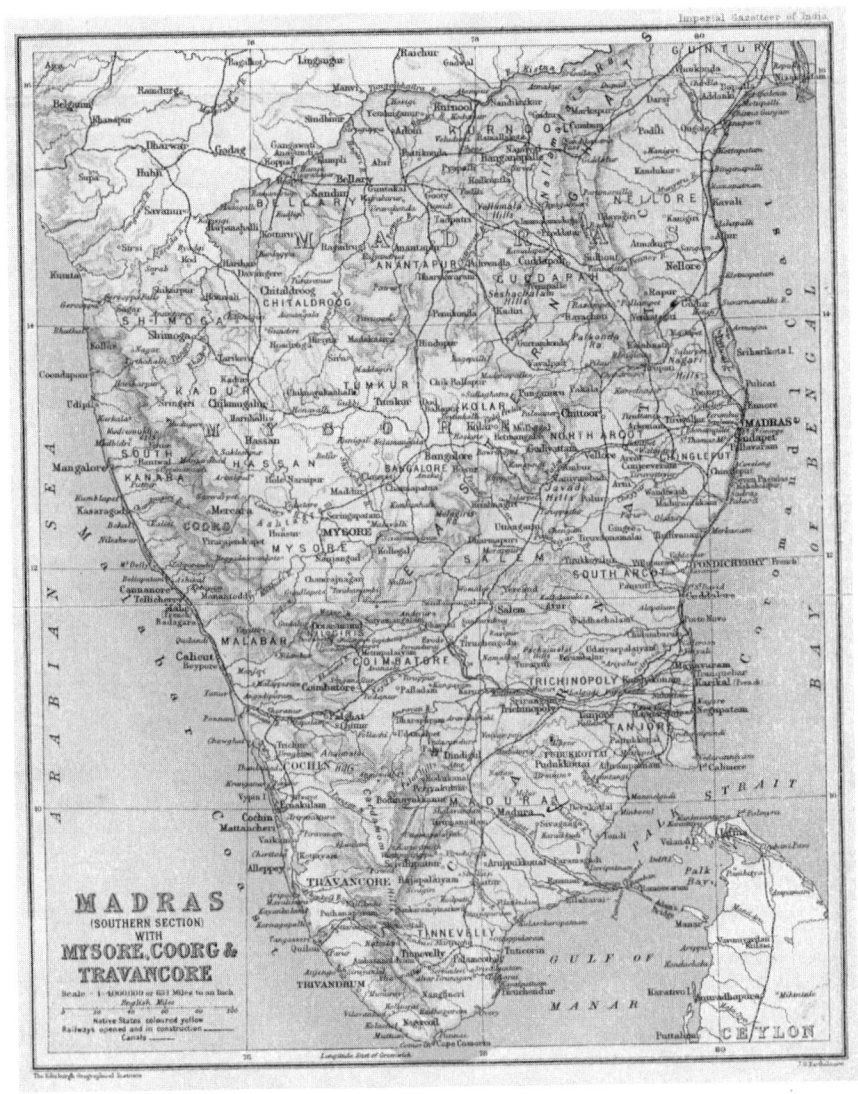

Map of southern Madras Presidency, 1909

Source: John George Bartholomew, 'Madras (Southern Section)', in *The Imperial Gazetteer of India*, vol. 18 (Oxford: Clarendon Press, 1909) (public domain via Wikimedia Commons).

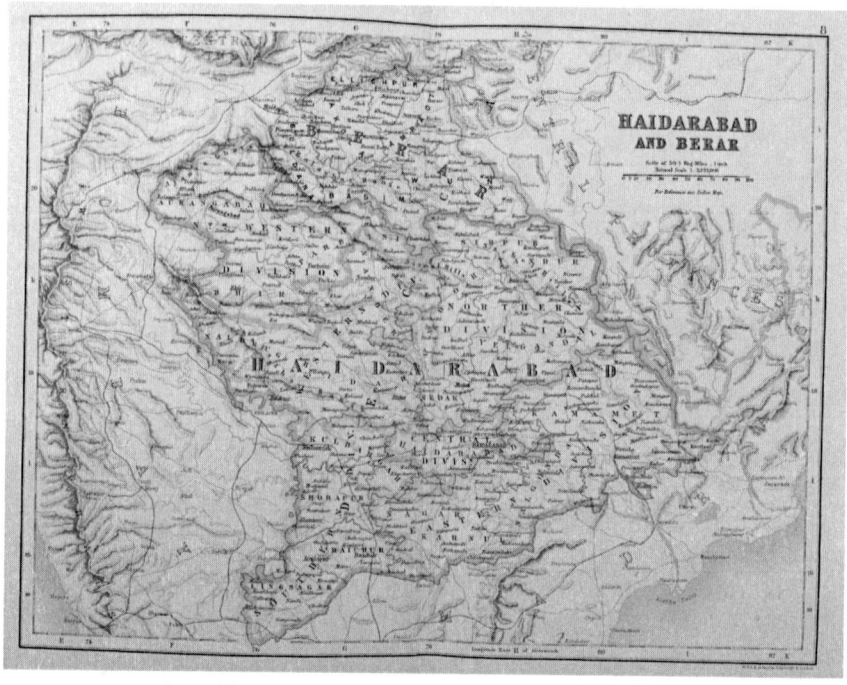

Map of Hyderabad and Berar, 1894

Source: W. & A. K. Johnston, 'Haidarabad and Berar', in *Atlas of India: Containing Sixteen Maps and Complete Index, with an Introduction by Sir W. W. Hunter* (Edinburgh and London: W. & A. K. Johnston, 1894) (public domain image courtesy of the Newberry Library, Chicago, IL).

Introduction

Self-Determination, Federation, and Civil Liberties in Twentieth-Century South India

Anti-colonial thinkers at the turn of the twentieth century already had a long history of grappling with concepts of liberty, equality, and self-rule in British India. Ever since the beginning of colonial rule, Indians had been debating the varied meanings of liberty,[1] from Rammohun Roy who called for a free press as early as 1823 to G. Lakshmanarasu Chetty who established the English newspaper *Crescent* in 1844 in the colonial city of Madras to specifically represent Hindu interests organizing against the growing influence of Christian missionaries on British colonial policy. From this early period to the late nineteenth century, when Indian National Congress (INC) leader Bishan Narayan Dhar declared, 'There is more of the revolutionary spirit in our vernacular novels and fugitive political and social tracts than in all the reports of the INC put together',[2] it was a testament to the vibrancy of vernacular public spheres in the provinces and presidencies of British India at the turn of the twentieth century. Indeed, anti-colonialism emerged from provincial archives as a force that was by nature transformational. Anti-colonialism not only encompassed movements organized against empire and colonial rule, but it also unleased revolutionary imaginaries of remaking colonial societies and mapping democratic futures. However, it was not until the early decades of the twentieth century that political demands intensified for the British colonial government to expand representative institutions towards the realization of the ideal of self-rule. Indeed, the language of liberty and self-determination used by Anglo-American statesmen, such as Woodrow Wilson as well as Vladimir Lenin to describe the ideological struggle of World War I, impacted colonized peoples' perception of their rightful place in a world of 'free' nation states, as argued by Erez Manela.[3] The language of liberty and self-determination was not entirely new to anti-colonial thinkers at this time. Rather, the interwar period saw a dramatic rise and intense *circulation* of discourses of self-determination which had a profound effect on anti-colonialism. In scholarship on British colonial rule in India, what has been relatively unexamined is the impact that these discourses had on shaping a range of political imaginaries, including, for example, growing demands for provincial autonomy in British India and autonomy for Indian 'native' states (or the hundreds of princely states of India) in any future political arrangement after the withdrawal of the British Empire. By 'political imaginaries', I mean to signal the emergence and circulation of a variety of political aspirations, ideologies, and mobilizations during the nationalist era.

This book revisits this period at the height of anti-colonial nationalism to chart the history of how democracy and democratic institutions began to establish roots in south India, particularly in the Telugu-speaking districts of the Madras Presidency and the neighbouring princely state of Hyderabad. The Telugu region has most often been linked to the rise of linguistic nationalism and the linguistic reorganization of states in post-independence India. However, there is a more complex history behind the origins of Telugu nationalism. By delving into the archives of provincial politics, I examine how anti-colonialism in the form of varied demands for self-determination, political and regional federations, and civil liberties came to shape democratic institutions in this region. Globally, anti-colonialism involved several parallel trajectories. The most prominent one is the trajectory of national self-determination that dominated the first half of the twentieth century. However, there are two other dimensions to the history of anti-colonialism in South Asia: first, the role of anti-colonialism in forging international solidarities after empire and efforts to remake the global order; and, second, how the politics of anti-colonialism helped *democratize* the region, giving rise to movements demanding provincial autonomy. This latter history is what I want to recover in this book.

The transition from empire to nation is most often associated in the historiography with an insular nationalism—a nationalism that is solely focused on shaping national identity and newly demarcated national borders.[4] While this period undoubtedly was dominated by questions of national borders and identity, discourses of internationalism and anti-imperialism dropped out of view after the emergence of the nation state to primacy in the age of decolonization in the post-war period. Recent scholarship has brought to the foreground the international face of anti-colonial nationalism and argued that these nationalisms were profoundly shaped by interwar internationalism and anti-imperialism.[5] However, what has not been given sufficient attention is the diverse internal face of anti-colonialism via the democratization of the region or province. The book draws attention to political debates and movements during this period that envisioned society and politics after empire—movements that were anticipating British withdrawal from the subcontinent and cultivating new democratic futures.

Recent scholarship on the French colonial experience has charted an alternate history of anti-colonial thought through a reading of African and Afro-Caribbean intellectuals who proposed models of imperial federation that attempted to address the colonial subject's desire for citizenship and individual rights without severing ties to metropolitan France.[6] The proposal was to have divisible sovereignty negotiated between metropole and colony after the dissolution of empire. Frederick Cooper and Gary Wilder offer different reasons for why Afro-French intellectuals offered up visions of imperial federation. Their studies drawing on the French in Senegal and the West Indies suggest that anti-colonial thinkers challenged empire and colonial domination to be sure, but also recognized the dangers and limitations of the nation-state form. Adom Getachew in her recent book, *Worldmaking after Empire: The Rise and Fall of Self-Determination*, recasts African activists' quest for federation as an attempt to shape the global order after empire.[7] And Erez Manela and Susan Pederson's work on the League of Nations and the discourse of self-determination has opened up lines of inquiry for colonial studies to revisit anti-colonial nationalism and explore other strands of political thought, including ideas of federation.[8] If for Afro-French thinkers the idea of federation after empire was meant to foster political and economic stability in former colonies, histories of British India, by contrast, have tended to narrate a single-minded focus on an independent nation state. Partha Chatterjee, for example, argues that the INC insisted on the establishment of the nation state as a necessary precondition for guaranteeing a common set of citizenship rights.[9] The idea that the goal of anti-colonial nationalism of the INC was to achieve popular sovereignty first and then seek freedom and equality as a nation with other nations and global cooperation has become near canonical within the history of British India and its aftermath.[10] My research suggests that this picture is incomplete because even within the confines of INC nationalism, provincial politics were being reformed in democratic directions that were neither strictly national in form nor starkly centralized.

It is within this context of the seismic global transformations of the early twentieth century wrought by two World Wars, the rise of international institutions, and the crisis of the imperial order that this book is situated. It examines the period between empire and nation in colonial India—a period that, I argue, was defined not only by the rise of the nation state and debates over a new global order, but also by the expansion of democratic participation in defining and negotiating political futures, by a heightened era of liberal thinking and the increased use of discourses of political rights and self-government. The book braids together narratives of civil societal discussions on political life and citizenship with proposals for federated arrangements and calls for provincial autonomy using the particular case of the princely state of Hyderabad and the emergence of provincial nationalism in the neighbouring Madras Presidency. The success of anti-colonial nationalism in establishing two sovereign nation states in the aftermath of the World Wars has obscured the complex political landscape of pre-independence India. Fortunately, there has been a noticeable shift in historical scholarship on colonial India from a preoccupation with nationalism's ascendance in the colonies to a critical examination of a broader landscape of political imagining formulated at the height of anti-colonialism. The moment between empire and nation in the decades leading up to Indian independence from British imperial rule offers a unique opportunity to examine the circulation of alternative political visions that competed with discourses of nationalist self-determination.

The princely state of Hyderabad was home to a unique confluence of political debates, combining questions about the future of Muslim sovereignty and states in the subcontinent with discussions of post-colonial arrangements of federation. Hyderabad in the 1940s was a multilingual and multi-religious society, a predominantly Hindu society governed by a Muslim king (the opposite of Kashmir where a majority Muslim population was governed by a Hindu monarch). What arose in Hyderabad in the colonial period was an emergent critique of monarchy along with an explicit desire for the continuance of the Hyderabad polity—either as a federated unit of India or as an independent state—after the withdrawal of the British as an imperial force from South Asia. Previously, the history of linguistic nationalism that led to the formation of the first regional state of Andhra Pradesh in post-independence India has been analysed without consideration of the history of the dissolution of its powerful neighbour, the princely state of Hyderabad. This produced a gap in the historical literature that overlooks the varied political aspirations incubating in the erstwhile Hyderabad state that were broader than the triumphalist nationalism of the INC. The historical literature as it now stands can be divided into political histories of the success of linguistic reorganization schemes during the Nehruvian period, historical and anthropological literature on linguistic nationalism and its cultural symbols and sentiment (Mother Tamil and Mother Telugu), and finally histories of the former princely state of Hyderabad focused on the political history of the Hyderabad state and its internal dynamics.[11] This literature, however, paints a skewed picture of provincial nationalism (and the adulation of the mother tongue) colliding with an 'ancient regime' cosmopolitanism in the emergence of Andhra Pradesh in 1956. The politics of twentieth-century south India, particularly Hyderabad and the Madras Presidency, were much more complex and reflective of a broader political landscape. This book charts that landscape by analysing the parallel development of public life, political activism, and democratic futures in British India and the princely state of Hyderabad. Some were coordinated efforts, others were parallel, but all were in dialogue with larger international and national discourses of self-determination, self-rule, and federation that sought to imagine democratic futures for a people-centred government in Britain's South Asian colonial territories.

Princely States: Debating Sovereignty and Democracy

The historiography on the princely states in colonial India reveals a diversity of political opinion—ranging from attempts by princes to reclaim sovereignty through negotiation of colonial treaties to debates over federating with an independent Indian union of states. In his vast and rich scholarship on the princely states and their relationship with British India, Ian Copland has meticulously documented the diverse political ideologies harboured by the princes who were far from agreement on the goal of political reforms introduced by the British.[12] In the second decade of the twentieth century, Copland argues that while angling for more influence, many princes were also working towards greater autonomy for their states. For the most part, these princes were not necessarily in favour of making the principle of self-rule a goal, even as Edwin Montagu made the pledge of self-government in 1917 the ultimate goal for India. Instead of embracing the principles of self-government and representative institutions, some princes translated the idea of self-rule and self-government into their desire for more autonomy from the British and colonial governments.[13] By the 1920s, princely Hyderabad had firmly committed itself to resisting internal political reforms that the administration deemed would interfere with what they safeguarded as internal sovereignty. In other words, what we see in the case of princely Hyderabad is that those concerned with questions of sovereignty (mainly the state administrative elite) were at loggerheads with those proposing the introduction and expansion of representative institutions (the professional elites). Amongst the hundreds of princely states, Hyderabad was undoubtedly a unique case. Not only was it one of the larger princely states, but it was also a Muslim state that had a unique status in India and globally after the dismantling of the Ottoman Empire in the 1920s.[14]

An earlier generation of scholars whose research centred on the princely states of India examined the complicated role of both the INC and the All-India Muslim League (AIML) and the impact they had in shaping princely politics, especially during the crucial decades leading up to Indian independence. This historiography was fuelled by an interest in drawing connections between studies of Indian nationalism and those of princely states. There was also an interest in unpacking the links between the INC and the AIML and their efforts in forging connections with the peoples of the princely states.[15] While this literature addressed the political history of the INC and the AIML and the intricate ties they established with the princely states, what does not get much attention is the political aspirations or imaginaries that emerged from social and political movements within the princely states which were distinct from the larger British Indian anti-colonial movements. In recent years, a new generation of historians working on princely states have argued compellingly that the princes sought to retain kingship as an alternative to democracy.[16] In Hyderabad this idea of holding onto monarchy—as a constitutional monarchy—was floated in the decades leading up to Indian independence. This recent turn in scholarship has led to rethinking princely politics in a broader national and international context alongside anti-colonialism, interwar internationalisms, and proposals for federation after British imperial withdrawal from South Asia.[17]

With regards to the princely state of Hyderabad, the scholarship has been similarly rich and expansive. Eric Beverley's and Kavita Datla's pivotal works on princely Hyderabad brought to the fore cross-border movements and connections between Hyderabad and British India.[18] Datla's work most importantly highlights the migration of the Muslim intelligentsia from north India to Hyderabad to work in the Nizam's administration—a revered Muslim polity that was the inheritor of Mughal legacy in the Indian subcontinent. For instance, Akbar Hydari, an important figure in Hyderabad politics connected to the Bombay industrial baron Badruddin Tyabji by marriage, headed to Hyderabad in 1905, after being appointed as chief accountant in the administration.[19] The establishment of Osmania University, the first vernacular university in colonial India—and its commitment to making Urdu, a prestigious language associated with north Indian literati, the language of education—brought many prominent Muslim scholars from northern India to Hyderabad. Once in the Hyderabad administration, Hydari rose to prominence quickly and was soon involved in the planning for Osmania University. In 1915 he addressed the Hyderabad Education Conference and made a compelling case for the use of the vernacular for educational purposes.[20] Convinced by arguments that Urdu would be a more worthy medium for education over classical languages such as Persian and Arabic, the Nizam approved the proposal for Osmania University in 1917.[21] Having a university teach modern subjects, including the sciences, in Urdu was expected to not only instill pride of language but also make Urdu itself more dynamic. The idea of Osmania University not only institutionalized secular modern education in Urdu, but also gave rise to what Kavita Datla calls Urdu nationalism in Hyderabad and in colonial India more broadly. This research undoubtedly brought Hyderabad to the centre of studies of anti-colonialism as articulated by the INC and the AIML. Beverley's work tracking cross-border movement of ideas and people between Hyderabad and the Bombay Presidency calls into question scholarship that limits its analysis with respect to national and provincial boundaries. Rather, Beverley proposes tracing Muslim internationalism that Hyderabad tapped into by cultivating transnational connections through a dynamic Muslim public sphere.[22] Beverley goes on to argue that Hyderabad managed to forge these particular international links through existing Muslim networks (transnational, pan-Islamism, Muslim internationalism) and with other 'sub-imperial' polities. This work on cross-border movement of ideas from recruitment of north Indian Muslims by the Hyderabad administration gives us a richer account of Hyderabad politics and culture.

Furthermore, there has been considerable focus on questions of sovereignty and international law in recent work on the princely states.[23] While the status of princely states was debated in the talks leading up to the Government of India Act of 1935, which urged a federation to consolidate smaller princely states with the British provinces, the colonial administration did not make similar pronouncements on internal political reforms in the princely states, thus enabling the idea of a federalism that allowed for sharing sovereignty. The princes routinely cited Bhulabhai J. Desai's legal opinion that the princely states had a right to hold onto their sovereignty at the end of empire in South Asia. This opinion was embraced by those princes who hoped to regain their autonomy after British withdrawal. Desai's opinion was that the princely state, according to international law, was a monarchical state, thus giving the prince the right to part with 'his sovereignty at his own free will'.[24] This also meant the prince could hold onto that sovereignty and not give it up to the future Indian Union. This is where my research intervenes to highlight that these maneuverings led to the unenviable position that Hyderabad found itself in 1947–1948 as debates over sovereignty did not take sufficient account of community leaders and political movements within Hyderabad to produce a consensus between the Nizam, the administration, and the various political groups.

Starting in 1928, Jawaharlal Nehru, as an internationalist socialist, however, made it known that the INC would exert pressure on the native princes to introduce a responsible government based on representative institutions. At the All India Congress Committee's Jubbulpore session, on 24–25 April 1935, the committee declared that the INC was just as concerned with the interests of the people of the native Indian states as with those of the people of British India.[25] Nehru insisted:

It would be, in our opinion, a most one-sided arrangement if the Indian States desire to join the federation, so as to influence by their votes and otherwise, the policy and legislation of the Indian Legislature, without submitting themselves to common legislation passed by it. It would be a travesty of the federal idea.[26]

In short, the idea of an Indian Union that accorded different sets of rights and institutions to the people of different states was unacceptable to Nehru and the INC leadership. While some princes such as the Nizam of Hyderabad sought to recover their sovereignty, the INC insisted on a common constitution guaranteeing rights of citizenship to all peoples of the proposed federated union. Unravelling the arguments made by the princes, Datla explores the intricacies of international law that the Hyderabad administration tapped into in order to assert the legitimacy of colonial treaties and their negotiation for autonomy in any proposed union of states.[27] Questions of sovereignty in the scholarship on princely Hyderabad inevitably lead to discussions of the forces of internationalism that shaped twentieth-century Muslim politics[28]—the fall and dissolution of the Ottoman Empire in the aftermath of World War I and the global rise of pan-Islamism-fuelled 'Muslim internationalism' in Hyderabad. In particular, the rise of pan-Islamism, combined with the Khilafat movement, profoundly impacted Hyderabad in the early decades of the twentieth century. The Khilafat movement looked to the Nizam and his polity as representative of a Muslim polity that would take on the mantle of the caliphate after the dismantling of the Ottoman Empire. This same energy and passion of pan-Islamism fed into the establishment of Osmania University.[29]

While princely Hyderabad advanced its own interests in regaining sovereignty and autonomy through treaty negotiations, there was a distinct popular movement that took on the task of representing Muslim political interest and made strides towards rethinking sovereignty after British withdrawal.[30] This signalled the emergence of Muslim politics in princely Hyderabad. The Majlis' politics differed from the Nizam administration's position in that they approached the subject of representative government in two distinct ways. A. Suneetha and M. A. Moid argue that the Majlis first 'sought to mobilize the Muslim subjects of the State from the non-elite sections as Muslims wherein the category was articulated as a cultural, social and political entity, not a theological one', and then 'through the elucidation of the principle of popular sovereignty, albeit of Muslims, it buttressed the idea that sovereignty needed to be grounded in people's support'.[31] In other words, the movement attempted to articulate a conception of popular sovereignty alongside other civil societal associations in Hyderabad.[32] The distinct contribution they made was to identify

Muslim interest with the survival of the Hyderabad state and the figure of the Nizam. The dismantling of the Ottoman Empire created a global crisis in the interwar period. This not only fuelled the Khilafat movement in British India, but also attracted renewed attention to Hyderabad as the inheritor of Mughal or Muslim sovereignty.[33]

Just as the INC extended its connections in the princely states to build a political base, the AIML, too, sought out political leaders there to generate and build a diversity of political opinion. However, the AIML was late to show interest in the fate of the princely states, and this lateness may have contributed to the fact that Pakistan was not able to persuade more princely states to side with them after partition.[34] One distinct concept that the AIML fostered in princely Hyderabad was the idea of Muslim sovereignty or the assurance of Muslim heritage reflected in any political reforms proposed in Hyderabad towards representative government. This is because if left to the workings of a representative government, the Muslim community in Hyderabad, made up of the administration and a segment of the overall population, would be reduced to a 'minority' with diminished political power—similar to the situation in which the Muslim community of north India found itself. The AIML and its Hyderabad representative, the Majlis, worked to retain political power for the Muslim community as they saw the Hindu elite and leadership wholeheartedly embracing representative democracy as a way to shore up political power in their favour and assert Hindu dominance. Finally, there has been a shift in scholarship on Hyderabad to understanding the upheaval at the moment of independence and its immediate aftermath as one of violent rupture and not a smooth transition.[35] In this narrative, Hyderabad becomes central.[36] This book turns to the different civil societal movements in Hyderabad to understand how their inability to forge a consensus on what Hyderabad should look like after Indian independence ultimately led to the break-up of the princely state of Hyderabad in the 1950s. My frame of analysis shifts to Hyderabad's dynamic civil society to trace debates that were taking place in the public sphere to make a case for analysing political movements and activism and to offer an alternative perspective from the standpoint of the administration and the Nizam.

Madras Presidency: Rethinking the Rise of Provincial Politics

As I have suggested, most analyses of Indian politics during the first half of the twentieth century have been dominated by the national frame. In this literature, not only princely states but also the provinces remain relatively marginal.[37] This book attempts to correct that lacuna by shifting our scale and foci of analysis to consider the political dynamics of provinces, princely states, and the region more generally as overlapping spaces in which discourses of self-rule and self-determination circulated in distinct and productive ways. The space of the region also allows one to bring in both the princely states and British Indian provinces into dialogue. While the turn of the twentieth century saw the rise of democratic politics based on liberal ideas of reason and debate, the expansion of representative institutions and the extension of the franchise at the provincial level led to some important developments in the northern Madras Presidency. I ask how the discourses of self-determination and federation shaped the idea of the province and the debates over federation in the broader politics of late colonial south India. Importantly, I suggest that the region or province was not merely a space for the consolidation or replication of the nation and national sentiments. The region indeed has its own distinctive political dynamics, aspirations, and movements.

An earlier generation of scholarly work on the Madras Presidency, and more generally on south India, was very attuned to the rise of a new type of politics (with the entry of new political actors) after devolution in the early decades of the twentieth century. This scholarship also paid attention to the rise of Dravidian nationalism. However, much of the politics that was examined was dominated by Tamil actors.[38] The so-called Cambridge School (as it was referred to by the Subaltern Studies Collective who came to prominence in the 1980s) also studied the larger region through the broad lens of the politics of the Madras Presidency as setting the stage for the rise of provincial politics.[39] This scholarship offered a fresh perspective on the colonial political system at the turn of the twentieth century and reframed it in terms of a history of politics at the local level. That shift enabled a generation of historians to examine the impact of the Government of India Act of 1919 and how the ensuing administrative reforms instigated the expansion of native participation in the Madras government, providing new opportunities for Indians to take part in the provincial government.[40] The new system of dyarchy instituted by the colonial government allowed for Indian ministers to share responsibility for the provincial government with the Governor in Council,[41] an opportunity opened up by Montagu's announcement promising the 'gradual development of self-government'. Far from being an act of charity, Montagu's intention was to introduce pragmatic reforms in order to make the government more efficient with Indians taking on administrative burdens but not executive power.[42] Things changed dramatically with the institution of the Montagu–Chelmsford reforms, also known as Montford reforms, and district-level politicians came to Madras to influence colonial bureaucracy. Christopher Baker writes, 'The protagonists of the new politics in Madras City were the men who understood the principle of gaining power and influence in a state that was essentially bureaucratic, and who were equipped—largely through knowledge of the English language—with the skills necessary for promoting the interests of a wide clientele in the corridors of government.'⁴³ Baker argues that new groups emerged vying for political power equipped with skills gained from colonial-era educational institutions. This new politics was defined by provincial elites coming to Madras to gain employment in the government but with the language skills also to vociferously demand their entry into the colonial administration. This, the Cambridge School argued, instigated political activism in Madras, though primarily for personal gain rather than a genuine commitment to an idea of political freedom. To support this argument about the instrumentality of the provincial elite in Madras, Baker quotes C. R. Reddy from Chittoor who observed this new politics in a 1922 article published in the *Indian Review*: 'The general politics of press and platform hardly affect the voting. The landlord, the merchant, and the lawyer have their clientele, and every man has his tribe, clan, or creed behind him who follow with sheepish fidelity. In this medievalism, political conviction counts for little.'⁴⁴ Reddy is scathing in his assessment of the professional elites pouring in from the provinces into the colonial city for advancing their own individual careers and their group (caste or religion) rather than cultivating democratic sensibilities and be schooled in liberal politics. Another proponent of the Cambridge School, historian Robert Frykenberg, wrote on local government and colonial administration in the Guntur district, a Telugu-speaking district in the northern Madras Presidency, and suggested a collaborative theory of politics that focused on native Indian participation and cooperation at the level of the district.⁴⁵ The theory sought to argue that political devolution and greater native participation in the government did not necessarily lead to Indians fully grasping the liberal idea of democracy.

The picture that emerges from these scholars is of south Indian politics being shaped by native English-speaking elites who were vying for their own political position by accommodating with colonial power. The new politics does not, in their view, express new political ideologies—that is, genuine ideas and aspirations tied to conceptions of freedom and democracy. In other words, when scholars searched for signs of anti-colonial nationalism and were unable to find them, they came to the conclusion that until the last decade of the nineteenth century no prominent leaders in Madras took on the task of shaping nationalist politics.⁴⁶ What they missed in their search was that the political reforms they analysed did in fact give rise to a new politics, but they did so precisely by focusing on the region. In fact, the new politics also gave rise to a range of political ideologies and political imaginaries centred on the region. While offering a new historical method for the study of colonial politics, this generation of historians viewed the rise of democratic politics in colonial India as the gradual incorporation of

Indian elites into the expanding institutions of self-government built by the colonial government. Implied in this understanding of Indian politics is that individuals and groups used political power to benefit themselves rather than espousing new political ideologies laying the groundwork for democratic futures.

It is important to note that while the Cambridge School illuminated the power dynamics of this period, it paid scant attention to the broader cultural politics that emerged in the early decades of the twentieth century. When Baker did extend this theory to the rise of new political parties such as the powerful Justice Party, again his analysis implied that the appearance of this new party and its members were motivated by political calculation to gain power and promote their particular group interests. The Justice Party was formed in 1916 when a group of non-Brahmins came together to form a political association that opposed the INC Home Rulers in the Madras Presidency.[47] There was a gradual shift away from this approach when historians based in American universities began to examine Tamil nationalism and the Dravidian movement. However, even these historians did not offer an alternative framework to understand the emergence of these new political parties and politicians.[48] But the shift did highlight the cultural component of the new emergent regional nationalisms. Tamil nationalism and the Dravidian movement no doubt received far more attention than neighbouring Telugu nationalism. Amongst these historians, Eugene Irschick's pioneering work on the Non-Brahman movement and the Justice Party laid the basis for understanding the critique of caste and brahminical dominance and the emergence of democratic politics under conditions of colonial rule in the Madras Presidency. Irschick also discussed the tensions in provincial politics between the northern Telugu districts and Tamil-dominated politics of Madras and how that tension impacted the politics of the Justice Party movement. What Irschick's work revealed was a rift between Tamil and Telugu speakers in the emerging Non-Brahman movement. If we move away from Madras-centred politics to the northern coastal districts, we see that Telugu nationalism was quite distinct in its historical origins and goals from Dravidian nationalism.

After the emergence of the Subaltern Studies Collective and its impact on the study of colonialism and nationalism, historical scholarship moved towards novel approaches in understanding the complexities of Tamil and Dravidian nationalism. This next generation of historians whose research was deeply influenced by the Subaltern Studies Collective and their rethinking of the Cambridge School and nationalist school of historiography—both of which offered analyses of colonial rule and the rise of anti-colonial nationalism—turned to excavate the cultural components of nationalism in south India. One important voice from this shift was M. S. S. Pandian's intervention in the debate over how to understand the rise of non-Brahmanism in Madras. In his pivotal article 'Beyond Colonial Crumbs', Pandian launched a critique of Baker's work, describing it as a 'faction school of history' fuelled by patron client politics—a form of politics that was purely instrumental with no legitimate ideologies associated with political parties.[49] For Pandian, Baker's analysis failed to frame the rise of new political movements, such as the Justice Party and Periyar's Self-Respect movement, in relation to caste politics, let alone recognize such politics as having legitimacy of their own.[50] Baker's dismissal of politics in Madras as 'faction' politics was based on that fact that non-Brahmin castes comprised the newly formed Justice Party who were economically well off compared to the Brahmins. This view of the Justice Party as lacking in legitimate political ideas failed to understand the emerging new political movements (including Periyar's Self-Respect movement) that would go on to profoundly shape south Indian politics. Pandian provides a fresh perspective of this new politics by examining public organizations that formed to articulate political interests for different communities such as the Justice Party and the Self-Respect movement. He outlines an alternative public sphere in which oppositional caste politics emerged, effectively producing multiple publics with competing articulations of the political as shaped by new social movements and new social conditions.[51] When we turn to the Telugu region, however, we see that non-Brahmanism unfolded very differently there. It did not take hold with the same force as it did in the Tamil-speaking regions and in the city of Madras where the Justice Party and non-Brahmanism prepared the ground for the emergence of the Dravidian movement.[52] Another difference with Tamil politics is that in the Telugu region, a focus on language becomes primary for political organizing as we will see with the Andhra movement in the Madras Presidency and in princely Hyderabad.

Language Politics as a Politics of Self-Determination

The emergence of both Tamil and Telugu nationalism was profoundly shaped by the rise of the vernacular orator (politician) starting from the 1920s.[53] In this critical decade, with the popularity of the Swadeshi agitation in the Madras Presidency, there is a shift in the history of modern Tamil oratory towards speech directed at the people, as forcefully argued by Bernard Bate, which in turn urged them to participate in the political process. This shift was predicated on a profound new idea of 'the people' that cut across divisions of class and caste. While the Cambridge School highlighted the important role of English-speaking politicians in provincial politics, the turn to language, culture, and region allowed scholars of Tamil nationalism to understand this novel conceptualization of the people in the 1920s mobilized by the *vernacular* politician. If the Cambridge

School offered broader understandings of the Madras Presidency as they analysed provincial politicians who used English to conduct debate (coming from different regions), scholars of Dravidian nationalism offered perspectives that diverge from that school by turning to Tamil politics and the emergence of the Dravidar Kazhagam (DK) and the Dravida Munnetra Kazhagam (DMK) as challengers to the dominance of the INC in colonial and post-colonial Tamil Nadu.[54] The latter scholars reframe the region as a linguistically constituted space that gave rise to distinctly regional–cultural politics. For the northern districts of Telugu speakers in the Madras Presidency, there has been little scholarship that covers that region's political landscape. However, one can take cues from the critical work of David Washbrook, Baker, and especially Irschick's analysis of tensions in the Justice Party in order to chart broader trends in the Presidency and delve into the new politics that emerged in the Telugu region. While the southern Telugu districts of Rayalseema were intricately connected with Madras political and public life—especially to the Justice Party—the northern coastal districts saw the rise of a different set of associational politics.[55]

For the northern Telugu-speaking region, two lines of scholarship emerged that were concerned with critically important themes running throughout nineteenth-century colonial India. Both colonial philology and social reform dominated the historical scholarship on this region. The latter was primarily concerned with the work of the famed nineteenth-century social reformer Kandukuri Viresalingam and the influence of social reformism on Telugu culture and society, especially in the northern coastal districts of the Madras Presidency where Viresalingam's activism was visible. The other line of research focused on the work of the nineteenth-century philologist Charles P. Brown who engaged extensively with the Telugu language and literature. Scholarship on Brown and Viresalingam delved into how cultural politics under colonial rule shaped the region, especially the northern coastal districts which received the most attention in scholarship on Telugu.[56] Broadly, this scholarship demonstrated that the social and cultural change that took place in the nineteenth century was primarily the transformation of Telugu as a language in the colonial and modern era. The focus on language in the research on Telugu and its history was a result of the prominence of Telugu intellectuals, both scholars and writers, debating how to teach Telugu in educational institutions from the primary to the university levels.[57] Particularly, the spoken language movement spearheaded by the educationalist Gidugu Venkata Ramamurti and the poet Gurzada Appa Rao in the early decades of the twentieth century sparked discussion about how best to not only teach Telugu in modern schools but also write in Telugu for modern media, from novels to newspapers.[58] This set into motion a century of debate in Telugu literary circles regarding the place of modern Telugu in a rapidly changing society in the decades leading up to independence and after.[59] Lisa Mitchell's research combining historical and ethnographic methods of analysis focuses in particular on how Telugu as a language was transformed (and monologized) in the long nineteenth century.[60] She begins with the premise that the transformations that Telugu (like other regional languages) underwent were radical in the nineteenth century and that they prepared the way for linguistic nationalism to take hold. Her work then traces the origins of Telugu nationalism to the transformations in language and foregrounds the cultural components of Telugu nationalism and the affective ties that it produced in forming a community.[61] Building on this earlier work, my research centres on the activities of the Andhra Mahasabha (AMS) and the activists who led the Andhra movement to illuminate the profound impact that they had in both the Madras Presidency as well as princely Hyderabad. However, diverging from this earlier scholarship on Telugu as a language, my work reveals that a more complex set of motivations was informing debates about the formation of a separate province for Telugu speakers. A narrow focus on the language debates obscures the larger political transformations that were taking place. What the early leaders of the Andhra movement and the subsequent debates in the Madras legislative assembly (MLA) and documented in the newspapers show is that the movement was profoundly shaped by interwar discourses of self-government and self-rule. These discourses shaped a new politics in south India, as I argue throughout the book, that gave rise to civil societal activism and an impetus in organizing the people into a political community.

The AMS, which was formed in the northern coastal districts of the Madras Presidency and in princely Hyderabad, had an enduring and powerful life in the first half of the twentieth century. It provided an important forum for nurturing Telugu culture and politics on both sides of the border between the Madras Presidency and princely Hyderabad. However, the AMS was much more than a cultural organization, despite representing itself as such many times, especially in the Hyderabad state. Rather, after research into the principal activists and their writings on the Andhra movement, what I argue is that the AMS became a dynamic forum that politicized the northern Madras Presidency and the Telangana region (the Telugu-speaking region in princely Hyderabad). The AMS took up a whole range of issues that were pedagogical by nature to questions of political representation.[62] Formed in 1913 in the northern coastal districts, the organization brought together a dynamic group of Telugu activists and intellectuals such as J. Gurunatham, whose activism and writings form the central subject of Chapter 1, and more prominent members such as Konda Venkatappayya, a Gandhian and member of the Andhra Provincial Congress Committee (APCC).

Other AMS supporters included the prominent Nyapathi Subba Rao, one of the founders of the national English language newspaper *The Hindu* based in the city of Madras, who began his activism in public life through social reform work with Kandukuri Viresalingam and his organizations based in Rajahmundry in the latter half of the nineteenth century.[63] In the neighbouring Hyderabad state, such stalwarts as M. Narsing Rao, the editor of the Urdu newspaper *Raiyat*, and Suravaram Pratapa Reddy, the founder and editor of the Telugu newspaper *Golkonda Patrika*, were both active members of the AMS. As the AMS took up cultural and social issues for its members to debate, it inevitably brought politics to the fore for its members. To get a sense of the range of political ideologies represented within the organization, one need only look at the political affiliations of Konda Venkatappayya, who was active in the INC; G. Venkatasubba Rao, who began the Andhra Swarajya Party (ASP) (to voice a conservative agenda set apart from the INC); and Ravi Narayana Reddy, who eventually turned away from an affiliation with the INC to the Communist Party of India (CPI) as he began to organize in the Telangana countryside.

The precursors to the AMS in the Madras Presidency took the form of district conferences that disseminated news and information on the political organizing at the national level and created forums for local activists to gather and debate both nationalist politics and their implication for the region and the district. Besides the district conferences, there was a proliferation of caste organizations in this period.[64] A notable one that challenged dominant Telugu nationalism came from the Adi Andhra Maha Sabha, which organized Dalits in Andhra.[65] Under the umbrella of the AMS, the dominant caste Hindu groups came together to advocate for Telugu representation. With Telugu nationalism, it was the cultural component that was most critical in creating the links that cut across district boundaries as well as across political ones with Hyderabad. The AMS conferences brought a diverse set of leaders—ranging from lawyers, students, and scholars—to annual meetings to deliberate on Andhra history, literature, educational and social reform issues, and the state of economic development at the district level. The turn to the vernacular was indeed significant in bringing about new attention to language and the opportunities it afforded to nurture a political community. As Bate has argued with regards to Tamil, the turn to vernacular oratory brought new energy to the politicization of the region. The AMS organizing was clearly enabled by this shift while still paying attention to national politics. In the Hyderabad state, the AMS presented its public face as a cultural organization that specifically drew attention to social reform issues within the Telugu-speaking community. While the AMS in the Madras Presidency put pressure on the INC and the Madras legislature to take up the issue of creating a separate province for Andhra, the AMS in Hyderabad worked to push educational and social reforms in the princely state and later supported the extension of civil liberties within the Hyderabad state and political reforms that would move the princely state towards a representative government. While divergent in political goals, both AMS branches sought to politicize their bases, using language and cultural bonds to disseminate and debate civil liberties, self-representation, and self-determination to bring attention to the region.

Moreover, the AMS in Hyderabad received support from the INC through its regional outfit, the Hyderabad State Congress. From the 1920s onwards, the INC and its supporting institutions pushed for political reforms in the princely states that mirrored changes taking place within British India. In pushing for these reforms, the INC sought out peoples' movements to align themselves with and to advocate with. The Hyderabad state administration, however, saw this influence of British Indian ideas as a direct threat and sought to curtail it at all costs. The INC worked similarly in British Indian provinces, creating local affiliations and associations and aligning regional agendas with national ones. In this way, the INC sought an equilibrium of its radical and conservative forces in order to attain the goal of self-rule. While self-rule at the national level meant independence and freedom from colonial rule, at the provincial level self-rule or self-determination signalled democracy and representative government that was only possible through cultivating language to form a political community. In aligning with regional units, the INC gave full support to the use of vernacular languages in politicizing regions and to expand their organizational structure. In that way, language became important for the region since it provided the mechanism to create not only an affective community but also the ability to build a democratic infrastructure.

꼬 꼬 꼬

The period that I cover in this book experienced great global change and the region I focus on underwent dramatic shifts with respect to fluctuating political boundaries after empire. The regions of Telangana, Northern Circars (the northern coastal districts of the Madras Presidency), and Rayalaseema (also part of the Madras Presidency) had a much more complex history than what colonial political and territorial boundaries reveal. The Telugu-speaking regions tell the story of the greater Deccan (from the early modern era) of shifting political boundaries, of layers of land tenure systems, of rivalries between Deccan sultanates and the Mughal Empire to European rivalries that made and remade the region. The regions that span from the northern reaches of Adilabad in Telangana to the northern coastal town of Srikakulam to the southern reaches of

Srikalahasti were knitted together through the connection of a common spoken and written language, Telugu. The idea of a common singular language (and the standardization of the Telugu language) is certainly the creation of modernity in that before this period Telugu circulated in many spoken dialects (and continues to as a dynamic living language) and in a variety of literary forms. Nineteenth-century colonial philology worked to produce a singular language through the production of grammars and dictionaries that standardized the teaching of Telugu in modern schools. In the contemporary period, the consensus of Telugu as a language acting as a binding force that would hold together a province and a regional state started to unravel in 2013 with the creation of the separate state of Telangana. This transformative political event manifested itself most dramatically in the toppling of statues in the city of Hyderabad—installed by the Telugu Desam Party (TDP) founder, N.T. Rama Rao.[66] The TDP emerged as a regional party in the 1980s, contesting the domination of the INC in Andhra Pradesh, and became a vehicle for Telugu pride. It can be seen as the culmination of Telugu nationalism as conceived by the Andhra movement from the first decade of the twentieth century. When the Telangana movement resurfaced in the first decade of the twenty-first century, it contested the assumed consensus of the Andhra movement, once again undermining the idea that language in itself can be the cohesive glue for a robust regional identity. This should give us pause as historians of linguistic nationalism to question whether earlier understandings of language movements had other agendas and goals. One such agenda was the attempt to define and identify the Telugu people and their political interests. Thus, the history I uncover of the Telugu region is that the experiment with democracy began during the anti-colonial struggle but intensified at the provincial level. By examining the formation and workings of the AMS in Telangana (princely Hyderabad) and in the Madras Presidency, my book argues that discourses of civil liberties, self-determination, and federation emerging out of Telugu publics revealed diverse political imaginaries crossing territorial boundaries between British India and the Hyderabad state.

Structure of the Book

It is vital to put the interwar period in a global framework in order to understand the rise of nationalisms and internationalisms that profoundly shaped politics at the regional level in British India. This book looks at discourses of self-determination and the debates over federation in order to open up the field of political discourse and examine its complexities and tensions. An important consideration will be to tease out strands of debate around ideas of self-rule and self-determination, as well as conceptions of people's government. What did self-determination and self-rule mean to various political actors and groups? How was self-determination interpreted at the level of the region in terms of representative government? How and why did associations organized around language become vocal in arguing for democracy or the democratic transformation of the region? Another key set of debates centred around how the region connects with the nation. Here debates over federation became central in thinking through issues of how to organize the region. Should the Telugu-speaking districts be all brought together under a single province? What is the future of the Hyderabad state in the aftermath of British withdrawal? Should Hyderabad retain its historical borders and distinct identity connected to its monarchical heritage?

Throughout the book, I will be attuned to a key conundrum—that despite these wide discussions and mobilizations, we have to consider why federation debates failed to provide a real alternative to or challenge the centralized nation state in India? It is clear that the nation state won out in late colonial India because ultimately both conservative and progressive forces came together to promote it—conservatives because it gave them control over a state to enforce majoritarian culture and invest in a state with its own imprint; progressives because the nation state promised possibilities for social equality and the eradication of longstanding hierarchies. However, this was hardly inevitable, especially at a time when political federalism was being proposed to counter the dangers of majoritarianism of the centralized nation state (the threat of ethnic expulsion and cleansing, and so on). My research suggests that the political impasses of princely Hyderabad pushed political movements to radicalize and pursue competing agendas, and, in the end, there was little incentive to align with one another in order to achieve a common goal.

In Chapter 1, I begin with a discussion on the emergence of regionalist discourses of self-government and self-rule (*swaraj*) that energized activist intellectuals in south India, prompting them to shift their attention from a focus on the nation to fostering local and regional democratic institutions. The rise of liberal democratic thought entailed both progressives and conservatives to come together to organize at the regional level on the basis of language. In the emerging Telugu publics, we can see debates form around competing discourses of social reformism and the politics of self-rule. Telugu activists assessed the work of social reform during the long nineteenth century and attempted to understand its relation to political discourses of self-representation and self-determination. The chapter centres on the founding of the enduring Telugu association, the AMS, in the northern coastal districts of the Madras Presidency for the purpose of cultural revival of the Telugu language and literature as well as building a political community that would make a demand for a Telugu province.

Chapters 2 and 3 lay emphasis on conceptions of federation broadly in south India—in princely Hyderabad and the Madras Presidency. Chapter 2 examines discourses of federation and the debates over self-government and self-determination as they shaped politics in the Madras Presidency broadly in relation to the emergence of competing political movements. In particular, the chapter asks how the Madras Presidency navigated both the Andhra demand for a separate province and the concomitant proposals of federation. Why did the INC leadership in the south resist the creation of the Andhra province in the decades before independence? The discourses of federation and self-determination contributed to a vibrant movement towards the creation of a separate province and provincial autonomy that challenged the INC emphasis on the political goal of a centralized nation state. Chapter 3 examines the meaning and implications of federation in late-colonial India broadly, as well as anti-colonial nationalism's engagement with federation more specifically. Was federation a break with the past or a continuation of empire? In this chapter, I argue that emergent political movements within the princely state of Hyderabad were anti-monarchical, threatening the integrity of the Hyderabad state. I examine how, in the interwar period, a dynamic anti-colonial nationalist movement led by Nehru and Mohandas K. Gandhi confronted and negotiated with what they clearly saw as alternative political imaginaries arising from uneven forms of rule instituted by British colonial rule—imaginaries that had to be disciplined by the INC's own version of an effective anti-colonial nationalism. The problem of federation as posed by the hundreds of princely states included their reluctance to give up their sovereignty. It became clear that the federation proposals from the princes and their administrators did not harbor emancipatory politics. There were distinct political interests that divided the goals of the Hyderabad state's administration against the states' people's movements. The latter were working towards a federated Indian Union and were committed not simply to Hyderabad as a sovereign political unit but rather to the extension of citizenship rights to the people therein and the building up of institutions for a robust representative government.

Chapters 4 and 5 turn to public associations in Hyderabad and the Madras Presidency and how they navigated the new political terrain of mass politics. Chapter 4 interrogates what is distinctive about the 1930s in Hyderabad. How do we understand the politics of the period through an examination of its public organizations and vernacular publics? Such framing of the question is needed in order to step back from the volatile politics of the 1940s when INC-led anti-colonial nationalism, the Majlis-e-Ittehadul Muslimeen's call for a popular monarchy and independent status for Hyderabad, and the emerging strength of the communist revolution in the Telangana countryside clashed with one another, producing a political impasse in 1947. Analysing debates about civil liberty within the burgeoning public sphere, this chapter attempts to uncover the complex set of relations (antagonisms as well as overlapping concerns) between the Hyderabad administration, civil societal organizations, and print publics. I track the discourse of civil liberty as employed by the most vibrant public organizations in the 1930s in order to see how it impacted conversations more broadly regarding political representation within a reformed and potentially independent Hyderabad.

Finally, Chapter 5 further explores the broader sociopolitical conditions for civic life in the Madras Presidency and delves, in particular, into the conditions for the rise of the AMS and the political imaginaries it enabled. The AMS arose simultaneously in princely Hyderabad and in the Madras Presidency as a dynamic cultural organization that ultimately engendered conflicting political ideologies. In essence, the AMS became the primary site for politicizing Telugu-speaking intellectuals, writers, and activists who entered civil societal institutions and sought to prepare themselves for democratic politics. After two decades of its existence, the members of the AMS began to splinter into opposing political ideologies. The book's concluding chapter turns to the immediate post-colonial period to reflect on the broader discourses of citizenship and political modernity that defined the politics of the region—from its emergence in the colonial and nationalist periods to its post-colonial afterlives. How did the post-colonial Indian Union after British withdrawal approach the question of regional autonomy and the redrawing of provinces and states after the breakdown of federation options in the 1930s? The chapter considers the precarious position of the Indian Union in the immediate aftermath of independence and the logic and momentum of the linguistic reorganization of states in the 1950s.

Notes

1. See C. A. Bayly, *Recovering Liberties: Indian Thought in the Age of Liberalism and Empire* (Cambridge, UK: Cambridge University Press, 2012).
2. Bayly, *Recovering Liberties*, 7.
3. See Erez Manela, *The Wilsonian Moment Self-Determination and the Origins of Anticolonial Nationalism* (New York: Oxford University Press, 2007).
4. From the important early work of Partha Chatterjee, particularly his *The Nation and Its Fragments* (Princeton, NJ: Princeton University Press, 1993), to more recent work on anti-colonial nationalism in British India such as Sunil Purushotham's *From Raj to Republic: Sovereignty, Violence, and Democracy in India* (Stanford, CA: Stanford University Press, 2021).

5. See Michele L. Louro, *Comrades against Imperialism: Nehru, India, and Interwar Internationalism* (Cambridge, UK: Cambridge University Press, 2018); Manu Goswami, 'Colonial Internationalisms and Imaginary Futures', *American Historical Review* 117, no. 5 (2012): 1461–1485; Manu Bhagavan, 'Princely States and the Making of Modern India: Internationalism, Constitutionalism and the Postcolonial Moment', *Indian Economic and Social History Review* 46, no. 3 (2009): 427–456.
6. See Frederick Cooper, *Citizenship between Empire and Nation: Remaking France and French Africa, 1945–1960* (Princeton, NJ: Princeton University Press), Kindle edition; and Gary Wilder, *Freedom Time: Negritude, Decolonization, and the Future of the World* (Durham, NC: Duke University Press, 2015).
7. Adom Getachew, *Worldmaking after Empire: The Rise and Fall of Self-Determination* (Princeton, NJ: Princeton University Press, 2019). See also Christopher Lee, *Making a World after Empire: The Bandung Moment and Its Political Afterlives* (Athens, OH: Ohio University Press, 2010) for work on post-imperial solidarities connecting African and Asian anti-colonial leaders.
8. See Manela, *The Wilsonian Moment Self-Determination* and Susan Pederson, *The Guardians: The League of Nations and the Crisis of Empire* (New York: Oxford University Press, 2015).
9. Partha Chatterjee, 'Nationalism, Internationalism and Cosmopolitanism', *Comparative Study of South Asia, Africa and the Middle East* 36, no. 2 (2016): 320–334.
10. See Bhagavan, 'Princely States', 427–456.
11. See Sumathi Ramaswamy, *Passions of the Tongue: Language Devotion in Tamil India, 1891–1970* (Berkeley: University of California Press, 1997) and Lisa Mitchell, *Language, Emotion, and Politics in South India: The Making of a Mother Tongue* (Bloomington: Indiana University Press, 2009).
12. Ian Copland, *The Princes of India in the Endgame of Empire, 1917–1947* (Cambridge, UK: Cambridge University Press, 1997).
13. Copland, *The Princes of India*, 339–340.
14. The royal family of Hyderabad intermarried with the last Ottoman emperor in the twentieth century, which illustrates the importance and continuity of the symbolic ties between the two in the post-World War I world. It is worth noting that no constitutional monarchy emerged after the dismantling of the Ottoman Empire.
15. Ian Copland and Barbara Ramusack were early pioneers in exploring the roots of peoples' movements that challenged monarchical authority within princely states. See Ian Copland, 'The Princely States, the Muslim League, and the Partition of India in 1947', *International History Review* 13, no. 1 (February 1991): 38–69 and Barbara Ramusack, *The Indian Princes and Their States*

(The New Cambridge History of India) (Cambridge, UK: Cambridge University Press, 2007).

16. See Bhagavan, 'Princely States', 427–456; Janaki Nair, *Mysore Modern: Rethinking the Region under Princely Rule* (Hyderabad: Orient Blackswan, 2011). Bhagavan has written eloquently about Jawaharlal Nehru's vision of fundamental rights being extended to the princely states and integrating those states into the Indian Union despite their resistance. Nair has examined the princely state of Mysore, known for being uniquely progressive. She examines the workings of indirect rule in princely Mysore, specifically looking at the shaping of what she calls a 'monarchical modern' form of power at the height of anti-colonial nationalism in British Indian provinces. Her analysis of how the institution of monarchy underwent sweeping changes during this period is useful in understanding the princely states as dynamic spaces rather than static old-world autocracies.

17. See Sunil Purushotham, 'Democratic Origins III: Violence and/in the Making of Indian Democracy', in *Indian Democracy: Origins, Trajectories, Contestations*, edited by Alf Gunvald Nilsen, Kenneth Bo Nielsen, and Anand Vaidya, 39–50 (London: Pluto Press, 2019); Taylor Sherman, *Muslim Belonging in Secular India: Negotiating Citizenship in Postcolonial Hyderabad* (Cambridge, UK: Cambridge University Press, 2015); Sarah Ansari and William Gould, *Boundaries of Belonging: Localities, Citizenship and Rights in India and Pakistan* (Cambridge, UK: Cambridge University Press, 2019); Purushotham, *From Raj to Republic*.

18. See Eric Lewis Beverley, *Hyderabad, British India, and the World: Muslim Networks and Minor Sovereignty, c. 1850–1950* (New York: Cambridge University Press, 2015) and Kavita Datla, *The Language of Secular Islam: Urdu Nationalism and Colonial India* (Honolulu: University of Hawaii Press, 2013).

19. Margrit Pernau, *The Passing of Patrimonialism: Politics and Political Culture in Hyderabad 1911–1948* (New Delhi: Manohar, 2000), 107.

20. Datla, *The Language of Secular Islam*, 47–49.

21. Shefali Jha draws attention to the irony of founding a vernacular university in Hyderabad, a state whose major spoken languages were Telugu, Marathi, and Kannada rather than Urdu. A Hyderabadi sociologist, Amir Ali, who Jha writes about, suggests that this emphasis on Urdu education (as opposed to English education) may have further alienated the bulk of the population and the professional elites. See Shefali Jha, 'Democracy on a Minor Note: The All-India Majlis-e-ittehad'ul Muslimin and Its Hyderabadi Muslim Publics', PhD dissertation, University of Chicago, 2017, 54.

22. Beverley, *Hyderabad, British India, and the World*, 49. See also Faisal Devji, *Muslim Zion: Pakistan as a Political Idea* (Cambridge, MA: Harvard

University Press, 2013). Devji has written persuasively about how Muslim nationalism and internationalism emerged within empires as the imperial form itself was being called into question.

23. See Datla, *The Language of Secular Islam*; Beverley, *Hyderabad, British India, and the World*; and Purushotham, *From Raj to Republic*.
24. All-India States Peoples' Conference, *Mr. Bhulabhai J. Desai and The Peoples of the States* (Bombay: All-India States' People's Conference, 1947), 6.
25. All-India States Peoples' Conference, *Mr. Bhulabhai J. Desai*, 19.
26. All-India States Peoples' Conference, *Mr. Bhulabhai J. Desai*, 22–23.
27. See Kavita Datla, 'The Origins of Indirect Rule in India: Hyderabad and the British Imperial Order', *Law and History Review* 33, no. 2 (May 2015): 321–350; and Kavita Datla, 'Sovereignty and the End of Empire: The Transition to Independence in Colonial Hyderabad', *Ab Imperio* 3 (2018): 63–88. Also see Sarath Pillai, 'Fragmenting the Nation: Divisible Sovereignty and Travancore's Quest for Federal Independence', *Law and History Review* 34, no. 3 (August 2016): 743–782. Bharati Ray traces the political history of the emergence of the princely state of Hyderabad and its relations with the British from the first treaty in the late eighteenth century to discussions leading to Indian independence. See Bharati Ray, *Hyderabad and British Paramountcy, 1858–1883* (New York: Oxford University Press, 1988).
28. See Pernau, *The Passing of Patrimonialism* and Beverley, *Hyderabad, British India, and the World*.
29. Margrit Pernau's most important contribution, however, centres on the workings of patrimonialism in Hyderabad and political reforms encouraged by the British. Beverley suggests a tension between a culture of patrimonialism and the emergence of modern bureaucracy in Hyderabad after the reforms initiated by Salar Jung I in the latter half of the nineteenth century. Both Pernau and Carolyn Elliot develop the thesis of patrimonialism and how it shaped Hyderabadi politics. For Elliot, patrimonialism was a sign of the lack of political parties voicing a diversity of political opinion. See Pernau, *The Passing of Patrimonialism*; Beverley, *Hyderabad, British India, and the World*; and Carolyn Elliot, 'Decline of a Patrimonial Regime: The Telangana Rebellion in India 1946–1951', *Journal of Asian Studies* 34, no. 4 (November 1974): 27–47.
30. See John Roosa, 'The Quandary in the Qaum: Indian Nationalism in a Muslim State, Hyderabad, 1850–1948', PhD dissertation, University of Wisconsin–Madison, 1998; and Lucien Benichou, *From Autocracy to Integration: Political Developments in Hyderabad State (1938–1948)* (Chennai: Orient Longman, 2000). Benichou and Roosa both examine the tumultuous period of the early twentieth century by tracing politics on the ground as they emerged.

Their work is pivotal in understanding popular movements and politics in Hyderabad from the 1930s until Hyderabad's forcible merger with the Indian Union in 1948. Their work importantly laid the groundwork to explore in depth the rise of democratic politics in the decades leading to Hyderabad's merger with India. A. Suneetha and Moid in their article on the historical role of the Majlis place them squarely in the rise of representative democracy in Hyderabad. Suneetha and Moid's contribution is notable in the scholarship on Hyderabad as it shifts to a consideration of civil societal associations and their aspirations rather than a focus on the administration and its negotiations with the British government. See M.A. Moid and A. Suneetha, 'Rethinking Majlis Politics: Pre-1948 Muslim Concerns in Hyderabad State,' *Indian Economic and Social History Review* 55, no. 1 (2018): 29–52. For further discussion of the Majlis and its transformation into a political party in post-independence India, see Shefali Jha, 'Democracy on a Minor Note'.
31. Moid and Suneetha, 'Rethinking Majlis Politics', 32.
32. For more discussion on the Majlis, see Chapter 4.
33. For the Hyderabad context, see Moid and Suneetha, 'Rethinking Majlis Politics'. For a broader understanding of Muslim sovereignty in a global context based on a reading of Muhammad Iqbal and Sayyad Qutb, see Sherali Tareen, 'Narratives of Emancipation in Modern Islam: Temporality, Hermeneutics, and Sovereignty', *Islamic Studies* 52, no. 1 (Spring 2013): 5–28.
34. Ian Copland, 'The Princely States'.
35. Taylor Sherman's research investigates violence and the state in colonial India, more specifically the aftermath of the 1948 police action when the Indian army forcibly integrated Hyderabad. Sherman's work reveals the ways in which the Muslim community in Hyderabad were 'integrated' into the larger national conversation, thereby producing a 'trans-regional' idea of a Muslim minority—a particularly important point to think through when considering the politics of the Majlis. See Taylor Sherman, *State Violence and Punishment in India* (London: Routledge, 2009) and Sherman, *Muslim Belonging in Secular India*.
36. Sunil Purushotham's work similarly offers an analysis of violence as foundational to the making of the Indian nation state by connecting the violence of police action in Hyderabad and the communist-led insurgency in Telangana in 1947–1948 to the larger history of partition and the exchange of populations at the moment of independence. See Sunil Purushotham, 'Destroying Hyderabad and Making the Nation', *Economic and Political Weekly* 49, no. 22 (31 May 2014): 29–33 and Purushotham, 'Democratic Origins III'. Purushotham's work builds on A. G. Noorani, *The Destruction of Hyderabad* (London: Hurst, 2014) and Srinath Raghavan, *War and Peace in Modern India* (London:

37. My previous research centred on the Madras Presidency—the area of British India under direct rule—and particularly the work of Colin Mackenzie, a Scottish surveyor, in producing cartographic and historical knowledge of the territories conquered by the British after the defeat of the southern Indian ruler of Mysore, Tipu Sultan. See Rama Sundari Mantena, *The Origins of Modern Historiography in India: Antiquarianism and Philology, 1780–1880* (New York: Palgrave Macmillan, 2012). My work on British colonial archives of the Madras Presidency led to questions concerning language and provincial politics in relation to the nationalist movement. These questions, when extended beyond the borders to the neighbouring princely state of Hyderabad which shares language and culture across the boundaries of its territory, led to this book. Clearly, there were parallel developments in the realms of both civil society and political culture.

Palgrave Macmillan, 2009). Both Raghavan and Noorani revisit the Standstill Agreement between the newly independent Government of India and the Hyderabad administration and trace the events that led to an unleashing of violence during Operation Polo, or the forcible merger of the princely state with India.

38. A number of historians worked on the Non-Brahman movement and provincial politics focusing on Tamil sources. Some early influential studies of non-Brahminism were Eugene F. Irschick, *Politics and Social Conflict in South India: The Non-Brahman Movement and Tamil Separatism, 1916–1929* (Berkeley: University of California Press, 1969); Marguerite Ross Barnett, *The Politics of Cultural Nationalism in South India* (Princeton, NJ: Princeton University Press, 1976); M. S. S. Pandian, 'From Culture to Politics: The Justice Party', in *Brahmin and Non-Brahmin: Genealogies of the Tamil Present*, 144–186 (New Delhi: Permanent Black, 2007).

39. This includes pivotal work of David Washbrook on the Madras Presidency and Christopher John Baker's work on south Indian politics in the two decades following M. K. Gandhi's entrance onto the national political stage. Both set the groundwork for understanding the rise of provincial politics in south India. In his pivotal work, *The Emergence of Provincial Politics*, Washbrook examines the intricate colonial bureaucracy built throughout the nineteenth century. See David Washbrook, *The Emergence of Provincial Politics: The Madras Presidency 1870–1920* (Cambridge, UK: Cambridge University Press, 1976) and Christopher John Baker, *The Politics of South India 1920–1937* (Cambridge, UK: Cambridge University Press, 1976).

40. See Baker, *The Politics of South India* and Washbrook, *The Emergence of Provincial Politics*.

41. Baker, *The Politics of South India*, 1.

42. Baker, *The Politics of South India*, 20.
43. Baker, *The Politics of South India*, 23.
44. C. R. Reddy, 'Dyarchy and After', *Indian Review* 23, no. 5 (May 1922): 294–304.
45. Robert Eric Frykenberg, *Guntur District, 1788–1848: A History of Local Influence and Central Authority in South India* (New York: Oxford University Press, 1965).
46. Madras was often depicted in nationalist historiography as a provincial backwater until Annie Besant politicized the region by introducing nationalist politics.
47. The Home Rule movement was led by Bal Gangadhar Tilak and Annie Besant. For a discussion of the tension between the INC and the Justice Party in the Madras Presidency, see Pandian, 'From Culture to Politics', 149.
48. See Irschick, *Politics and Social Conflict in South India* and Barnett, *The Politics of Cultural Nationalism in South India*.
49. M. S. S. Pandian, 'Beyond Colonial Crumbs: Cambridge School, Identity Politics and Dravidian Movement(s)', *Economic and Political Weekly* 30, nos. 7–8 (February 1995): 385–391.
50. The Self-Respect movement was led by E. V. Ramasamy, or Periyar, in the 1920s after breaking with Gandhi and the INC for their conservatism and their refusal to take into discussion his proposal of 'communal representation' of non-Brahmins in the legislatures. M. S. S. Pandian, 'The Brahmin as a Trope: The Self-Respect Movement', in *Brahmin and Non-Brahmin: Genealogies of the Tamil Present* (New Delhi: Permanent Black, 2007), 190.
51. See M. S. S. Pandian, 'One Step outside Modernity: Caste, Identity Politics and Public Sphere', *Economic and Political Weekly* 37, no. 18 (4 May 2002): 1735–1741.
52. Gundimeda Sambaiah argues that non-Brahmanism does not take hold in Telugu regions because the lower castes organized under the 'Adi' ideology rather than Dravidianism because the non-Brahmin castes, such as the Reddys, Kammas, Kapus, and the Rajus, were in fact dominant castes. Sambaiah further argues that the non-Brahmin groups in Andhra were not really critiquing brahminical power as such, but rather they were seeking to gain that cultural and symbolic power—in other words, very different politics from anti-caste movements. See Gundimeda Sambaiah, 'Mapping Dalit Politics in Contemporary India: A Study of UP and AP from an Ambedkarite Perspective', PhD thesis, Department of Politics, SOAS, University of London, 2013.
53. The work of anthropologists—specifically Bernard Bate's work—provides another framework to reconsider early-twentieth-century politics in south India.

See Bernard Bate, *Tamil Oratory and the Dravidian Aesthetic: Democratic Practice in South India* (New York: Columbia University Press, 2009).

54. The Justice Party and the Self-Respect movement initiated the Dravidian movement in the Madras Presidency. The movement began as a recognition of the dominance of the Brahmin caste in the colonial administration, educational institutions, and finally the INC. See Irschik, *Politics and Social Conflict in South India*; Pandian, 'The Brahmin as a Trope'; and Bate, *Tamil Oratory and the Dravidian Aesthetic*.
55. Irschick, *Politics and Social Conflict in South India*, 244.
56. See John Greenfield Leonard, 'Kandukuri Viresalingam, 1848–1919: A Biography of an Indian Social Reformer', PhD dissertation, University of Wisconsin–Madison, 1970; and Peter Schmithenner, *Telugu Resurgence: C.P. Brown and Cultural Consolidation in Nineteenth-Century South India* (New Delhi: Manohar, 2001).
57. See Velcheru Narayana Rao, ' Print and Prose: Pundits, Karanams, and the East India Company in the Making of Modern Telugu', in *India's Literary History: Essays on the Nineteenth Century*, ed. Stuart Blackburn and Vasudha Dalmia, 146–166 (New Delhi: Permanent Black, 2004).
58. See Rama Sundari Mantena, 'Vernacular Publics and Political Modernity: Language and Progress in Colonial South India', *Modern Asian Studies* 47, no. 5 (2013): 1678–1705.
59. See Gautham Reddy, 'The Andhra Sahitya Parishat: Language, Nation and Empire in Colonial South India (1911–15)', *Indian Economic and Social History Review* 56, no. 3 (2019): 283–310.
60. Mitchell, *Language, Emotion, and Politics*.
61. What these interventions in Telugu cultural history neglect, however, are the different historical trajectories for Telangana and the Telugu districts of the Madras Presidency. Benjamin Cohen's work on the 'little' kings, or *samasthan*s, of princely Hyderabad delves into their unique political formation and their cultural, economic, and political ties to the pre-colonial kingdoms of the Kakatiyas and the Vijayanagara Empire. Cohen argues that as a princely state, Hyderabad was built on pre-colonial institutions from the Kakatiyas to the Qutb Shahis and that the Nizam state saw itself as a multiethnic polity. See Benjamin B. Cohen, *Kingship and Colonialism in India's Deccan: 1850–1948* (New York: Palgrave Macmillan, 2007).
62. Pandian, in his analysis of the Justice Party and their politics, explains that the Justice Party movement was the coming together of various organizations who were concerned with both questions of representation and social questions— what Pandian calls the pedagogic. The AMS clearly lines up with what Pandian

  describes in Madras and the emergence of the non-Brahmin critique, though for the AMS there was no real caste critique even as caste reform was taken up. See Pandian, 'From Culture to Politics', 157.
63. See R. Suntharalingam, *Politics and Nationalist Awakening in South India, 1852–1891* (Tucson, AZ: University of Arizona Press, 1974).
64. Sambaiah, *Mapping Dalit Politics*, 214.
65. Sambaiah, *Mapping Dalit Politics*, 217.
66. 'Tank Bund Statues Thrown into Lake', *Asian Age*, 10 March 2011.

1
Liberalism and Anti-Colonialism in South India

In his sweeping history of Indian liberalism, *Recovering Liberties*, C. A. Bayly argues for the need to reassess a broad range of nineteenth-century Indian thought in pursuit of political and social liberty. Bayly draws attention to the complexities of studying liberal thought in colonial India even as liberalism was quite obviously constrained and compromised by what Eric Stokes had earlier identified as authoritarian in its colonial career.[1] The contradictions of liberalism and empire have been recently explored by a broad range of scholars.[2] Despite the complexity of imperial politics and the contradictory career of liberalism in the colony, Indian liberal thought emerged, Bayly argues, in the nineteenth century into a powerful political and social discourse arguing for a set of personal freedoms in pursuit of political and social liberties.[3] While the language of liberalism offered Indians a way to argue for political and social liberties, under the constraints of colonial rule, the ways in which they formulated demands for rights and freedoms cannot be folded into the historical trajectory of classical liberalism. The rise of new political discourses that re-energized public spheres (particularly with the expansion of vernacular public spheres) at the turn of the twentieth century brought forth new political activism and debates over freedom, individual rights, and civil liberties. In essence, what we see at the turn of the twentieth century is the rise of political imaginaries shaped by ideas of self-rule and self-determination, which in turn led to a deepening of Indians' commitment to institutions of democracy alongside the rise of nationalisms. Furthermore, during the early decades of the twentieth century, there were competing political imaginaries pulling intellectuals and activists from an exclusive focus on the nation to that on conceptualizing the region and interests specific to the region. The turn to the region, I argue, shifts the story of nationalism in the colony to a story of democracy. What does a turn to building democratic institutions mean at the regional level? With the Government of India Act of 1919 and the devolution schemes that enabled local governing, there also emerged regional discourses of self-government and self-rule that energized activist intellectuals, prompting them to shift their attention from building nationalist solidarity (to aid anti-colonial nationalism) to expanding local and regional democratic culture.[4] While an earlier historiography laid emphasis on devolution schemes as instigating a competition among elites, I turn to the region to see how the idea of self-rule helped to shape democratic practices and institutions. Within this context, we see a debate fomenting around discourses of social reformism and the emergent politics of *swaraj* (self-rule). Regional activists in the northern Madras Presidency began to assess the work of social reform throughout the long nineteenth century alongside its relation to political discourses of self-representation and self-determination. This chapter traces the shift from public debate being centred on social reform that dominated the nineteenth century to conceptualizing and building political community. How did this shift to building political community shape the region? In order to understand how public debate and political activism in this period shifted in this direction, one must turn to the region.

From the standpoint of the region, what we see is that alongside social reform activism (and the expansion of progressive politics) arose an enduring form of Indian conservatism. Not merely a defence of 'traditional' or customary practices, conservative thought sought to limit reformist intervention to religious practice and institutions.[5] The attempt to limit reformism dates to the early nineteenth century with colonial debates over legislating Hindu practices of widowhood. While tracking the rise of liberal thought, it might be useful to begin by disaggregating the disparate strands of liberalism in colonial India, thereby distinguishing liberal conservatives and their work to preserve the 'home' or the private sphere from being tainted by the 'alien' colonial state and, by extension, by radical social reformers who attempted to address caste, gender, and other social inequalities.[6] It is within this context of the rise of a new liberal politics and institutions embraced by regional activists alongside the rise of conservatism and progressivism—specifically with regards to the kind of social change that should accompany freedom from colonial rule—that I turn to the life and work of J. Gurunatham, an intellectual who spearheaded the Andhra movement, a regionalist movement in British India in the northern Madras Presidency. The movement emerged in the late colonial era but only really erupted onto the national stage immediately after independence. I argue that the Andhra movement was more than an ethnic regionalist movement; rather, it was a complex sociopolitical one that brought together cultural and political conservatives, progressives, and radicals to make an argument for the formation of a linguistic province and, later in the post-colonial era, a regional state. However, the motivations for arguing for a linguistic province, especially in the decades leading up to independence, were more complex than the scholarship on linguistic nationalisms or subnationalisms have led us to understand. Articulations of cultural revival or linguistic and ethnic identity were accompanied by arguments about regional autonomy, self-determination, and building of democratic institutions and culture. Regional movements, such as the Andhra movement, at critical moments were strategically inclusive of both conservative and progressive elements. Gurunatham was crucial to the Andhra movement in its initial years, and his writings give us a lens into a particular kind of cultural politics in late-colonial south India that set the region on the path to a democratic future. In one of the few publications attributed to Gurunatham, he launched a scathing critique of the famed reformer Kandukuri Viresalingam and the practices of social reformism itself, and crafted a position that sought to balance a critique of Hinduism with a what he saw as the need for a robust politics stemming from the standpoint of the region.[7] Anti-colonialism gave rise to a broad range of political responses in British India as it emerged from colonial domination, and for Gurunatham the politics of social reform was limited in its scope. In other words, social reform in itself as a broad regional and national movement, Gurunatham argued, was not capable of envisioning or animating a broader political response that was critical in the anti-colonial struggle. His conception of regional autonomy that would give rise to a robust politics was held together by an idea of a federated India made up of provinces organized around language.

Bayly persuasively argues that Indian liberalism was an embattled political ideology throughout the nineteenth century that often faced critique from conservative forces, from the landed gentry, including the native princes and religious nationalisms, as well as from progressive forces such as Gandhian nationalists and Indian communists.[8] During the nationalist era, conservatives saw political challenge from liberals and socialists such as Jawaharlal Nehru, whose commitment to social change, whether pertaining to caste or gender inequality, would lead to the potential erosion of Hinduism, Hindu institutions, and the upholding of the Hindu social order and upper-caste dominance.[9] The self-avowed conservative party, the Swatantra Party, emerged after independence in 1959 to represent the political interests of the conservatives who wanted gradual change and accepted that change had to be sought through liberal democratic institutions to represent the interests of the electorate—even if those interests conflicted with the moderates' own political goals. With a shared commitment to liberal institutions, both conservatives and progressives within the Indian National Congress (INC) embraced the idea that rational exchange across political lines was possible to produce consensus or accommodation.

The Hindu nationalists, however, came from a different trajectory altogether. They diverged from the INC's strategy of forging a multi-religious and multiethnic national identity and sought to uphold Hindu identity as the dominant national culture supported by Hindu institutions. In the wake of the formation of the (AIML) in 1906, Hindu organizations came together to assert majoritarian politics. Hindu nationalism had different strands at its origins—ranging from quite radical reformist agendas to removal of untouchability (a platform that the Arya Samaj took up, for example) to more majoritarian agendas of asserting Hindu dominance (the Hindu Mahasabha, for example).[10] As documented by many scholars, the Hindutva movement, as conceived by V. D. Sarvarkar, drew its inspiration from European fascist politics.[11] In the immediate independence period when political parties had to test their strength and reach as they participated in the electoral process, the Rashtriya Swayamsevak Sangh (RSS)—the extreme wing of Hindu nationalists—was banned from participating in the political process after the assassination of Mohandas K. Gandhi in January 1948 by one of their enthusiastic supporters. Keeping in mind the various trajectories of anti-colonial politics, this chapter tracks political life in colonial Andhra, the Telugu-speaking districts comprising the northern coastal districts of the Madras Presidency. In particular, it charts the emergence of liberal political discourses giving rise to both conservatism and progressivism. It also tracks how those discourses animated regionalist aspirations such as the Andhra movement from the 1910s to the 1950s and defined provincial politics in the colonial era.

According to historian Howard L. Erdman, Indian conservatism confronted great challenges throughout the nineteenth century from social reformists who advocated radical proposals for dramatic changes with regards to caste and gender inequality in traditional Hindu society.[12] If a kind of conservatism was taking shape in the midst of nineteenth-century social reformism, how do we track it and identify its core elements? The familiar history is that the long nineteenth century saw the rise of dynamic social reform movements led by reformers (regionally and locally situated) who questioned customary religious practices that shaped the status of Hindu and Muslim women and lower-caste communities. Parallel to these movements arose what were called 'traditionalist' responses to these radical proposals. The most famous was of the formation of the Dharma Sabha in early-nineteenth-century Bengal as a response to the colonial attempt to abolish the practice of *sati* in the 1820s. The abolition movement found an ally in a Bengali intellectual and reformer, Raja Rammohun Roy. Thus, social reform from its origins in early-nineteenth-century colonial India has been depicted in the historiography as a contest between modernizers and traditionalists couched in the discourse of modernization.[13] However, what we miss in this characterization of modernization is the emergence of colonial publics and liberal democratic institutions in the midst of the age of reform.[14] Viewed through this lens, we can see that Indian social reformists were in essence setting the stage for articulating a progressive politics in opposition to a growing conservative response, which sought to defend inherited customs and traditions as integral to values and practices that sustained pre-colonial social and cultural life. In other words, if we recast the so-called radical and traditionalist responses as political responses that set the course of Indian politics on a democratic path, we have a framework to understand the rise of political conservatism (alongside progressivism) in colonial India.

Bayly wrote the history of the nineteenth century as the story of the rise of Indian liberalism. The age of social reform and ideas of social liberty clearly shaped Indian liberalism and gave impetus to the emergence of democratic politics that shaped not only anti-colonial nationalism but also the founding of the Indian republic in the aftermath of British imperial rule. Recasting this history with the objective of tracking different political ideologies, such as progressivism and conservatism, provides a more complex political history of the late colonial period in Indian history—one that does not reduce the multiplicity of political imaginaries to a singular nationalist narrative of anti-colonialism. Moreover, the conservative response was not simply Janus-faced in making the return to traditional life a primary goal. Rather, I argue that political conservatism also charted out a path in the framework of new democratic futures. Viewing the age of reform in the context of the rise of democratic politics gives us a more dynamic framework to understand the tensions that erupted in the nationalist era.[15]

A key factor that facilitated the gradual entrenchment of liberal institutions in British India was the rise of vibrant forms of publicity—in particular, the proliferation of vernacular language newspapers. New forms of publicity indeed prepared the way and created avenues for the emergence of a range of political ideologies from conservative to progressive. Both conservatives and progressives embraced forms of publicity and print in order to disseminate their political ideologies and strategies for shaping political futures of the region.[16] In addition, as Bernard Bate argues, novel forms of political speech entered southern India alongside the rise of anti-colonial nationalist agitation. It was in 1918–1919 that mass politics arrived in the Madras Presidency during the Gandhian phase of *swadeshi*. In particular, the organizing around the Rowlatt Act in Madras brought about this shift in politics characterized by political speeches specifically employing vernacular languages to directly address the people. Bate goes on to argue, 'The vernacular oratorical revolution ... entailed a new kind of agency on the part of an entirely new genre of political actor, the vernacular politician, who could now turn toward and evoke the participation of people formerly thought to be irrelevant at best and irrational and dangerous at worst.'[17] Thus, the emergence of the vernacular politician ushered in a new form of democratic politics because the vernacular politician could now directly address the people to appeal to their particular interests. Using regional languages to speak to a particular linguistic community rendered that community as distinct from neighbouring languages and communities.

In the Telugu-speaking districts, the Andhra movement gave rise to the vernacular politician who began to see the crowds as a community in need of political organization and started to use Telugu in speaking directly to the people. The Andhra movement began in the northern coastal districts of the Madras Presidency but spread far and wide into the princely state of Hyderabad and even threatened the integrity of the erstwhile princely state at times. The movement was significant in politicizing the Telugu-speaking community across borders. J. Gurunatham, a member of the Young Men's Literary Association (1903–1904) in Guntur, a teacher at the Christian College of Guntur, who later became secretary of the rajah of Kurupam (in Vizianagaram district), and finally a member of the Supreme Legislative Council, understood the necessity of training people to become citizens. He knew that this very much depended on expanding civic life for people to engage in, which would eventually prepare the way for the people to organize into a political community. Only then would communities from the region be able to imagine their place in a democratic future. In organizing a regional political and cultural movement, Gurunatham's project was largely to extend democratic reforms and institutions in the Telugu-speaking districts of the Madras Presidency. Not surprisingly, the use of the vernacular at the turn of the twentieth century enabled visions of a new democratic society based on ideas of equality and individual freedom. This rights discourse was not only circulating internationally with the onset of World War I and the subsequent formation of the League of Nations, but also within colonial India in the form of growing calls for the expansion of liberal reforms and self-government. An illustration of this new mode of politicization at the regional level, the Andhra Mahasabha (AMS), the primary organ of the Andhra movement, was created because Telugu speakers felt uncomfortable in a Tamil-dominated colonial administration and in an INC unit. The initiative to begin another association for the political, cultural, and social work of Telugu speakers identified language as the cohering and potentially radicalizing element. The turn to the vernacular language rather than English made possible the articulation of the distinct concerns of the different districts—forming into a region—and voicing their unique social, cultural, and political viewpoints. This is what the organizers of the AMS envisioned. This turn to the vernacular in political organizing and activism energized the movement for a separate Andhra province, but it also drew attention to a new democratic politics that viewed direct communication with its people as of primary importance.

Gurunatham was firmly rooted in local associational life in the northern coastal districts of the Madras Presidency. He wrote frequently for *The Hindu* on matters of advancing the cause of the Andhra movement. He came to be regarded as one of the founders of the Andhra movement, which soon began to agitate for establishing a separate province for Telugu speakers that would break up the bigger province of Madras. The Andhra movement was indeed the culmination of earlier nineteenth-century cultural and literary associations that mobilized around the Telugu language.[18] Before the founding of the AMS, Gurunatham wrote a fascinating biography of the towering nineteenth-century reformer Viresalingam, based in Rajahmundry, in 1911, which offers insight into the political debates taking place in the early decades of the twentieth century in the northern coastal districts of the Madras Presidency.[19] The biography of the most famous social reformer in the Telugu-speaking region allowed Gurunatham to tease out the advancements that were made by nineteenth-century associational life with regards to the Telugu language and culture while also drawing out the inadequacies of social reformism. Gurunatham observed significant social and political changes taking place at the turn of the twentieth century. However, the primary object of critique offered in his book on Viresalingam was directed at the agendas of social reformism. To sum up his arguments, he viewed social reform and reformists as lacking clear political vision and that their progressive politics remained limited to the superficial change of Hindu customs and practices, without addressing the underlying economic and political conditions that needed improvement; the latter would lead to the improvement of the Telugu people as a community. Gurunatham argued that social reformers were well-intentioned in their efforts to instil critical scepticism towards Hindu rituals, but they did absolutely nothing to politicize the region and organize the people, let alone proposing changes to transform the regions economically and politically. Most importantly, social reformism did not organize the community and move them towards a liberal democratic future. The reforms did not lead people to creatively imagine new democratic futures. Gurunatham argued that in order for the Telugu people to perceive themselves as a political community with specific interests that needed to be represented and thereby take part in the march towards self-government, something had to change. In essence, Gurunatham saw that the ground had to be prepared for representative institutions to take hold. Towards that end, he called for the Telugu people to orient themselves towards building political community in the region or province to garner political aspirations. In that sense, for Gurunatham, political reform was more crucial than social reform at this critical juncture in colonial history. Political reform encompassed a great deal—from fostering civil societal institutions centred on the development of the region and appreciation of developments in the field of language and literature to conducting public debates on what a responsible government would entail for the region. Gurunatham outlined these concerns in his recounting of the colonial history of Andhra and its embracing of social reformism—a discourse he characterized as alien to the internal dynamic of the Telugu-speaking region.

Gurunatham argued that Andhra (the Telugu-speaking coastal districts) was particularly underprepared for democratic change and democratic reform, in distinct contrast to the Bengalis, the Marathas, and the Punjabis. The three linguistic groups he references were all active in not only nationalist politics but also religious and social reform activism throughout the nineteenth centuries. Andhra, however, emerged from different political and social conditions. This was so, he argued, because the latter groups (the Bengalis, Marathas, and Punjabis) all had to contend directly with British armies when their territories were violently conquered. The Telugu people, on the other hand, had their districts transferred from the Nizam of Hyderabad to the British, thus effecting a change in the head of state without any violent confrontation, and therefore technically not conquered. The Nizam of Hyderabad, himself a breakaway governor from the withering Mughal imperial state, ruled the region passively (as an absentee landlord of sorts) as long as the people paid their taxes. Gurunatham elaborates this point:

> The Telugu country was merely transferred to their rule by means of an *inam*, or free gift. It was wholly in a disorganized and disunited condition. The military classes had vanished, the learned classes also had sunk into the background; the roots and the traders who formed really the vast bulk of the population enjoyed no peace and security; and were easily at the mercy of every freebooter and superstition-monger; while the whole country was under the sway of the Zamindary system.[20]

The sociopolitical conditions, he writes, were in disarray when the British arrived to fill a political vacuum. Not only was there no political cohesion or resistance to the turning of political fortunes, but the learned elite was also marginalized and the economic elite were left with little security. Gurunatham's pointing to superstition is noteworthy in that he singles out the cultural impact of the political conditions. His identifying of superstition as cultural decay is revealing in that his own religious commitments were presumably firmly grounded in reason (the opposite of superstition). He argues that the inertia that Andhra society fell into, which was then fostered by the Hyderabad state and the *zamindars* (landlords) (through sheer neglect rather than active plunder), persisted during much of the eighteenth century before the arrival of the British. One can look at Gurunatham's representation of this period as an indictment of the monarchical state that deprived the people of investment in their own region. Gurunatham described the *zamindars* as 'a class illiterate, cruel and tyrannical; lived the most immoral and extravagant lives and encouraged, rather thrived by, an endless system of intrigue and deceit'.[21] He blasted the *zamindars* as a worthless lot who encouraged hangers-on and had little motivation to foster a vibrant political life for the people. Here, Gurunatham offered a fairly standard liberal critique of feudal society. However, it is important to note that the *zamindars* historically were, in fact, often patrons of Telugu literature, a role they continued into the nineteenth century.[22] Indeed, some *zamindars* welcomed change and participated in political debates such as the rajas of Venkatagiri and Bobilli. Nonetheless, these were the social and political conditions that, Gurunatham argued, gave rise to what he called the 'passive intellectual' in the Telugu-speaking districts. The British inherited the northern coastal districts from the Nizam and allowed the free rein of the *zamindari* system, which did not cultivate the conditions for liberal institutions such as a vibrant public sphere. Gurunatham did concede that the modern Telugu intellectual was also the product of British introduction of an educational system and the civil service system that rewarded the meritorious (through the exam system) rather than the sycophancy of the former *zamindari* system. But he still characterized the Telugu intellectual who arose to ascendency under these conditions during the nineteenth century as a passive intellectual.

What made the nineteenth-century Telugu intellectual passive for Gurunatham was his enthusiastic and often blind embracing of a critique of religious custom and habit without attempting to develop a corollary vision of a political future. Social reformers such as Viresalingam were preoccupied with reforming what they saw as superstition (something we know that Gurunatham too abhorred) rather than preserving traditional institutions that needed to be passed onto the next generation. It is interesting to note Gurunatham's concern with cultural preservation in contrast to the social reformers who seemed unaware of the impact that their reforms would have on Telugu and, in this case, Hindu society. Studies of Viresalingam have routinely highlighted his embracing of reason and rationality in opposition to superstition and irrationality as a way to argue that the condition of women (and Hindu widows in particular) can be improved if Hindu practices, especially surrounding marriage and widowhood, were reformed.

Viresalingam's writings from his journalism to his literary endeavours are preoccupied with social reform and the cultivation of reason in the public sphere. Gurunatham's disagreement with Viresalingam was not with the use of reasoned debate to rethink Hindu custom but rather that religious belief needed to be understood in such a manner so as not to undermine religious morality. This underlying morality is what he believed was the glue that held Hindu society together. For Gurunatham, this short-sightedness of social reformism ran counter to the immediate necessity to organize the community and energize the public into political action with an eye towards a democratic future.

What, Gurunatham asked, were the true ends of the social reformist vision in Andhra? Because of the lack of political conditions that existed in the other regions such as Bengal and Punjab, the Telugu-speaking regions, he contended, saw the rise of a particular kind of intellectual who was by nature imitative rather than organic. Gurunatham argued that the passive intellectual did not imagine beyond the reformation of Telugu society in simple imitation of English society (as disseminated through the study of English literature and missionary teachings). When the British extended their sovereignty in the region, Gurunatham wrote, 'The introduction of English education and a public service tended to upset the old social equilibrium, without leading at the same time to any new adjustment of social and religious forces.'[23] He concedes that the dissemination of English education did the necessary work of upsetting 'the old social equilibrium' in as much as it instigated public life and the cultivation of civic virtue. His critique of social reform is not that it was simply an alien import because he actually welcomed English education. This is an important point because it undercuts the idea that social conservatives were uncritical adherents to tradition. Rather, we see that Gurunatham did not see the dissemination of English education as a threat. If English education did benefit Telugu society in that it upset 'the old social equilibrium', it did not do enough to cultivate democratic sensibilities in the people. However, the turn to public service did not lead to the realignment of what Gurunatham called the 'social and religious forces', which he believed was necessary for a vibrant polity. What a new adjustment of 'socio-religious forces' means in the context of his critique of Viresalingam is that reformists' attacks on Hindu religious custom and practice should lead productively to the formulation of new practices that would serve as a moral foundation for a new polity. Furthermore, Gurunatham sought to understand why social reformists limited themselves to the critique of social and religious customs and did not undertake a more ambitious critique that questioned the legitimacy of colonial rule. The latter would have indicated an interest in cultivating the new public- and civic-mindedness necessary to shape a new democratic polity.

Gurunatham's intellectual biography centred on the life and work of Viresalingam. Besides Madras, the northern coastal districts of Guntur, Rajahmundry, and Vizianagaram became vibrant centres of reformist and political activity in the nineteenth century. Viresalingam's reform work was primarily located in Rajahmundry, where he began the journal *Vivekavardhani* in 1874. The aim of the journal was twofold: the improvement of the Telugu-speaking people and the revitalization of the Telugu language. Viresalingam's social reform work also included the founding of the Rajahmundry Social Reform Association in 1878 and a Widows Marriage Association in Rajahmundry. His social reformism was driven by the idea of social improvement and mainly concerned with the eradication of what he saw as irrational customs that weighed on women in particular and Hindu society broadly. He was less concerned with reformulating Hindu religious practice and more with improving or modernizing as other religious reformists were committed to (such as members of the Arya Samaj or the Brahmo Samaj). Nyapathi Subba Rao, one of the founders of the prominent English newspaper *The Hindu*, in Madras, was also secretary of the Widows Marriage Association. At the association's public meeting held in 1888, Subba Rao declared:

> The 11th December 1881 is a red letter day in the annals of reform in the Madras Presidency, especially the Northern Circars, for on that day was inaugurated a reform dear to the heart of every one interested in the regeneration of our country and destined sooner or later to produce great results in the social fabric of the Hindu Society.... The reform is important.... [It] showed to the people at large that the reign of tyranny must come to an end and each institution must be judged by its fruits and judged by that standard.... To the friends of social reform, this movement is significant as it habituates the Hindu mind not to accept the order of things as they exist, simply because they have existed from time out of memory but to judge each institution on its own merits and ask whether it rightly serves a useful purpose.[24]

Subba Rao envisioned a vibrant public sphere where an individual could employ reason in debating the merits of each social institution. This, he argued, would lead to the regeneration of society—the opposite of what Gurunatham saw as leading to the eventual breakdown of Hindu and Telugu society. Subba Rao instrumentalized reason as a utilitarian tool that would measure each custom and practice on 'its own merits' and ask whether it serves any useful purpose in society. Viresalingam's prose writings are preoccupied with the cultivation of reason in the modern individual to question received tradition. Rajagopal Vakulabharanam has described this period of social reform in Andhra as inaugurating a new public sphere—a reformist public that enabled critique of Hindu-caste society by opening up customs and habits to public scrutiny.[25] The reformist public really enabled multiple public spheres, which opened otherwise closed communities to critique from caste 'outsiders'. What made the situation explosive was not the colonial gaze but the access other caste communities now had to scrutinize each community's private customs and habits. This opening cleared a path for a broader critique of caste and its place in Hindu society. Gurunatham, however, did not agree on this point with Subba Rao and Viresalingam—that just by opening up religious custom and habit to public scrutiny, enduring social transformation would follow. Rather, Gurunatham seemed to suggest there were limits to the discourse of public reason in that reason could only accomplish so much when confronting a religious community constituted on the basis of *moral obligation* and not rational discourse.

Viresalingam became prominent for not only his social reform activities but also his literary accomplishments. He wrote what is considered to be the first 'modern' Telugu novel, *Rajasekharacaritramu*, and the first autobiography in Telugu. In his autobiography, Viresalingam wrote that in order to improve the Telugu country and secure progress, 'we ought to work on all sides, for education, for social customs and practices and for moral and religious matters, without confining ourselves to politics alone'.[26] He went on to write, 'I thought that it was more advantageous to expose the evil acts of those who were with us, executing the laws of the Government than to criticise the laws and their makers who were somewhere far away from us.'[27] It is interesting to note in this passage that Viresalingam for all purposes resigned himself to remaining apolitical. Gurunatham highlighted these passages from Viresalingam's autobiography to point out that the latter's reformism was directed only at exposing 'evil acts of those who were with us'—it sought reform only within the community. To criticize the makers of laws far away seemed pointless to Viresalingam; the British were not just alien rulers but distant ones who had no impact on the daily lives of Indians. His essentially local and regional interventions sought to change the habits of one's community through appealing to existing customs. It is worth recalling Mahadev Ranade's broad conception of social change and the law. Ranade writes, 'All progress in social liberation tends to be a change from the law of status to the law of contract, from the restraints of family and caste customs to the self-imposed restraints of the free will of the individual.'[28] However, it was precisely this exclusive focus on Hindu custom in reformism practised by Viresalingam that Gurunatham opposed. For Gurunatham, it seemed an incomplete project to reform religious custom without addressing the social and political conditions that sustained those customs and habits.

Ultimately, Gurunatham's scathing critique of Viresalingam was that his reformism tackled only the external structure of Hinduism. Gurunatham also seemed to doubt Viresalingam's deep knowledge of Hindu texts, especially given his apparent lack of engagement with the Upanishads. Gurunatham wrote, 'Hinduism is the groundwork on which the national life of the people of the different parts of the country attained progress for hundreds of years.... Viresalingam Pantulu attacked the external organization of the religion, its theology based as it was on miracle and mystery and the expounded of this theology, viz. the priestly classes.'[29] Gurunatham faulted Viresalingam for formulating an external critique of Hinduism. He also suggested that Viresalingam got Hinduism wrong. In other words, instead of focusing on the external structures of Hindu ritual, why not examine the underlying set of beliefs that sustained what Gurunatham called 'national life'? Gurunatham charged that Viresalingam did not know Hinduism from its core texts. This clearly stands out as a strand of social conservatism expressed by Gurunatham to protect Hinduism from the onslaught of the social reformists. Gurunatham believed the reformists were flawed in their politicization of religion and that their critique was ultimately derivative, merely reacting to colonial public and missionary propaganda.

In Gurunatham's eyes, Viresalingam lacked 'historical imagination' too because he did not fully assess Hindu history and offered only a piecemeal form of moral and religious uplift.[30] This limited Viresalingam's understanding of the existing political conditions of the Telugu country. In fact, Gurunatham argued that social reformism was misplaced in Andhra because it did not arise from local social conditions at all but was rather transplanted from Bengal. The social conditions in Bengal were such that it necessitated the Brahmo movement. In colonial Bengal, England-returned Bengali men questioned the social customs of Hindus and were then cast out by the orthodox community. The Brahmo movement was radical but small in relation to the larger community of orthodox Hindus who were not receptive of these new religious reformers, whereas in Telugu country there was no such young class of England-returned Telugu speakers that sought social acceptance. Gurunatham saw the Brahmos as a strange breed because of these social conditions. These men invented peculiar new customs and new forms of religious expression, such as a prayer meeting imitating Christianity.[31]

While decrying the lack of political will in feudal India, Gurunatham reserved respect for Hinduism as a set of moral beliefs. This was so because, for Gurunatham, religion formed the moral foundations of Indian society since ancient times. He did, however, identify a new emergent morality that was advocated by social reformism—a public secular morality that became open for scrutiny by the people rather than a morality propagated and upheld by religious authority. This provided for him a sign of a new society and the need for a new politics:

> Morality, as we now understand it, is altogether of modern origin. Ancient societies were without it altogether. The power that moved and moulded the course of ancient communities came mostly from their religion, while at the present day the motive force for public conduct is to be found in the political or economic aspirations of the people.[32]

He writes that pre-colonial society in India was governed by religious authority, whereas in modern times, during the colonial era, morality was shaped by the 'political and economic aspirations' of the people. This was the liberal idea of the public that Gurunatham identified. Yet he did not include Viresalingam's social reform work within this purview of a morality that arises from public conduct. Gurunatham rather argued that Viresalingam's brand of social reformism only targeted the superficial aspects of Indian society—that is, the external structures of religion—when what was needed was the cultivation of a liberal public through the transformation of the underlying political and economic foundations of Andhra society.

What, then, was the new politics needed at this historical juncture? It is not that political activism itself was new to the Madras Presidency. R. Suntharalingam's classic study of development of political institutions and associational life in the Madras Presidency traces changes over the course of the nineteenth century from the establishment of George Norton's literary circle in the early part of the century to political discussions of the prominent Madras Native Association established in 1852.[33] However, at the turn of the twentieth century, there was a burst in political associations alongside social reform conferences. The cultivation of public reason shaped both social and political agendas of this generation of Telugu intellectuals. Social reformists and those advocating for political reforms shared an idea of the public as an arena for rational exchange and debate. For an example of this, we can turn to the *Voice of Progress*, a journal of the Madras Hindu Social Reform Association (established in 1892), which published an essay on the achievements of social reform. The persistent problem for social reformers, according to the essay, was how to persuade orthodox-minded Hindus of the necessity for social change. For its part, the Hindu orthodoxy organized together to resist social reformers from meddling in customs and rituals they deemed central to Hindu religious practice. Interestingly and importantly, however, there was an expectation that both sides would conduct debate in a rational public sphere.

The author of an essay titled 'Fifty Years of Reform in Southern India' wrote on the use and power of reason in public debate:

> The Prarthana Samajist may not attract the same following as does the Arya Samajist, but that furnishes no reason why he should pretend to be other than what he really is. The 'masses' may not take Reason as their sole guide, but all men, outside of the lunatic asylum, take it as one of their guides. The language of reason is a common language understood by men of all persuasions.
> —Sanatana and Arya, Brahmo and Agnostic.[34]

What is stark in this piece is its singling out of reason and rationality as the guiding principle in vernacular publics, whether for conservative or progressive ends. Social reformers and political reformers alike carved out and relied on a public sphere for critique and rational exchange to further their political and social agendas. The turn of the twentieth century was on the cusp of mass political mobilization by Indian anti-colonial politics. The overlap between the agendas of social and political reformers and the turn to political reforms were an important moment for activists to define what political futures they were committed to— thus, the shift from a focus on social to political reforms defined the anti-colonial moment. While social reform (impacting both caste and gender hierarchies) and religious reform produced divisions within communities between the progressives and the orthodox, the turn to political reform narrowed those divisions. When activists all agreed to commit to political reforms, it brought people of different ideological persuasions together, united in the goal of fostering institutions of representative democracy sustained by discourses of self-determination and self-rule.

Still, it is important to keep in mind that social and political reform movements were distinct from one another. The political movements sought to expand the participation of Indians in governing, while the social movements were committed to associational life that targeted the reform of social and religious customs, involving caste practices and the uplift of women in Indian society. There was much dialogue and overlap between the two sets of activists and associations, and one can read their responses to one another's critiques at this critical moment.[35] Gurunatham's intellectual biography of Viresalingam was written within this context, providing a compelling critique of social reform work and activism and declaring the necessity of a new framework for politics. At the First Godavery District Conference held in Coconada in 1895, president Rao Bahadur C. Jumbulingam Mudaliar addressed the conference by stating:

> ... your association is an excellent adjunct and solid groundwork for that stupendous organization, the Indian National Congress. True political life has just commenced among us, and the concessions for the practice of that life are no doubt granted in a very small degree with restrictions, which have been considered by the authorities necessary under the present circumstances of the country. It is for Associations like these, by their wise, moderate and practical discussion of public matters, and their study and healthy education of the masses in public matters, to convince the Government that we deserve a larger measure of political enfranchisement with fewer and fewer restrictions.[36]

Mudaliar singles out the work that associational life did at the local and regional level and in particular draws attention to political associations which tapped into the political concerns of the people. This work and efforts on the part of the associations would provide evidence to the colonial government that the people were prepared for increased involvement in matters of the government. Associational life would train a civic population in governing and convince the colonial administration that the people were prepared for self-government and that it was necessary to expand enfranchisement. The objectives of the association were:

> 1. By circulating pamphlets, leaflets, tracts or otherwise, and 2. By providing for the delivery and holding of lectures, exhibitions, public meetings and conferences, and thereby to foster among the people a healthy public opinion: To ascertain the actual wants of the District, and adopt constitutional and loyal measures in bringing them to the notice of the authorities concerned: To direct and control the working of the Village and Taluq Associations, now in existence, or may hereafter come into existence in the District, having objects similar to those of this Association and which may be affiliated to this Association: And to do all such other things as are incidental or conducive to the attainment of the above objects.[37]

The conference was the first of a series of conferences to bolster political involvement in the district of Godavari. There were similar ones in other districts as well. The publication of the minutes of the first Godavari conference lists a number of political associations active in the district: the People's Association of Tanuku, the Landholders' Association of Alamur, the People's Association of Akeed, the Bhimavaram Taluq People's Association at Bondada, the People's Association at Sivadevamchikkala, the Hume Club of Kopalli, the People's Association at Pittapore, and so on.[38] Dewan Bahadur Kanchi Krishnaswamy Rao Pantulu Garu, then then chief justice of Travancore, wrote:

I am very proud to find that Coconada, where I had the good fortune to spend a few years at a time when political ideas were slowly dawning on its educated residents, has, within the last 12 years, become the centre of political activity of a very healthy type, and is setting a good example to the Southern Districts of the Madras Presidency. Godavari was the first in Social Reform and is now the first in Political Reform.[39]

From the evidence of this list of political associations, one can conclude that these kinds of discussions shaped Telugu intellectuals' political imaginaries. At the beginning of the twentieth century, the political ground prepared by these associations and their politicization of the people sparked proposals to form a separate province comprising Telugu-speaking districts in the Madras Presidency.

Gurunatham took part in the initial discussions that led to the formation of the AMS in 1913. Even before the official establishment of the AMS, a meeting of different district conferences, the Godavari, Krishna, and Guntur, in 1912, combined their efforts to build a cohesive political community that would promote the broader region of 'Andhra'.[40] A group, including Gurunatham and Konda Venkatappayya, met at Bapatla in the Guntur district with the aim of founding a separate Andhra circle of the INC. Venkatappayya went on to push for the founding of the Andhra Congress Circle (ACC) and tried from the very beginning to argue for the separation of the Telugu-speaking districts into a province. He published an influential tract on the Andhra movement in 1913 (Figure 1.1) and a longer piece with the same name in 1938.[41] The idea initially was to build an independent voice distinct from what he perceived as the Tamil-dominated INC unit representing the Madras Presidency. With this in mind, the ACC was established on 8 April 1917. At the time, the Home Rule movement under the leadership of Annie Besant energized the Madras Presidency and made nationalist agitation available, bringing new recruits into the movement. Bhogaraju Pattabhi Sitaramayya, in his magisterial history of the INC, suggests that another success of the Home Rule agitation as it was spreading in the south was the recognition of the integrity of language areas and the organizing of the leagues, which 'adopted the linguistic principle as determining the provincial delimitations'.[42] The extension of anti-colonial nationalism into southern India demonstrated to the INC leadership the necessity of organizing along language. It is under these conditions that Gurunatham, along with his compatriot U. Lakshminarayana, prepared a map (see Figure 1.2) of the region of Andhra outlining the Telugu-speaking areas in the Madras Presidency, the Central Provinces, the Nizam's Dominions, and the Mysore state. The map illustrates a contestation of the arbitrary political boundaries of both the British and the

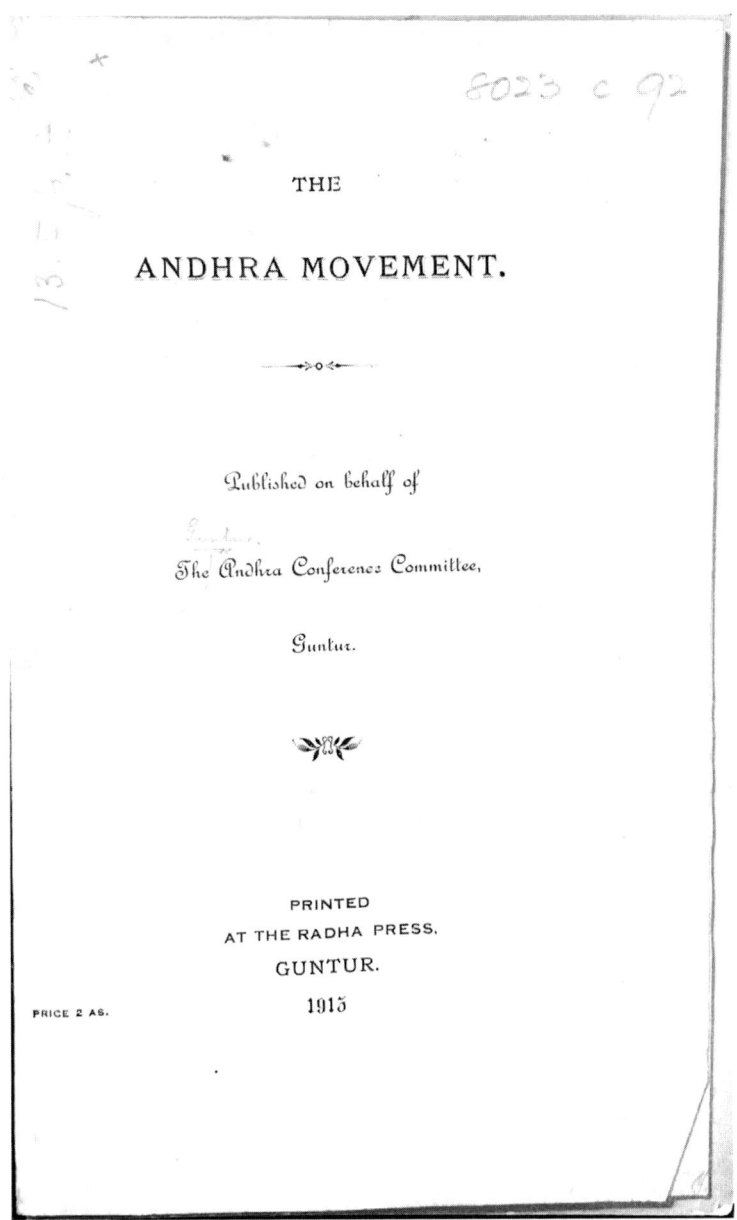

Figure 1.1 Cover page of the Andhra Conferences Committee's publication *The Andhra Movement*, 1913

Source: Andhra Conferences Committee, *The Andhra Movement* (Andhra Conferences Committee, Guntur) (Guntur: Radha Press, 1913).

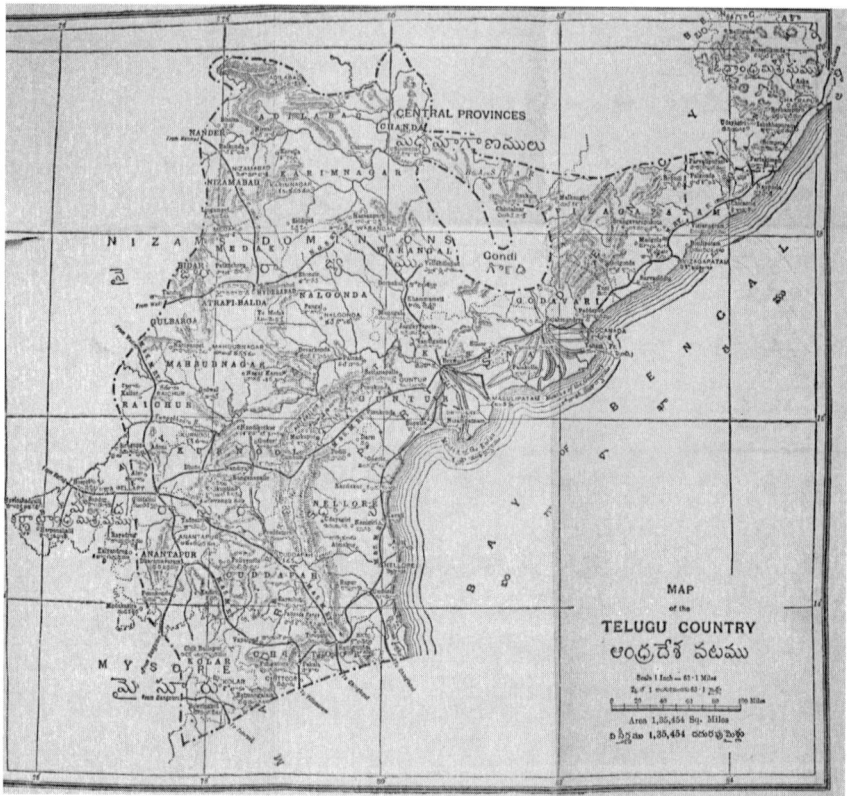

Figure 1.2 Map of the Telugu country from the Andhra Conferences Committee's publication *The Andhra Movement*, 1913

Source: Andhra Conferences Committee, *The Andhra Movement* (Andhra Conferences Committee, Guntur) (Guntur: Radha Press, 1913).

Nizam's Hyderabad state. The map re-envisioned a coherent and rationally delimited regional province on the basis of the Telugu language.

This, of course, raised concerns in the neighbouring princely state of Hyderabad that this young upstart movement had designs to incorporate the Telugu-speaking districts of the Hyderabad state with British Indian provinces. The idea that a regional movement would incorporate the Telugu-speaking districts of the Hyderabad state would be devastating to any political futures that the Nizam's administration envisioned. The formation of the ACC and the AMS was the initial step in the movement that ultimately demanded a separate linguistic state in post-independence India. Prior to this, however, there were organizations devoted to the patronage of Telugu literature and the writing of the history of Andhra. When he addressed the second Andhra Conference in Bezwada in 1914, Subba Rao acknowledged that Telugu literary endeavours, such as the *Vignanachendrika* series that came out of the city of Madras, *Andhra Pracharini Grandha Nilayam* of Nidadavole, and *Andhrabhashabhivarthini Sangham* of Masulipatam, enriched modern Telugu language and literature with the publication and circulation of Telugu prose works on science as well as fiction. The support given to Telugu language and literature through these endeavours had other repercussions besides giving strength to the Andhra movement. Alongside the territorial aspirations of the Andhra movement, there was parallel to this an equally dynamic language reform movement that sought to modernize and make Telugu accessible to a larger population.[43] The Telugu dictionary project, under the direction and guidance of Jayanti Ramayya Pantulu, was well underway with the support of the Telugu Academy, the Andhra Sahitya Parishad, and the patronage of the maharajah of Venkatagiri and the rajah of Pittapur.[44] At this point, the primary proposal of the Andhra movement was not exclusively the idea of separating Telugu-speaking districts into one province. It was only with trepidation that the Andhra activists argued the separation of a new province for administrative convenience. Rather, more importantly, Telugu activists encouraged political engagement on the part of the people. This desire to bring people into the political fold and civic engagement was also at the heart of social reformers such as Subba Rao. As the movement took on momentum, the Andhra activists made a case for why the creation of a province for Telugu speakers would be politically expedient. The Telugu newspaper *Krishna Patrika*, on 31 May 1912, reported the meeting of the Kistna District Conference held at Nidadavole:[45]

> It is the wish of some that the division of the country into provinces for administrative purposes should be determined by the language spoken. This desire was at the bottom of the agitation of the Bengalees which resulted in the abolition of partition of Bengal. The Beharees are jubilant.... The Uriyas of Ganjam wish that they should be placed under the Government of Orissa. An Indian nationality maybe an impossibility but there are signs of a federated Indian nationality based on differences of Language.... Unless the Andhras do their best to carry out this ideal, they cannot be said to have done their duty towards India.[46]

Inspired by influential Marathi social reformer and INC leader Gopal Krishna Gokhale, Venkatappayya began the *Krishna Patrika* and gave up his law practice to pursue the pedagogical mission of bringing about a dynamic civil society and public debate to the Telugu people. The *Krishna Patrika* provided a forum for nationalists in the Telugu-speaking districts, and it is not too surprising that they wrote favourably about the desire of the ACC to advocate for a new province based on language. On the other hand, Subba Rao, who was one of the founders of *The Hindu*, initially viewed the Andhra movement as divisive and called it a separatist movement. This revealed the divide in political discussion between the northern coastal districts and the city of Madras (where *The Hindu* was based). On the other hand, the English weekly *Andhra* from Guntur and the *Andhra Patrika* from Bombay were both supportive of the movement. The *Andhra Patrika* (a Telugu newspaper), started by Kasinadhuni Nageswara Rao in 1908 in Bombay, shifted its headquarters to Madras in 1914, when the Andhra movement came into public debate and prominence. Venkatappayya had this to say about the results of the initial discussions in 1912:

> This thought of a single movement in the interests of all Andhras took a definite shape in the discussions that were held at Guntur soon after the return of the delegates from Nidadavole. It was agreed that movement to be called, "the Andhra Movement" intended for the general advancement of the Andhras, including their educational and industrial improvement, and also for their proper representation in public services, should be started and a conference which might be termed, the Andhra Conference, "Andhra Mahasabha," be convened every year in important centres in the Andhra country.[47]

The resolutions proposed at the first conference held at Bapatla in 1913 centred around the call for the creation of a new province based on language. There was much resistance—not only from non-Telugu speakers in the Madras Presidency, but also within the region among the many who believed that talk of separation might harm the greater cause and goals of anti-colonial nationalism. Separation, it was feared, would splinter the national idea as well as introduce destructive competition between groups for government posts. While there was clearly a growing number of supporters of the Andhra movement, the resistance was considerable and came from important figures such as Subba Rao. As the founding editor of *The Hindu*, Subba Rao initially tried to keep distance from the movement and expressed scepticism. In a letter, dated 22 January 1913, addressed to the editor of *The Hindu*, the joint secretaries, K. Ventatappayya and V. Bhavanacharlu, of the Andhra Conference, wrote that the movement did not get its fair treatment in the newspaper and was being mischaracterized as politically irresponsible. They insisted that the Andhra movement was in reality an organic culmination of advances in education and the burgeoning Telugu press in the nineteenth century:

> The strenuous labors of Mr. Viresalingam Pantulu in the cause of social reform and the liberal ideas and high ideals of life which he preached in his vigarous writings and which were exemplified in his remarkable life roused the Telugus from their lethargy and helped to create in them a love for public life and a degree of public spirit which, with the advance of English education amongst them and with the example of noble lives in other parts of India and elsewhere, has been gradually growing in strength and showing itself in the various institutions started in the country for the development of literature and education and for the amelioration of their social and political conditions.[48]

Subba Rao, Venkatappayya, and Sitayamayya debated the timeliness of the movement and what it could achieve. Venkatappayya, as the most vocal proponent of the movement, expounded on the benefits that resulted from Telugu associational life—not only giving sustenance to Telugu language and literature but also pushing for educational advancement for Telugu speakers with the founding of colleges and universities where Telugu could be enriched. Reacting to this plea, Subba Rao reconsidered the Andhra movement and published several exchanges between himself and Sitaramayya. Subba Rao needed convincing that the Andhra movement would not be the beginning of the proliferation of separatists' movements dividing an already vulnerable nationalist movement. Far from it, Venkatapayya insisted, writing in *The Hindu*, that the Andhra movement gave renewed energy 'for the love of public life' and the cultivation of a 'public spirit' for the Telugu people.

After his initial scepticism, Subba Rao soon took on the mantle of presiding over the second Andhra Conference that took place in April of 1914 in Bezwada.[49] Those who were hesitant were convinced that the movement could be productive. They were also convinced that the movement was aligned with the political climate of the time when there was greater movement towards self-government and self-determination. Indeed, at the first conference, the issue was raised that the 'aspirations of the Andhras were legitimate and the demand for a separate province was in consonance with the Viceroy's despatch relating to provincial autonomy and to the ideal of self-government on colonial lines which was the chief plank of the Indian National Congress'.[50] In the initial stages, the Andhra activists had to navigate the fine line between appearing to be working against the nationalist cause (which was contesting colonial rule) and making a legitimate case for political mobilization of the Telugu-speaking community.

It was a safer subject to advocate for the greater use of Telugu in public life and foster a Telugu renaissance of sorts to counter what was perceived as disrespect for Telugu—not only in Hyderabad but also in Madras, the political centre of anti-colonial agitation in southern India. Subba Rao, in his speech from the second Andhra Conference in Bezawada in 1914, declared, 'There is an awakening among the Andhras and a renaissance in Telugu literature, comparable to the days of Krishnadevaraya, less dependent on the favor of princes and more firmly based on the appreciation of the people.'[51] The declaration acknowledged the new democratic aspirations undergirding the revival of Telugu literature based upon what Subba Rao called 'the appreciation of the people'. This renaissance was driven by a thriving press publishing newspapers and books that shaped new literary tastes. The Telugu library movement was organized in the Telugu-speaking districts to foster this renaissance and made accessible printed books and newspapers to the public in villages, towns, and cities. Subba Rao went on to suggest that there was a general awakening to the fact that a national system of education was better suited for Indian conditions than simply clamouring for educational institutions in the West. In fact, he suggested, an educational system suited to the actual life of the Indian people would produce even greater results: 'It is felt that if there is to be real improvement in the condition of the people, the present system of education should be placed on a better footing and instruction imparted through the vernacular.'[52] Viresalingam, who was also present at the meeting in Bezawada, declared, 'This Conference views with gratification the attempts set on foot to perpetuate the memory of national poets, like Nannaya, Pothana and Tikkana, and urges the adoption of necessary measures to conserve ancient monument of historic interests in the Telugu country.'[53] Viresalingam's resolution was a response to another member moving a resolution that the Andhras should be compelled to extend their patronage to the arts, crafts, and other cultural productions in the region.

Most importantly, Subba Rao told members of the conference that in order to demand a separate state they had more work to do through the formation of a league devoted to forming public opinion on the subject, as it is not a demand that was obvious to all Telugu-speaking people. He said that it would be the duty of the league 'to educate public opinion in India as to the desirability of remodelling [sic] provinces on the basis of language and bring home particularly to the different parts of the Telugu districts the immense benefits that would accrue to them from the formation of an Andhra Province'.[54] On the second day of the second Andhra Conference, a debate erupted between those who advocated for a separate province and those who opposed it. M. Suryanarayana of Vizianagaram moved the resolution, calling for the reorganization of provinces on a territorial basis of provincial administration. He denied that this demand would put the larger goal of nationalism in danger and foster exclusiveness on the part of the Telugus rather than their brotherhood with Tamilians and other Indians. The discussion ended in a stormy debate, as reported in the proceedings.[55] Venkatappayya then published a letter in *The Hindu*, on 1 June 1914, that responded to the idea of an Andhra province, even though it was not agreed upon to make it a platform for the AMS at their first or second conference. Venkatappayya emphasized that it was not an easy task to advocate for a separate province, nor was it the goal to do so. Rather, he wrote, such a political goal would require an unceasing constitutional agitation for years. He went on to say:

> They aim at education and enlightenment of the people on the subject not merely by occasional addresses at one meeting here and a conference there but steady work carried on for years' end to years' end and through leagues and associations established in all centres in the country and by lecturing tours and distribution of literature.'[56]

This was nothing less than an impassioned call for the extension of civic institutions for nurturing Telugu political life and public spirit. The second conference did endorse the patronage of Telugu publications and institutions to further Telugu public life. It called for the Telugu people to support The Andhra Jatheeya Kalasala based in Masulipatam and the Andhra Sahitya Parishad in Madras. It also drew attention to the establishment of the National School in Rajahmundry, singled out the *Andhra Patrika* as an important new publication in Telugu, and, interestingly, urged the establishment of an English daily in order to further the cause of politically uniting Telugu speakers. The conference finally also gestured towards the important social reform issues concerning early marriage and the dowry system.[57] The turn to the vernacular—the use of Telugu for public life and in particular political speeches—was critical for the Andhra movement to succeed. With the start of the Andhra movement, political meetings began to be conducted in Telugu exclusively. Venkatappayya wrote:

> There has been unprecedented awakening amongst the masses. The message of Swaraj was delivered to them in their mother tongue. Speeches and writings in the vernaculars roused their patriotic instinct and created in them boundless enthusiasm for the cause of the country. Thousands of men and women rushed into the movement and made marvelous sacrifices which staggered even our opponents.[58]

The use of Telugu for political speeches effectively aroused nationalist passions. Just like Gurunatham, Venkatappayya, too, knew that a movement had to reach the people and implore them to take up organizing civic life and political community. This was, in a sense, a novel experiment that urged people to prepare for democratic reforms and take up the call for self-government. It sought to instil among Telugu speakers an understanding of the everyday practice of governing, which involved not only a cultural renaissance of sorts but also a call for public spirit. Gurunatham, in his book on Viresalingam, articulated this quite clearly by mentioning not only the virtues of public life but also the cultivation of civic life to produce a viable political community.

In the Telangana region of the Hyderabad state as early as 1901, the Sri Krishnadevaraya Andhrabhasa Nilayamu (Sri Krishnadevaraya Andhra Language Association) was established in the city of Hyderabad by prominent members of the community there.[59] M. Hanumantha Rao, an important Telugu intellectual in Hyderabad, joined the association in 1912, when he came to the city to study law. He witnessed the burgeoning of these organizations when he resided in the city. There was a clear revival of Telugu language and literature taken up by activists and associations in the Madras Presidency as well as in princely Hyderabad. However, the motivations were slightly different in Hyderabad in that the tension did not stem from the dominance of Tamil as it did in the Madras Presidency. In Telangana, the public acknowledgement of Telugu was imbued with political relevance even though the Telugu activists had to present their organization as purely cultural. The activists in Telangana promoted Telugu libraries which were opened in and around Hyderabad to give prominence to the language and literature. At this time, Telugu newspapers such as *Nilgiri*, *Golkonda*, the *Tenugu Patrika*, and *Sujata* were in circulation in Telangana. In 1921, the first meeting for the Andhra Janasangham took place after what Hanumantha Rao explained as a particularly jarring incident. A gathering of Urdu, Marathi, and English speakers were giving speeches in their respective languages. But when one speaker began to speak in Telugu to address the crowd, the gathering yelled to put a stop to it. This was, to say the least, disturbing to the Telugu intellectuals and inspired Telugu youth in the city to begin organizing themselves to carve a public space for Telugu.[60] A similar story of Telugu intellectuals and activists feeling that their language was not given due respect in the public sphere arose in the Madras Presidency. The Janasangham in princely Hyderabad met as a group four times before the establishment of the AMS in 1930. Suravaram Pratapa Reddy, the founder of the prominent newspaper *Golkonda Patrika*, chaired the AMS's first meeting in Jogipeta (Medak district in Telangana). The purpose of the association was to bring together Telugu intellectuals for the common goal of promoting Telugu in and around the Hyderabad state. Prominent members of the newly formed AMS included M. Narsing Rao, Pratapa Reddy, Hanumantha Rao, Burgula Ramakrishna, and Ravi Narayana Reddy.

At the fourth AMS meeting in Sirisilla in Karimnagar district, Hanumantha Rao laid out an agenda for the association that included subjects like promoting Telugu learning in Hyderabad and advocating for the mother tongue in schools and universities. He also spoke of the need to tackle the problem of child marriage, the rights of peasants, and the question of girls' schooling—all typical social reform issues that dominated British India as well. In particular, the issue of promoting Telugu and using it in the public sphere was brought up as of utmost importance for the AMS. Because Urdu was the language of the Hyderabad state and administration and the medium of education at its premier education institution, Osmania University, Telugu intellectuals felt the Telugu language needed to be promoted, especially in early and higher education.[61] There were Telugu newspapers in circulation in the state, but this was not sufficient. The Telugu library movement, promoted by the AMS in the Madras Presidency, inspired the AMS in Hyderabad to encourage the founding of libraries and the circulation of Telugu books and newspapers in villages and towns in Telangana.

The meetings explicitly avoided issues of overt political nature.[62] From the very beginning, the AMS in Telangana had to seek permission to hold meetings and assure the administration that they were not conducting political discussion that would undermine the integrity of the state, as the Hyderabad administration did not allow political gatherings and any gathering or meeting had to be approved by the administration.[63] Hanumantha Rao was also a member of the Gasthi 53 Committee, which did agitate to lift the infamous Gasthi 53 that was put in place in 1929—a circular that placed limitations on public political discussion and public gatherings. The Hyderabad state kept a watchful eye on political discussions conducted by civil societal organizations that were expanding in the state during the 1920s and the 1930s. The AMS was being closely monitored and scrutinized by the administration, as was Pratapa Reddy's prominent Telugu language newspaper, the *Golkonda Patrika*. Hanumantha Rao was a critical participant in the vibrant public life in Hyderabad and was both involved in the AMS and simultaneously agitated to expand political reforms in the Hyderabad state. In 1937, he appealed to the Nizam government and argued that restrictions placed on free speech as they were in Hyderabad would hinder the growth of public life and political discussion in the state and stunt the development of an informed public.[64] He formulated a sophisticated critique on the necessity of public life and the role that it would play in educating the people so that they become aware of their rights.

The AMS in Telangana carried on its cultural activities and clandestine political discussion, especially in the 1940s, when, along with the centrist liberals, there were prominent socialists and communists who posed challenges to their leadership. AMS activists worked along with the Hyderabad State Congress to discuss political reforms in the state. The AMS continued in this manner until 1944, when the association splintered into two groups, neither of which continued to share the political position of the liberal centre. The AMS in Telangana went through dramatic shifts in the 1940s. In March 1940, Jayaprakash Narayan, along with the Congress Socialist Party's (CSP) national executive, declared at the Ramgarh meeting that the CSP would expel members of the Communist Party of India (CPI) from its organization since they were in effect undermining the CSP and its stated political goals to work with the INC.[65] These radical changes were felt throughout British India, but it was especially interesting how they manifested themselves in princely Hyderabad. The 1930s and the 1940s brought to the fore intense political debate in Hyderabad that polarized members of the AMS by the end of the 1930s. By 1940, there was already a vocal group within the AMS that was sympathetic to the communist movement in British India and attempted to organize the association into a militant organization.[66] As the group split into two, one faction—the liberal one—was led by Narsing Rao, the prominent editor of the Urdu newspaper *Raiyat*, while the other faction was taken up by the leadership of Narayana Reddy, who transformed it into a communist wing in Hyderabad. Thus, the Andhra movement in Hyderabad took on different political trajectories, encompassing both progressive socialists, conservatives, and, later in the 1940s, radicals. All the while, both the liberal and communist factions supported the activities of the AMS in promoting Telugu language and literature in public life.

Meanwhile, in the Madras Presidency, the Andhra Swarajya Party advanced a more conservative ideology that steered away from the INC ministries after the 1937 elections. *The Hindu* reported that the Andhra Swarajya Party (ASP) began to agitate for council entry after G. Venkatasubba Rao wrote an article titled 'Hyderabad Reforms' in the English newspaper *Andhra* in 1939 on the reforms proposed by the Nizam of the princely state of Hyderabad for functional representation.[67] Venkatasubba Rao wrote that they were welcome reforms, received with approval by Sarvarkar and the Aryan League. Functional representation, he insisted, was not borrowed from fascist Italy: 'The ancient tradition of the Indian Social system itself has been built upon Vrithi (functions). Cautilya, the great authority on Mauryan Polity, describes the Science of Politics as Ardha Shastra and even in the present-day West the Science of Wealth is called Political Economy.'[68] He decried the INC ministry and its policy of destroying 'ancient Indian aristocracy' and reasoned that Akbar Hydari's scheme should be welcomed because it 'is a well-balanced whole between the rich and poor, the prince and peasant, Pattidar and tenant, educated and uneducated and even the unwanted journalist will probably find a place in the New Hyderabad Assembly'. He argued that the village *panchayat* system was built on economic foundations and that Nehru himself urged Indians to base political action on economic interests in order to defuse communal tension. The conservative members, such as Venkatasubba Rao, who supported the INC while also criticizing its tactics believed there were alternatives to the political imaginaries offered by the leadership. In defending functional representation as put forward by the Reforms Committee in Hyderabad in 1938, Venkatasubba Rao upheld a vision of an Indian aristocracy that could and should be preserved as compatible with the formation of an Indian Union and its traditions. Venkatasubba Rao, in his alignment with Hindu nationalists, upheld an ancient 'aristocracy' as tradition. Gurunatham, at an earlier moment, articulated a conservative politics that involved a critique of social reformism and the damage that it could unleash. If we recall, Gurunatham in 1911 criticized Viresalingam and his brand of social reformism and laid out what it lacked in terms of a politics. However, Gurunatham was firmly committed to a transformation of Indian society along liberal lines and to the dismantling of feudal remnants such as the *zamindari* system. Gurunatham's conservatism was distinct from Venkatasubba Rao's. The latter's ideology, as discerned from his numerous writings, was aligned with the Hindu majoritarian politics of Hindutva. However, Gurunatham did not live to witness the rise of Hindu nationalism, and we will never know how he might have shifted his politics with the burgeoning of political ideologies in the 1930s. Venkatasubba Rao's defence of the aristocracy and the monarchy is interesting in striking contrast to Gurunatham's often scathing critique of the landed aristocracy. In tracing the proliferation of political imaginaries in British India and Hyderabad, one can see that there was further splintering of political ideologies in the 1930s and the 1940s, from conservatism to communism, advocating for different visions of a future state and society.

The multiple colonial publics in British India as well as in the princely state of Hyderabad were clearly fraught with contention between competing ideologies—ranging from caste critique to the politics of gender, family, and place of religion.[69] Bayly argued that this desire to bring about a critical public through the cultivation of civil society institutions is at the heart of the history of nineteenth-century Indian liberalism.[70] Telugu liberal intellectuals, from the nineteenth-century social reformer Viresalingam to the Andhra activists in the first half of the twentieth century, were all positioning themselves to critique the colonial state while at the same time questioning traditional sources of authority that legitimized hierarchical caste and gendered practices. This led to the formation of a progressivism that shaped regional politics as much as national. The latter set of progressive activists were driven by the desire to confront customs and practices that they considered out of sync in modern societies and socio-religious practices that perpetuated social inequalities. All the while, the elaboration of a critical public had to negotiate and contend with those who argued for a moral obligation to community and the reassertion of caste community, as well as those who explicitly supported Hindu majoritarianism, such as in the work and activism of Venkatasubba Rao, especially in the 1930s and the 1940s. The elaboration of public life and political imaginaries took place in the Hyderabad state alongside the Madras Presidency in the Telugu-speaking districts. By crossing borders between the princely state of Hyderabad and the Madras Presidency, one can see that a broader liberal democratic project was at work through civil societal activism and the extension of political life by one of the pre-eminent institutions in the Telugu region—the AMS. The AMS has been rightly studied as the primary organ of the Andhra movement and the AMS' important political demand for the reorganization of provinces using the criteria of language to demarcate borders. The movement has been scrutinized for understanding the rise of a regional form of nationalism and the formulation of an ethnic identity based on language. However, as the writings of Gurunatham, Venkatappayya, and other contemporaries illustrate, the movement encompassed much more than a narrow ethnic nationalism. Of course, there were indeed passionate language enthusiasts who saw the formation of a regional province or state for Telugu speakers as a natural birth right.[71] Others who were driven by new discourses of self-government and self-rule made the demand for a regional province based not on language as a natural right but rather on the notion that language would be the ideal tool to democratize and politicize the region and empower the people. Giving prominence to the regional language would create mechanisms to disseminate new democratic practices. The AMS in both the Madras Presidency and in the Hyderabad state provided a forum that would advocate the Telugu language for schooling, for literary innovation, as well as for public speaking. While politicizing the community through their public meetings and publishing the goals of their movement in English and Telugu newspapers, the AMS took on the task of political and social reforms in order to further cultivate democratic sensibilities in the Telugu people.

Notes

1. Eric Stokes, *The English Utilitarians and India* (Delhi: Oxford University Press, 1982).
2. See Uday Mehta, *Liberalism and Empire: A Study in Nineteenth-Century British Liberal Thought* (Chicago: University of Chicago Press, 1999); Jennifer Pitts, *A Turn to Empire: The Rise of Imperial Liberalism in Britain and France* (Princeton, NJ: Princeton University Press, 2009); Karuna Mantena, *Alibis of Empire: Henry Maine and the Ends of Liberal Imperialism* (Princeton, NJ: Princeton University Press, 2010); Andrew Sartori, 'The British Empire and Its Liberal Mission', *Journal of Modern History* 78, no. 3 (September 2006): 623–642; Partha Chatterjee, 'The Curious Career of Liberalism in India', *Modern Intellectual History* 8, no. 3 (2011): 687–696.
3. C. A. Bayly, *Recovering Liberties: Indian Thought in the Age of Liberalism and Empire* (Cambridge, UK: Cambridge University Press, 2012), 1.
4. R. Suntharalingam, in his *Politics and Nationalist Awakening in South India, 1852–1891* (Tucson, AZ: University of Arizona Press, 1974), writes on the rise of all presidency-wide political associations in nineteenth-century Madras and the Madras Mahajana Association's efforts to bring local associations together to deliberate on larger questions of self-representation. Suntharalingam traces the politicizations of the educated classes in the Madras Presidency. He also points to the push from the Indian Association (Calcutta) and the Brahmo Samajists, who travelled through the Madras Presidency to draw attention to all-India political issues. In other words, in the last decades of the nineteenth century, as associations such as the Indian Association and the Indian National Congress (INC) tried to reach out to the other presidencies to create an all-India political consciousness, Suntharalingam points out how within Madras there were efforts to reach out to local associations and create a broader politics. In the early decades of the twentieth century, however, there was another dramatic shift—this time the focus shifted from national politics to the region in south India.
5. The literature on religious reform in the nineteenth century is vast. Some notable works are David Kopf, *British Orientalism and the Bengal Renaissance* (Calcutta: Firma K. L. Mukhopadhyay, 1969); T. Raychaudhuri, *Europe Reconsidered: Perceptions of the West in Nineteenth-Century Bengal* (Delhi: Oxford University Press, 1988); Brian Hatcher, *Idioms of Improvement: Vidyasagar and Cultural Encounter in Bengal* (New Delhi: Oxford University Press, 2001); J. Barton Scott, *Spiritual Despots: Hinduism and the Genealogies of Self-Rule* (Chicago: University of Chicago Press, 2016).
6. The idea of 'home'—the space carved out for the preservation of tradition in Indian nationalism—was theorized by Partha Chatterjee. While I agree with

the conception of the inner sphere, clearly it was not a space that confined women. Women, too, were social reformers and political activists who traversed those boundaries to further their own progressive and conservative agendas. See Partha Chatterjee, *The Nation and Its Fragments* (Princeton, NJ: Princeton: Princeton University Press, 1993).
7. See J. Gurunatham, *Viresalingam: The Founder of Telugu Public Life* (Rajahmundry: S. Gunneswararao Bros., 1911).
8. Bayly, *Recovering Liberties*, 5.
9. See Tanika Sarkar's 'A Prehistory of Rights: The Age of Consent Debate in Colonial Bengal', *Feminist Studies* 26, no. 3 (Autumn 2000): 601–622 and Srimati Basu's *The Trouble with Marriage: Feminists Confront Law and Violence in India* (Berkeley: University of California Press, 2015). Basu's chapter 'Construction Zones: Marriage Law in Formation' discusses the much-debated and controversial Hindu Code Bill of 1949, which sought to introduce radical social change but was met with resistance.
10. See John Zavos, *The Emergence of Hindu Nationalism in India* (New Delhi: Oxford University Press, 2000) for the early organizing that the Hindu Sabha movement did and the transformations it underwent in the early decades of the twentieth century. Also see Christophe Jaffrelot, *The Hindu Nationalist Movement and Indian Politics: 1925 to the 1990s: Strategies of Identity-Building, Implantation and Mobilisation (with Special Reference to Central India)* (London: Hurst, 1996) and Thomas Blom Hansen, *The Saffron Wave: Democracy and Hindu Nationalism in Modern India* (Princeton, NJ: Princeton University Press, 1999).
11. Marzia Casolari, 'Hindutva's Foreign Tie-up in the 1930s: Archival Evidence', *Economic and Political Weekly* 35, no. 4 (22 January 2000): 218–228.
12. Howard Erdman, *The Swatantra Party and Indian Conservatism* (Cambridge, UK: Cambridge University Press, 1967).
13. See classic accounts of social reform by Kenneth Jones, *Socio-Religious Reform Movements in British India* (Cambridge, UK: Cambridge University Press, 1989); Hatcher, *Idioms of Improvement*; and Partha Chatterjee, 'A Religion of Urban Domesticity: Sri Ramakrishna and the Calcutta Middle Class', *Subaltern Studies* 7, no. 7 (1992): 40–68.
14. In his study of Hindu reform, J. Barton Scott suggests that the liberal ideal of the self-governing individual as it emerged in the context of colonial rule in India needs to take into account the construction of religious subjectivity. Furthermore, he suggests that modern Hinduism should be understood in relation to empire rather than in relation to conceptions of pre-colonial tradition. He argues that colonial governmentality shaped notions of liberal selfhood and individuality and that religious reform was central to these constructions. See Scott, *Spiritual Despots*.

15. See Scott, *Spiritual Despots*.
16. See Chinnaiah Jangam, *Dalits and the Making of Modern India* (New Delhi: Oxford University Press, 2017); Rama Sundari Mantena, 'Vernacular Publics and Political Modernity: Language and Progress in Colonial South India', *Modern Asian Studies* 47, no. 5 (2013): 1678–1705; Veena Naregal, *Language Politics, Elites, and the Public Sphere: Western India under Colonialism* (New Delhi: Permanent Black, 2001); Francesca Orsini, *The Hindi Public Sphere, 1920–1940: Language and Literature in the Age of Nationalism* (New York: Oxford University Press, 2002); Bernard Bate, *Tamil Oratory and the Dravidian Aesthetic: Democratic Practice in South India* (New York: Columbia University Press, 2009); and Bernard Bate, 'The Ethics of Textuality: The Protestant Sermon and the Tamil Public Sphere', in *Ethical Life in South Asia*, ed. Anand Pandian and Daud Ali, 101–115 (Bloomington: Indiana University Press, 2010).
17. Bernard Bate, *Tamil Oratory*, 162.
18. See Rama Sundari Mantena, 'Vernacular Futures: Colonial Philology and the Idea of History in Nineteenth-Century South India', *Indian Economic and Social History Review* 42, no 4 (2005): 513–534; Lisa Mitchell, *Language, Emotion, and Politics in South India: The Making of a Mother Tongue* (Bloomington: Indiana University Press, 2009); Velcheru Narayana Rao, 'Print and Prose: Pundits, Karanams, and the East India Company in the Making of Modern Telugu', in *India's Literary History: Essays on the Nineteenth Century*, ed. Stuart Blackburn and Vasudha Dalmia, 146–166 (New Delhi: Permanent Black, 2004).
19. Gurunatham, *Viresalingam*. For early historical studies of Viresalingam's reformist activities in coastal Andhra, based in the city of Rajamundry, see John Greenfield Leonard, 'Kandukuri Viresalingam, 1848–1919: A Biography of an Indian Social Reformer', PhD dissertation, University of Wisconsin, Madison, 1970, and Vakulabharanam Ramakrishna, *Social Reform in Andhra (1848–1919)* (New Delhi: Vikas Publishing, 1983).
20. Gurunatham, *Viresalingam*, 9.
21. Gurunatham, *Viresalingam*, 11.
22. Interestingly, Gurunatham served as secretary to the rajah of Kurupam—one of the principal *zamindar*s in the Northern Circars. For a description of these *zamindar*s and how their families and traditions persisted after the English East India Company took control of those regions starting in the eighteenth century, see A. Vadivelu, *The Aristocracy of Southern India* (Madras: Vest and Co., 1903).
23. Vadivelu, *The Aristocracy*, 21.
24. Rajagopal Vakulabharanam, 'Self and Society in Transition: A Study of Autobiographical Practice in Telugu', PhD dissertation, University of Wisconsin, Madison, 2004, 114–115.

25. Vakulabharanam, 'Self and Society in Transition', 114.
26. Gurunatham, *Viresalingam*, 31.
27. Gurunatham, *Viresalingam*, 31.
28. See Mahadev Ranade, 'Introduction to "A Collection by Mr Vaidya Containing the Proceedings which Led to the Passing of Act XV of 1856"', in *Miscellaneous Writings of the Late Hon'ble Mr Justice M.G. Ranade* (New Delhi: Sahitya Akademi, 1992), 82.
29. Gurunatham, *Viresalingam*, 131. See Scott, *Spiritual Despots* on how Hindu reform groups such as the Brahmo Samaj and the Arya Samaj looked towards the *vedanta* tradition for teasing out pure Hindu concepts that should be revived in the colonial present to reinvigorate Hindu society.
30. Gurunatham, *Viresalingam*, 133.
31. Rajagopal Vakulabharanam writes of Kasibhatta Brahmayya Sastri who wrote a critique of Brahmoism. See 'Anti-Reform Discourse in Andhra: Instance of Failed Cultural Nationalism?' In *Ritual, Caste, and Religion in Colonial South India*, ed. Heiko Free, Michael Bergunder, and Ulrike Schroder, 310–329 (Delhi: Primus Books, 2011).
32. Vakulabharanam, 'Anti-Reform Discourse in Andhra', 173.
33. See Suntharalingam, *Politics and Nationalist Awakening in South India*.
34. 'Fifty Years of Reform in Southern India', *Voice of Progress* 1, no. 2 (November 1901): 1–4.
35. For instance, see *The Voice of Progress*, a monthly journal conducted by a Committee of the Madras Hindu Social Reform Association 1, no. 1 (October 1901). In an article titled 'A Complaint against the Social Reformers', the reformer is accused of not defending Hinduism from the onslaught of attacks from enemies. It declares that these reformers are not patriotic and nor are they versed in Hinduism. Furthermore, the article goes on to say, 'A social reformer as such is no an oriental scholar, living in an atmosphere of habitual admiration of ancient wisdom. He lives and acts in the living present' (p. 6). To the charge of unpatriotic stance of the reformist, the author writes that 'it is no duty of the reformer's to wink at the country's ills, for the sake of the people's applause' (p. 7).
36. *Report of the Second Godavery District Conference Held at Rajahmundry, on the 8th 9th and 10th June 1896* (Rajahmundry: Vivekavardhani Press, 1897), 5–6.
37. *Report of the Second Godavery District Conference*, 34.
38. *Report of the Second Godavery District Conference*, 37.
39. *Report of the Second Godavery District Conference*, 36.
40. M. Venkatarangaiya (ed.), *The Freedom Struggle in Andhra Pradesh (Andhra)*, vol. 2: *1906–1920 A.D.* (Hyderabad: AP State Archives and Research Institute, 1969), 79.

41. Konda Venkatappayya, *The Andhra Movement* (The Andhra Maha Sabha Publication, series no. 1) (Madras: Andhra Maha Sabha Publication, 1938).
42. Bhogaraju Pattabhi Sitaramayya, *The History of the Indian National Congress*, vol. 1: *1885–1935* (New Delhi: S. Chand, 1969), p. 130.
43. See R. S. Mantena, 'Vernacular Publics'.
44. Subba Rao's presidential address at the Andhra Conference at Bezawada, 11 April 1914. 'Proceedings of the Second Andhra Conference', *Madras Mail*, 11 April 1914, in Venkatarangaiya, *The Freedom Struggle in Andhra Pradesh (Andhra)*, vol. 2, 382.
45. Venkatappayya, *The Andhra Movement*, 16.
46. K. V. Narayana Rao, *The Emergence of Andhra Pradesh* (Bombay: Popular Prakashan, 1976), 37.
47. Venkatappayya, *The Andhra Movement*, 16–17.
48. 'A Letter of the Joint Secretaries of the Andhra Conference Committee, 22nd January 1913', in Venkatarangaiya, *The Freedom Struggle in Andhra Pradesh (Andhra)*, vol. 2, 359.
49. 'Proceedings of the Second Andhra Conference', 379.
50. 'Resolution on the Andhra Province at the First Andhra Conference', in Venkatarangaiya, *The Freedom Struggle in Andhra Pradesh (Andhra)*, vol. 2, 371.
51. 'Proceedings of the Second Andhra Conference', 382.
52. 'Proceedings of the Second Andhra Conference', 383.
53. 'Proceedings of the Second Andhra Conference', 387.
54. 'Proceedings of the Second Andhra Conference', 385.
55. 'The Andhra Conference Final Proceedings', *Madras Mail*, 14 April 1914, in Venkatarangaiya, *The Freedom Struggle in Andhra Pradesh (Andhra)*, vol. 2, 391.
56. 'K. Venkatappayya's Letter on the Andhra Province and the Ceded Districts', *The Hindu*, 1 June 1914, in Venkatarangaiya, *The Freedom Struggle in Andhra Pradesh (Andhra)*, vol. 2, 395.
57. Venkatarangaiya, *The Freedom Struggle in Andhra Pradesh (Andhra)*, vol. 2, 392–393.
58. Venkatappayya, *The Andhra Movement*, 34.
59. Madapati Hanumantha Rao, *Telangana Andhrodyamamu* (Telangana Andhra Movement) (Hyderabad: Telugu Viswavidyalayam, 2000 [1949]), vii.
60. M. H. Rao, *Telangana Andhrodyamamu*, viii.
61. For a fuller discussion of language policies in princely Hyderabad, see Tariq Rahman, 'Urdu in Hyderabad State', *Annual of Urdu Studies* 23 (2008): 36–54.
62. M. H. Rao, *Telangana Andhrodyamamu*, xii–xiv.

63. 'Andhra Mahasabha: Jogipeta', *Andhra Mahasabha Proceedings* (Hyderabad: Golkonda Press, 1936), 5. See Chapter 4 on the fight for civil liberties in princely Hyderabad.
64. *Hyderabad Bulletin*, 21 September 1937.
65. Gene D. Overstreet and Marshall Windmiller, *Communism in India* (Bombay: Perennial Press, 1960), 179.
66. P. Sundarayya, *Telangana People's Struggle and Its Lessons* (New Delhi: Foundation Books, 2006 [1972]), 12.
67. G. V. Subba Rao Papers, vol. 33, Telangana State Archives (TSA), Hyderabad. See G. V. Rao's 'Hyderabad Reforms'.
68. G. V. Rao, 'Hyderabad Reforms'.
69. There is a rich body of literature on the colonial public sphere in South Asia. C. A. Bayly's *Empire and Information: Intelligence Gathering and Social Communication in India, 1780–1870* (Cambridge, UK: Cambridge University Press, 2000) set the framework to rethink the rise of the public sphere in the nineteenth century. On regional and vernacular publics, see Naregal, *Language Politics*; Orsini, *The Hindi Public Sphere*; Bate, *Tamil Oratory*; and Bate, 'The Ethics of Textuality'; and R. S. Mantena, 'Vernacular Publics'. More recently, Brannon Ingram and Scott have taken on the task of offering an assessment of the important work on colonial publics in relation to religious reform efforts; see Brannon Ingram and J. Barton Scott, 'What Is a Public? Notes from South Asia', *South Asia: The Journal of South Asian Studies* 38, no. 3 (2015): 357–370.
70. Bayly defines liberalism as the pursuit of political and social liberty: 'Its common features were a desire to re-empower India's people with personal freedom in the face of the despotic government of foreigners, embodied traditional authority and supposedly corrupt domestic or religious practices.' Bayly, *Recovering Liberties*, 1.
71. This is evocative of the idea of the mother tongue as almost a biological attribute. Lisa Mitchell, in her work on Telugu, explores 'how languages came to be viewed during the twentieth century as primary and natural foundations for the reorganization of a wide range of forms of knowledge and everyday practice'. See Mitchell, *Language, Emotion, and Politics in South India*, 11.

Part I

Federation

2
Self-Determination, Federation, and the Provinces

After the reversal of the 1905 partitioning of Bengal that inspired the first broad-based mass agitation against colonial rule, the Swadeshi movement, the colonial government of India began to put forward proposals for the devolution of power, gradually moving British India towards self-government. This became a catalyst for different political groups to imagine political futures in which the Indian states would be self-governed. One prominent structure being floated around at the time was a federation, or a federated union of states. By the late 1920s and the 1930s, an all-India federation was proposed as a working idea and especially took force after the Round Table Conferences that were to foster dialogue between the British government and the Indian nationalists (and their various political affiliations) along with the native states (the princes). Even before these political developments, Chittaranjan Das, a prominent member of the INC and the founder of the Swaraj Party, in his 1922 book, *Freedom through Disobedience*, wrote of the necessity—indeed, the inevitability—of a great Asiatic federation. This was at the height of Pan-Asianism and Pan-Islamism and speaks to the prevalence of federation as an ideal alongside the nation state emerging at the end of European empires.[1] The federation idea spoke to the reality that multiple states would emerge at the end of empire, which would have to rely on mutual cooperation. Furthermore, the idea resonated with an emergent internationalism based on transnational affiliations. Taking his cue from the prominence of Pan-Islamism at the time, Das forecasted an 'Asiatic Federation' as the wave of the future after the fall of the European empires:

> Even more important than this is the participation of India in the great Asiatic Federation which I see in the course of formation. I have hardly any doubt that the Pan-Islamic movement which was started on a somewhat narrow basis has given way or is about to give way to the great Federation of all Asiatic people. It is the union of the oppressed nationalities of Asia. Is India to remain outside

the union? I admit that our freedom must be won by ourselves, but such a bond of friendship and love of sympathy and co-operation between India and the rest of Asia, nay between India and all the liberty-loving people of the world is destined to bring about World Peace.[2]

In 1924, the Hindustan Republican Association (HRA) declared that it would make a 'Federal Republic of the United States of India' one of its political goals, along with universal suffrage. The HRA, unlike Das, was proposing a federated union of states within the subcontinent, including the hundreds of native states ruled by princes. The HRA was also committed to universal suffrage towards popular sovereignty. In a form of protest against the Simon Commission, in 1928, the Nehru report (named after Motilal Nehru, the father of Jawaharlal Nehru) was released, giving form to the idea of a united federation. Soon after, the AIML, under the leadership of Muhammad Ali Jinnah, formulated 'Fourteen Points', which included a commitment to a federation with autonomous provinces. Unlike the ambivalent position of the native states with regards to federating with India, for the British Indian provinces the discourse of self-determination and self-government spoke directly to an idea of federation that combined ideals of anti-colonial nationalism alongside the desire for self-government at the provincial level. Even as late as 1942, the CPI envisioned a union of regional states, each with the right to self-determination and its own identity, coexisting without conflict. However, Gangadhar Adhikari, a prominent member of the CPI, imagined regional states to be able to choose complete autonomy. Adhikari's tract *Pakistan and National Unity*, published in 1944, argued in favour of the idea of a federation, specifically giving force to the growth of nationalities at the regional level. The discourse of self-determination gave impetus to the idea of providing more autonomy to the regions in order for them to self-direct, develop their resources, and provide for their people. In other words, the region would not only provide a territorial identity but also allow a conceptualization of the 'people' entitled to self-government.[3]

This chapter takes a closer look at what the discourse of federation brought to the provinces of British India and the debates over self-government and self-determination, specifically in the Madras Presidency during the height of anti-colonial nationalism and the politics it enabled. The aim is to delineate the forces that shaped the political community in the early decades of the twentieth century—the political community imagined not as an exclusive ethnic community but as a regional community in which to enact liberal democratic reforms. How did discourses of self-government and self-determination impact the region? When we delve into the particular ways in which the discourses of rights, civic responsibility, and political representation emerged at the regional level in post-independence India, we begin to get an understanding of the unique social, cultural, and political dynamics that constituted the region, distinct from the dynamics of nationalism and national identity. The region and regional politics were not simply a mimicking of nationalist politics; rather, they constituted a distinctly new form of politics. With this in mind, I examine the dynamics of the new regional political discourse in twentieth-century south India, primarily in the Telugu-speaking districts of the Madras Presidency. Thus, this chapter explores how national and international discourses of self-determination, federation, and language shaped the region in early twentieth-century south India.

Swadeshi in Andhra

The push towards self-government intensified early in the first decade of the twentieth century. That decade saw the partitioning of Bengal and the rise of *swadeshi* politics in its aftermath—a turn to agitational politics, including mass boycotts. *Swadeshi* also provided a political language for people to take up in crafting new demands from the colonial administration at the national and provincial levels. After the failure of the Morley–Minto reforms (1909), the Montagu–Chelmsford reforms (1918) expanded native participation in the Madras provincial government. Christopher Baker, in *The Politics of South India 1920–1937*, argues that the impact of the reforms was dramatic,[4] setting into motion new political currents, such as the rise of non-Brahmanism in the Madras Presidency. Baker's argument is that dyarchy, as it was instituted by the colonial government in the 1920s, fostered the growth of regional parties, provincial politics, and liberal–political institutions, and ultimately expanded the government to include greater native participation. This led to discussions about how best to break up big provinces that were constituted during the colonial era without gauging native Indian opinion. The push was a result of arguments that rested on the idea of administrative convenience to break up big provinces, leading, in turn, to the challenge from regional parties that language should determine provincial divisions. For instance, the 1920 Nagpur meeting of the INC allowed for the redistribution of Congress committees on a linguistic basis.[5] The spread of the Swadeshi movement into south India and of the Home Rulers, led by INC leader Annie Besant in Madras, was challenged by the emerging Non-Brahman movement through the establishment of the Justice Party. Also established at this time was the AMS, which created an alternative forum for Telugu speakers to organize themselves and to lobby the INC to represent their regional interests. While the AMS included members from the INC, the Justice Party emerged as an opposition party contesting the dominance of the INC in the Madras Presidency.

Like Baker, David Washbrook, too, argues that a new politics emerged at this critical juncture, but beyond new political demands, Washbrook argues there was a qualitative shift in politics that shaped the modern Indian political system.[6] Illustrating this shift towards a new politics, the *Krishna Patrika*, a Telugu-language newspaper, published an informative article titled 'On the Duty of Candidates' in 1920:

> The era of passing resolutions has gone and that of carrying them out has dawned. A new epoch has commenced when dissensions in the Legislative Councils have to be given up, and the reconstruction of the Indian nation taken up. Political life has been a sport, a source of enjoyment, a stepping stone to honourable appointments. Skill in disputation and eloquence were adopted as the means. All that has passed away now, and with it must go the veterans that have been trained in it. Politics, hereafter, does not consist of the patch work of the external machine. It does not mean winning the praises of the foreigners or gaining the favor of the rulers. *Politics means reconstruction of the nation, an evolution of the society, the cementing of the Hindu-Muhammadan union, the adoption of national education, the preservation of our traditions, and the adoption of Swadeshi goods.*[7]

The sentiment expressed in this article reflected the great political transformations taking place in the first two decades of the twentieth century. Politics, now an arena for public life, was something entirely different from before. No longer externally oriented or conditioned by the relations of colonial rule, politics became the means through which the region and the nation were to be reconstructed and the citizen-subject was to be educated to take up civic responsibilities.[8] To understand the depth and nuance of these overarching changes, let us take a closer look at the Swadeshi movement and how it impacted the Telugu-speaking northern coastal districts of the Madras Presidency.

Drawing on ideals of native self-reliance, the Swadeshi movement erupted in Bengal in response to the partitioning of Bengal by the then viceroy of India, George Curzon (1898–1905), in 1905. The movement was fuelled by young radicals such as Aurobindo Ghosh, animated by a new fervour for nationalist organizing. Besides the ideal of self-reliance, the Swadeshi movement promoted a constructive programme that included a conception of national education or curriculum and encouraged the use of regional (rather than English) languages for educational purposes as well as for politics. This also coincided with the emergence of a passionate cultural nationalism in British India, which involved the cultivating of cultural and religious symbols to mobilize the population towards a broad political movement questioning the legitimacy of British colonial rule.

Self-Determination, Federation, and the Provinces

The Swadeshi movement began to make inroads in the Telugu-speaking districts of the northern Madras Presidency starting immediately in 1905. On 9 September 1905, *The Hindu* published an editorial commenting on the Swadeshi movement and its rapid spread beyond Bengal, despite emerging first in response to specific political grievances in that province:

> The Swadeshi Movement is spreading rapidly everywhere. From Bengal it has now extended to every province, in the Punjab, Upper India, Western and Central India and down in the South, the movement has seized hold of the minds of the masses. Swadeshism is not a new exotic idea imported from the West. It is purely indigenous growth and the outcome of circumstances entirely Indian.... [T]he causes that have made it so rapidly popular in every part of India are to be found in the general political and industrial condition of the country.[9]

The Swadeshi movement was launched in Calcutta in August of 1905 and soon spread to other parts of India, in large part through the efforts of Bipin Chandra Pal and his lecture tours, which made a long-lasting impact on the Madras Presidency. For instance, in Rajahmundry, a town in the northern coastal district of West Godavari (part of the Madras Presidency), a Swadeshi meeting was held on 31 October 1905, in the local Town Hall, where men from various backgrounds gathered to discuss how to encourage local industries and arts. The men represented professions of the educated classes—from lawyers and teachers to landholding and merchant classes.[10] Another meeting was held in the coastal town of Masulipatam on 5 October 1905, where the concern was with the revival of the weaving industry.[11] It was also reported in the *Madras Mail* that Parsi traders from Bombay were attempting to get rid of their stock of English goods through their participation in the Swadeshi movement. In the city of Madras, K. Krishnaswamy Rao gave a speech on 24 February 1906, in which he defined what *swadeshi* was and why it would shape politics by pointing out that 'Swadeshism is nothing but self-help and self-improvement'.[12] He emphasized that *swadeshi* was more than just the revival of native industries—local arts and crafts—and that it was also a necessary beginning of a political revival. He went on to state that this was a politics that would emulate the rest of the 'civilized' and prosperous nations in the world. It was a call for Indians to take charge of their own industries and take part in a global trend in 'self-improvement'. Harisarvottama Rao, a student from Madras Christian College, urged people towards what he too called 'self-help'. These young activists encouraged people to take ownership of their locale or region and industries by taking up agitational politics against British colonial rule. In doing so, they hoped to contribute to the reshaping of national culture and politics from the standpoint of the region. Implied in the idea of *swadeshi* is that colonial rule or British rule was an alien import. To spread the message of *swadeshi*, the 'Swadeshi League' sent Nyapathi Subba Rao, the co-founder of *The Hindu*, and Venkataramana Rao to tour the northern coastal districts of the Madras Presidency. C.Y. Chintamani, who was the assistant secretary of the Indian Industrial Conference along with Subba Rao, delivered speeches in English and Telugu in cities such as Nellore, Guntur, Coconada, Vizagapatam, and Vizianagaram.[13]

The Hindu reported several incidents of Vande Mataram processions, including one in Rajahmundry that took place on 14 February 1907.[14] The newspaper reported that the procession included the 'leading gentlemen' of the town as well as students who held up banners reading 'Bande Mataram' as well as 'Allaho Akbar'—illustrating that the idea of *swadeshi* transcended religious boundaries. At the end of the procession, C. Veerabhadra Rao and Harisarvottama Rao spoke to a crowd of 1,000 people. Later, in the summer of 1907, Bipin Chandra Pal toured Andhra, particularly the city of Rajahmundry, where his speeches inspired the people to establish a National High School.[15] Pal delivered lectures in Rajahmundry for five days to an audience largely consisting of students from the local arts college. These reports indicate the growing impact of *swadeshi* and the Vande Mataram movement on young people, especially students. It also began to appeal to the local population from merchants to new professionals, such as lawyers. *The Hindu* reported that Pal visited Masulipatam, in Krishna district, after his visit to Rajahmundry on 11 May 1907, and spoke about the necessity of boycotting as political action, the need to develop a national education, and the idea of *swaraj* (self-rule).

Self-Determination and Provincial Politics

While Swadeshi and the Home Rule movements brought into the Indian political discourse conceptions of self-reliance, self-help, and self-rule (*swaraj*)—clearly articulated by Indian nationalists and circulating in British India prior to World War I—there was also a push coming from internationalist discourses of self-determination during this critical period. Indians interpreted the language of self-determination and self-government circulating in the interwar period on their own terms, such as *swaraj* and *swadeshi*.[16] Charles Hardinge, the governor general during the interwar period, wrote what appeared to be a controversial despatch in which he mentioned self-government for the provinces in due time. The despatch, dated 25 August 1911, recommended changes that were interpreted by Indian nationalists as a movement towards self-representation. Hardinge wrote:

> ... it is certain that, in the course of time, the just demands of Indians for a larger share in the government of the country will have to be satisfied, and the question will be how this devolution of power can be conceded without impairing the supreme authority of the Governor-General in Council. The only possible solution of the difficulty would appear to be gradually to give the provinces a larger measure of self-government, until at last India would consist of a number of administrations, autonomous in all provincial affairs, with the Government of India above them all[.][17]

While Indians interpreted this as a gesture towards self-government, British politicians tried to repudiate such an interpretation and called into question whether Britain was ready to grant such governing powers to Indians as non-Europeans. They questioned, in short, whether Indians as a race were prepared to take on such an important role.[18] The secretary at the time, Robert Crewe, stated:

> ... to the inception in India of something approaching the self-government enjoyed by those colonies which have late years received the name of Dominion. It is vain to deny the existence of such a school. I say quite frankly that I see no future for India on those lines. I do not believe that the experiment—for it would be an experiment quite new, so far as my knowledge of history goes, in the wide world—of attempting to confer a real measure of self-government with practical freedom from Parliamentary control, upon a race which is not our own[.]...[19]

Meanwhile, as reported by the *Madras Mail* on 4 May 1915, Annie Besant declared reassuringly, 'There was no power anywhere which had the right to say to a nation that it was either fit or unfit for self-government.' She went on to say that Indians should demand to manage their own affairs and have 'complete control over every provincial concern'.[20] *The Report on India's Constitutional Reforms*, popularly known as the Montagu–Chelmsford reforms, noted that World War I had played a key role in popularizing such nationalist ideas. The language of liberty and self-determination used by American and British statesmen to describe the ideological struggle of the war impacted colonial peoples' perception of their rightful place in a world of 'free' nation states.[21] The report stated:

> ... the war has come to be regarded more and more clearly as a struggle between liberty and despotism, a struggle for the right of small nations and for the right of all people to rule their own destinies. Attention is repeatedly called to the fact that in Europe Britain is fighting on the side of liberty, and it is urged that Britain cannot deny to the people of India that for which she is herself fighting

in Europe, and in the fight for which she has been helped by India's blood and treasure.²²

The report pointed out that the Government of India was on a path towards greater responsible government in which Indians would be gradually introduced into the administration with greater responsibilities. It also concluded that the Government of India had been, until then, a system of autocratic government that was now due for change. There was a clear recognition that the old system could no longer continue, presumably because of Britain's ideological standing in the world of nations. Britain's reform-minded government introduced changes in the Government of India to foster the principle of 'self-determination' though considerably limited in colonial India. Edwin Montagu, who authored the report, expressed his views in the House of Commons in 1917 that India and Indians were prepared for self-government.²³ It was indeed this coming together of political discourse that began with the Swadeshi movement and the global language of liberty and self-determination taking shape during the interwar period that impacted the new politics we see emerging in provincial politics in British India.

In the northern coastal districts of the Madras Presidency, the Andhra movement began to take shape in 1910 after the impact of 'Swadeshism' through the conscious revival of regional industries and a gradual political awakening of the region's role in the nationalist struggle. While there was friction in previous decades between social reformists advocating for radical reform of caste and custom on the one hand and nationalists who advocated political reform on the other, the Andhra movement was able to incorporate aspects of both. M. Venkatarangaiya writes that the earliest expression of a call for the Andhras to unite was in an article published on 19 January 1910 in the Telugu-language newspaper *Deshabhimani*. The *Deshabhimani* was a nationalist newspaper publishing articles on *swadeshi* politics. In other words, it had a nationalist scope, but at this particular moment it began to shift its focus towards the region and towards the Andhras as a political community. The newspaper stated:

> Just as the body could not really develop unless the various organs develop in a healthy manner, so also Mother India cannot shine unless the various races of India, who are the various organs, develop themselves.... Unless in the beginning each race by itself endeavours to become united, there can be no real national union in India. Applying this test the Telugu people stand in an unenviable position. The fact that the Telugus go by a common name points to the possibility of their future union.²⁴

The author of this article laments that India as a nation depends on healthy 'organs', or regions, and that these regions need to work to develop themselves and keep up with the rest of the nation as it marches towards a 'real national union'. Fortunately, the author points out, because the Telugus have a common name or language binding them together, there is hope that they could produce a union. The author goes onto write that the Andhras were divided into four groups—those from the Northern Circars, the ceded districts, north and south Arcot, and, lastly, the Nizam's Dominions—all of which eventually became part of Andhra Pradesh in 1956 after the merging of the Telangana districts of the former princely state of Hyderabad. The article also declared that it was, however, lamentable that the Andhras were currently not more politically active in national politics and therefore they were not fully politically conscious. The call for unity was indeed a call for the Telugu-speaking people to become aware of their political conditions and to become motivated to organize their community. There was a general sense that the Telugu people were not advancing their community within the larger entity of the Madras Presidency and that the provincial conferences and meetings were not representative of Telugu political interests. The beginnings of the Andhra movement lie in the idea that the Telugu language had been artificially distributed across provincial and princely state borders. Thus, the AMS provided a forum to bring Telugu speakers together to nurture cultural organizations devoted to the cultivation of the Telugu language and history and thereby revitalize Telugu culture. The AMS would also provide an organized way to lobby the colonial government with demands for forming a new province out of disparate Telugu-speaking districts. The Andhra movement emerged around the same time that the Non-Brahman movement was taking shape in the Madras Presidency to give voice to those who felt left out of an expanding colonial public sphere that was becoming increasingly dominated by brahman voices. It was important for these groups to make their voices heard in order to shape the direction of the Presidency.[25] For the advocates of the Andhra movement, as voiced in the Telugu newspapers at the time, it was thought that a separate province for the Andhras would encourage greater politicization of the people.[26]

This shift in political discourse and the nature of political reforms under consideration by the colonial government and the nationalists prompted the proliferation of Telugu pamphlets and histories in print on the necessity of cultivating democratic institutions and sensibilities at the provincial level and urging Telugu-speaking subjects to take on the responsibilities of becoming citizens. An interesting, slim volume titled *Votu* (Vote) by Gadicharla Harisarvottamarao in Telugu appeared in print in 1923, clearly aimed at a

Telugu readership to disseminate the concepts of democratic participation and popular sovereignty. It was published by the Andhra Parishad in the politically active city of Bezwada (modern-day Vijayawada). Harisarvottamarao, who appeared earlier in records of the Swadeshi agitation during the years of 1906–1907 in the cities of Madras and Rajahmundry, acted as the president of the AMS when the meeting was held in Ananthapuram in 1919.[27] He argues in *Votu* that in world history, as monarchies began to transition to people-led governments, only those kings who were responsive to the people were able to keep their power. The implication here is that in the past, only those rulers who paid due attention to the needs of the people were able to retain their power. Harisarvottamarao documents the transition from monarchies to the rise of democracies globally to teach the Telugu readers that what they are witnessing in India is a global historical process of transition away from monarchical rule, and also, of course, the movement towards popular rule (or self-rule) meant a questioning of the legitimacy of British colonial rule. He writes that eventually *praja prabhutvam* (people's government) gained a prominent place in the history of political institutions globally.[28] It is significant that at this particular moment in British India, there was a growing consensus that the political future of India lay in popular sovereignty as articulated most vociferously by the INC.[29] Harisarvottamarao goes on to describe the necessity of self-rule or self-government, which he took as a lesson from American history. Self-rule, he declared, was related to the rights of every person—the right of individual freedom being the most important, for it leads ultimately to political freedom (*rajakiya svatantryam*). His idea that the root of political freedom lay in individual freedom is noteworthy. Harisarvottamarao goes on to state that there are two important freedoms in modern times—individual freedom and political freedom—and both are necessary for the support of any people's government. His elaboration of the meaning of freedom illustrates his understanding of and commitment to liberal democracy and bringing liberal democracy to not only India but also to the Telugu people. His short book was a primer of sorts to educate Telugu-speaking subjects on the history and practice of democracy so they could better adapt it to their own sociopolitical conditions. Telugu texts such as *Votu* aimed at the Telugu-speaking community fulfilled the important function of helping individual readers absorb liberal political discourse that was fast taking root in British India. Activists such as Harisarvottamarao saw the necessity of educating people in the political language of liberal democracy so they could better understand the political climate and eventually take on the task of making themselves into responsible citizens.

Swadeshi politics promoted the use of the vernacular language for precisely this reason of reaching out to the people and ensuring their investment in their own political future—in short, politicizing them. In the 1930s, numerous Telugu books focused on the political changes that British India was undergoing. The prolific writer Digavalli Venkatasivaravu published a number of Telugu books on British Indian history and the political history of the region, including the implications of dominion status for British India for a Telugu-speaking audience.[30] Venkatasivaravu published a particularly interesting text defining political terms such as 'democracy', 'direct democracy', 'referendum', 'federation', and the 'League of Nations'.[31] An interesting text by Kalluri Chandramouli, who was a member of the Constituent Assembly representing the Madras Presidency in 1946–1948, outlined a broader history of democracy, beginning with major political changes in the history of the West, starting with Thomas Hobbes and his social contract theory.[32] Chandramouli was an elected member of the Madras legislative assembly (MLA) in 1937 and 1946 and contested in the 1951 elections in post-independent India. He was also deeply involved in the nationalist movement, participating in Mohandas K. Gandhi's Salt Satyagraha and the Civil Disobedience movement. In his *Nanadesa Rajyanga Nirmanamulu* (An Account of Constitutions of Various Countries), he introduces important political terms such as 'state', 'law', 'sovereignty', 'civil liberty', and 'constitution' to a Telugu audience. These texts were published in the early 1930s when the Round Table Conferences set forth the goal of deliberating a new constitution for India. Konda Venkatappayya, one of the main activists in the Andhra movement and the co-founder of the AMS and the ACC, published a book on modern constitutions and the rise of democratic governments around the world during the interwar period.[33] Venkatappayya argues for a durable modern democratic constitution for India that would allow for differences (such as language and religion) to flourish while promoting the principle of equality. In Hyderabad, in 1938, Suravaram Pratapa Reddy, a prominent publisher of the Telugu-language newspaper *Golkonda Patrika* and an active member of the Hyderabad branch of the AMS, published *Prajaadhikaaranamulu* (People's Rights), with a preface written by Bhogaraju Pattabhi Sitaramayya, a prominent member of the INC. In this book, Pratapa Reddy discusses the history of statecraft in ancient Greece and Rome, India, Europe, and the Middle East, tracing the shift from monarchical power to people's power.[34] Importantly, he focuses on how World War I and Woodrow Wilson's Fourteen Points reshaped the global order. By tracing the rise of popular sovereignty from the Magna Carta to the American, French, and Russian revolutions as well as the Great War, Suravaram portrays the post-World War I world order as the culmination of that trajectory. The profound impact of the war, Suravaram writes, was the normalization of 'self-determination' on an international scale and especially so in the colonies.

Self-Determination and the Andhra Movement

The language of liberty and self-determination used by the British government and its absorption into Indian political discourse (as seen in the proliferation of Telugu pamphlets and books at this time), as well as the impact of the Swadeshi movement and its ideals of self-reliance and self-rule, not only had an impact on broader currents in Indian nationalism but also profoundly shaped regional conceptions of self-government. This directly led to two demands made by regional activists such as those who started the Andhra movement in the Madras Presidency: (*a*) provincial autonomy and (*b*) the redrawing of provincial boundaries based on a more rational basis than the historical accident of imperial borders in British India. The impact of the Montagu–Chelmsford reforms on provincial autonomy in south India has been dealt with by numerous historians, especially as it gave rise to the Justice Party and, more broadly, the Non-Brahmanism movement in the Madras Presidency.[35] However, the reforms also coincided with another critical development in south Indian politics in addition to the Non-Brahmanism movement. Regional political activists strengthened their call to redraw provincial boundaries using linguistic criteria—an argument that was spearheaded most vociferously by the Andhra activists through the AMS.

The Andhra movement was not the first broad-based movement in colonial India to demand the redrawing of provinces according to linguistic criteria. The Oriya (present-day Odia) language movement began in the 1860s, protesting the dominance of Bengali in the region and demanding the use of Oriya in vernacular schools.[36] This movement shifted to the call for a separate province for Oriya speakers in the early decades of the twentieth century. The Telugu intellectuals who spearheaded the Andhra movement made constant references to the other movements in order to legitimize their own grievances and set their goal as not only institutionalizing Telugu as a language of education but, more importantly, also pushing for representative institutions better suited to developing the geographic region of Coastal Andhra or the Northern Circars. In the 24 February 1913 issue of *The Hindu*, a letter from V. Subrahmanyam of Triplicane asks:

> Why did the dispatch of Lord Hardinge have such an impact on the Andhras alone and not on others, say, the Malayalis or Kannadigas? The condition of the Andhras in Madras Presidency resembled that of Biharis in the Bengal Presidency. They were the second largest group in the Presidency. They were the second largest group in the Presidency with similar grievances in matters of education and public service. Neither Malayalis nor the Kannadigas were numerous in the Madras Presidency comprising less than 10 percent and about

4 per cent respectively. The Kannadigas were more numerous in Bombay but still only about 10 percent. Further in the Madras Presidency, the literacy even in vernaculars of Malayalis and Kannadigas was high.... Consequently, the well-educated Malayali or Kannadiga in Madras Presidency had better chances for public service compared to their numbers and so were not aggrieved like the Andhras.[37]

The Andhra activists, through their primary organ, the AMS, founded in 1913, were busy comparing numbers, assessing majorities and minorities in the provinces, and making arguments about how best to develop their region, resources, and community. Strategies of colonial governmentality—specifically, strategies of enumeration, such as the census—helped forge community identities based on language, caste, and religion.[38] These communities were further refined and called forth in the early twentieth century, when new political technologies were being introduced at the regional level. The expansion of representative institutions as a result of constitutional reforms led to the formation of significant constituencies in south India: the Justice Party, the regional units of the INC, and the Self-Respect movement broadly in the Madras Presidency. In the Telugu-speaking regions of the Madras Presidency, equally significant were the Adi-Andhra Mahasabha in the northern coastal districts and the AMS that began in the northern coastal districts but expanded into the Hyderabad state.[39] As Baker has argued, the Montagu–Chelmsford reforms were to instigate greater expansion of native participation in the Madras government. However, Eugene Irschick and Baker link the reforms to the expansion and success of non-Brahmanism in the Madras Presidency.[40] One can extend this analysis to suggest that the expansion of representative institutions led to the growth of regional parties and provincial politics and institutions. For the Andhra activists, the expansion of representative institutions and proposals for provincial autonomy necessitated discussions about how best to break up big provinces such as the Madras Presidency and thus give greater powers and autonomy to significant regional or territorial constituencies within the Presidency. During the height of non-Brahmanism, however, the Andhra movement faced competition. As Telugu speakers were prominent in the Justice Party in Madras, they posed a political challenge for the Andhra activists who were primarily working with the INC. Venkatappayya, one of the founding members of the Andhra movement, initiated the separation of the ACC.

Within this complex set of political currents in the Madras Presidency, it is not unusual for language to become the basis for making demands on regional political autonomy. Civil societal activism that centred on language in British India went through successive periods in which language was the object of reform and revival throughout the nineteenth century. By the turn of the twentieth century, language increasingly became the basis for making a claim on territory and its resources (in the language of development and modernization).[41] While the processes of institutionalization of language began early in the nineteenth century, the latter phase was considerably shaped by the new politics unfolding in the early decades of the twentieth century. Venkatappayya, as one of the primary Andhra activists of this period, wrote on why new provinces must be rethought along linguistic lines:

> If the people living in those provinces are to have an organic growth and development, they must be constituted into separate, handy, compact and homogenous entities, so that the natural binding forces of society, such as, language and literature, custom and tradition, culture and sentiment, may have free play and promote unity, tolerance and responsibility and other noble qualities characterising a race or community entitled to self-government.[42]

Venkatapayya makes a case for the idea that a people or community of a region should be bound into linguistic units (though language is one important criterion along with literature, tradition, and sentiment that unifies a people) because that would make governing rational—especially *self*-government. Venkatappayya attributes the idea of provincial autonomy as the future of British India to John Bright, who, he argues, 'foreshadowed the political destiny of India in which "the different provinces shall ultimately form locally autonomous States with separate governments, separate armies, etc."',[43] though from this quote it is not clear what Venkatappayya makes of the political future of India conceptualized as regional autonomous states. The proposal is quite radical and would have been vehemently opposed by his contemporaries in the INC. Venkatappayya goes on to argue that this political destiny is gradually being realized in the aftermath of the agitation against the partitioning of Bengal as Indian people have become politicized and self-consciously agitate for their own individual and regional interests. Venkatappayya writes that the region of Andhra had been constituted historically before colonial rule: 'It is clear that the Andhra for ages had kingdoms of their own which were both extensive in territory and ruled by monarchs endowed with military genius and administrative capacity. Their language and literature have been highly developed.'[44] However, while Andhra formed into a single unit with a common history, tradition, customs, and language under a common and powerful king, Muslim rulers in the Deccan, he argues, split the region into divisions. Furthermore, with the advent of British rule, those divisions became even more entrenched as the presidencies were formed in British India.

Venkatappayya quotes Sitaramayya, who was a friend of the Andhra movement, that the creation of the Madras Presidency was particularly arbitrary and irrational as it was a 'pure chronological growth' and not at all based on any natural laws or on the influence of historical events or on the consideration of language.[45]

In his work on modern constitutions, Venkatappayya places importance on democratic constitutions worldwide and explains how it might work in British India. The devolution schemes of the colonial government gave greater levels of autonomy to local and regional governments, leading to the cultivation of liberal conceptions of citizenship and public life. Venkatapayya draws attention to the idea that self-government relies on a people committed to 'unity, tolerance and responsibility', and that only within a community bound by language and tradition could basic conceptions of citizenship be cultivated. Mrinalini Sinha recalls the interwar period in Indian history to draw attention to the emergence of the 'anticolonial mass subject' for new forms of civic solidarity.[46] In provincial politics, as Venkatapayya delineates, a sense of civic responsibility was being called forth. Intellectuals and activists hailing from different regions began to think of ways to foster community bonds and loyalty through the cultivation of civic mindedness. Local and regional literary societies took the lead in providing space for public discussion and debate over literary, social, and political issues at the turn of the twentieth century. Associations such as the Young Men's Literary Association of Guntur, the Vizianagaram Literary Association, and the Coconada Literary Association were a few such societies that were established in the Telugu-speaking districts to provide the space.[47]

The first Andhra Mahajana Sabha (later the AMS) meeting took place on 20 May 1913 and was presided over by B. N. Sharma, a member of the Legislative Council of Madras, who later became member of the Viceroy's Executive Council.[48] It was momentous in that the meeting brought together representatives from the Telugu-speaking districts of British India and from the princely state of Hyderabad. At the venue for the conference, twenty-two gates were constructed, each adorned with the names of poets, heroes, and heroines commemorating Andhra history. The proceedings began with the song 'Vande Mataram', which declared their allegiance and commitment to the nationalist movement, while the meeting was conducted in Telugu.[49] At the turn of the twentieth century, the impact of the shift to vernacular languages in public speaking cannot be underestimated.[50] Sharma told the audience at the conference that they were Indians first and sons of 'Mother Andhra' second, thus balancing their regional affiliations with the compulsions of nationalism.[51] This was a common refrain of the Andhra activists lest they be mistaken as working against the nationalist cause. But even as the Andhra activists clearly began to promote language as the basis for a territorial political community in the region, they nevertheless knew that the nationalist movement was primary. The goal of independence for the nation, as outlined by the INC, had to take precedence over regional identities and affiliations. Nevertheless, the Andhra activists felt that they could do both—cultivate their regional political identity all the while simultaneously working for the nationalist movement. In fact, the Andhra activists saw themselves as pioneers outlining a strategy for federated regional identities that would simultaneously uphold a national one. This idea the Andhra activists charted out as a path for regional identity based on language continued into the post-independence period when Andhra achieved separate statehood in 1953.[52]

At the first AMS conference, two resolutions were reached. The first was that

> to ensure efficient administration and the promotion of the best interests of the people of India, the Government will sooner or later have to make language areas, the territorial basis of provincial administration.[53]

And the second was that

> provincial administration, on such a basis, is necessary in order that both the self government [sic] on colonial lines pleaded for by the Indian National Congress and the provincial autonomy approved of by the Government of India, may develop on healthy and natural lines, this Conference Committee, now appointed, ascertain public opinion, on the question whether the government should be asked to constitute the Telugu districts into a separate province.[54]

The argument was based on the idea of administrative convenience which especially made sense as a common language would ease communication. The idea that representative government must be based on a shared language is part and parcel of the broader projects of political modernity. Furthermore, the Andhra activists believed it was in their interest to push for linguistically demarcated provinces. In his *Memorandum on Andhra Province* (1938), V. Ramadas Pantulu quoted the Standing Committee of the AMS on the relationship between a provincial identity and a national one:

> The moment we visualize each of the fifteen or sixteen provinces constituted on linguistic basis, functioning each in its own as, fostering its own language, promoting its own culture, imparting its own instruction and administering its justice through its vernacular language and dealing with its villages and their rural problems through the vernaculars of the heart, the very moment we visualize India as a nation whose nationalism is not the steam-road-rolled

product exhibiting a dull uniformity, but as a harmonious combination of diverse cultures exhibiting a fundamental unity.[55]

Indeed, the region became the primary locus for new aspirations of cultural pride. However, more importantly, I would argue that the region became the site for the elaboration of liberal civil societal institutions that would inculcate democratic virtues of citizenship. What these regional movements had in common, first and foremost, was an articulation of a civilizational defence of the region. Along with a civilization defence was the argument that their regional language was worthy as any other—articulating cultural pride. But even more important was their call for adequate political representational institutions for the region. The region was conceptualized and articulated as a territorial linguistic community, with the implicit argument being that language (transcending caste ideally) would act to bind the community together and inspire its speakers to work towards the political unit of the region. From this perspective, language was thus both a source of cultural pride and a site for political modernity.

At the first Andhra Conference, Sharma said that the Telugus needed to cultivate 'a spirit of brotherhood, a nationality based on common tradition, interests and aspirations, and towards uplifting themselves in the scale of nations by their education, character and wealth'.[56] Like other Andhra activists, Sharma recognized that linguistic pride or nationality based on a common language had to be cultivated in order to create a cohesive political community. Cultural cohesion fostered through linguistic provinces would help to further democratize politics in India. In 1913, Venkatappaayya went to the ceded districts of the Madras Presidency to speak to local leaders with the explicit purpose of convincing them of the benefits of amalgamating the Telugu districts into one province.[57] The Andhra activists recognized that there was no inherent natural community based on language that would lead to a political community. It had to be cultivated and constructed and made politically viable by producing consent amongst the various parties. Consent would come about by carefully addressing the needs of all the Telugu-speaking districts. The ceded districts were opposed to the demand for a separate Andhra province from the very beginning. Yet, despite the hurdles faced by the Andhra activists, language was clearly preferred over caste and religion as markers of a community since the latter were seen to be more divisive.

As for the liberal aspiration for developing civil societal institutions, the region became the ideal locus to conceptualize and cultivate the new citizen-subject required for a self-governing India. Venkatappayya wrote in 1913 that the 'Andhra movement is only an attempt to open their [that is, the Telugu people's] minds to their present backwardness and induce individual exertion as well as corporate action on their part to improve their condition'.[58] While Venkatappayya argued that Andhra constituted a region well before the advent of British colonial rule, there was much work to be done to compel Telugu people to think of themselves as liberal subjects capable of and responsible for self-rule. The work of the Andhra movement was to cultivate a love for education and culture, to motivate people to improve themselves and become better citizens, to create a spirit of cooperation and mutual trust, to educate people about the agricultural and commercial potential in the region and inspire them to work collectively towards its progress, and to cultivate Telugu literature in order to disseminate 'the principles of modern culture and enlightenment to the masses'. Again, the clearly stated goals of the early Andhra activists reflected the conscious effort that was being put into making a dynamic liberal civil society.

Two decades after the founding of AMS, there was a steady discussion of how to develop the provinces as British India moved towards self-government. The Andhra activists believed they were on a path towards a new province in the 1930s. Back in 1919, when Montagu was travelling around British India interviewing various leaders, Sharma put forward a motion in the Imperial Legislative Council for the creation of a separate province for Andhra. This was struck down at the time because of the more pressing issue of Gandhi's impending Non-Cooperation movement. It took them a series of compromises to make the case for a separate province from first convincing the Rayalseema districts that they would benefit by grouping with the northern coastal districts to form an Andhra state. However, after Andhra University was established at Waltair in the coastal districts in 1931, the Rayalseema districts were reluctant to join the coastal districts in agitating for an Andhra province. This then led to the demand to make Madras a joint capital for both the Tamils and the Telugus.

The twentieth session of the AMS, held on 8 October 1938, was preoccupied with this question of making Madras the capital of an Andhra province. First, the coastal Telugus had to be convinced that it would be beneficial for their province to have Madras as its capital. Pantulu writes that Andhra public opinion had come around to the idea that making Madras the capital for Andhra would aid industry, commerce, and banking in the province. The Rayalseema districts insisted on Madras, but the Working Committee of the Tamil Nadu Congress protested this new development. They needed to be convinced. The Andhra activists brought in Vavilla Venkateswara Sastrulu and Sarvepalli Radhakrishnan for the task. Sastrulu made a historical argument—that from the very beginning of English transactions in south India, Telugu brahmins were employed as translators and interpreters. There were also prominent Telugu intellectuals in Madras contributing to its public life, such as Kavali Borayya, the famed assistant of Colin Mackenzie, the first surveyor general of India. For these reasons, Sastrulu argued that Madras had always been a Telugu city from its very foundations. Radhakrishnan offered a more measured recommendation—that Madras remain the capital of an Andhra province. He cited C. Rajagopalachari speaking at the MLA on the question of an Andhra province. Rajagopalachari quoted the Montagu report on the idea that a common language is a 'strong and natural' basis for 'provincial individuality'. It was not, however, the only criteria; rather, race, religion, geography, and economic interests all needed to be taken into account. Beyond that, the most important goal was 'the largest possible measure of general agreement on the changes proposed, both on the side of which is gaining, and on the side, that is the area that is losing advantage'.[59] In other words, a consensus had to be reached (as far as possible) through public discussion and debate, reaching out to those who were sceptical of the benefits of unifying the Telugu districts and making Madras its capital. Rajagopalachari was approached by Andhra movement leaders, as quoted in an article, 'Separate Andhra Province: Madras Premier's View', published in the *Times of India* on 4 December 1937, in which he stated that it was clear that Andhra should eventually be reorganized on a linguistic basis. However, Rajagopalachari stated that it was not the right time to do so because if Madras was split into two units, they would be too small to be able to exert pressure on the colonial government. He instead urged everyone to 'focus public opinion on the major issues and attain the INC objective of independence'.[60] For INC activists like Rajagopalachari, the primary objective of achieving independence from British rule trumped any discussion of redrawing provincial boundaries. Whether new provincial boundaries were formed on the basis of language, ethnicity, religion, or geography, Rajagopalachari contended that the time was not right because it could jeopardize the nationalist struggle and the goal of independence.

The Andhra Movement and Ethnic Nationalism

In the midst of these intense and polarizing debates in the MLA, there were more aggressive stances taken up by political activists in the northern coastal districts who wanted an immediate resolution to the question of separate statehood for the Andhras. The news from Madras was met with firm resolve to push even harder for the formation of a separate province for the Telugus. Groups such as the Andhra Defence League (ADL) and the ASP came into the public arena to make these demands. The leading voice for an immediate separation of the province was G. Venkatasubba Rao, the editor of the journal *Goshti*, which was devoted to providing a cultural and political forum for political conservatives in south India. He was also the founder of the ASP. Venkatasubba Rao was a vocal and rather consistent critic of the INC and their equivocal support for the constitution of the Andhra province. Rao felt it was necessary to adopt radical measures to put pressure on the legislative debates. By appropriating nationalist political strategies of the Gandhian activists (all the while vehemently disagreeing with Gandhi and Gandhian politics), Rao called for *satyagraha*s and boycotts to create popular pressure towards the creation of an Andhra province. The ADL, formed by Venkatasubba Rao in the city of Bezwada, aimed to bring Telugu-speaking districts in the British provinces and the princely states into one singular Andhra province. By founding a separate organization from the AMS, it is clear that Rao felt a stronger voice needed to be heard that was uncompromising in the demand for a separate province. Rao did not hesitate to include the Nizam's territories in his maps and discussion of the future organization of linguistic provinces. Rao's political organization and activism centred on creating a political community out of what he saw as the *natural* bonds of language. In his English-language journal, *Goshti*, he writes that the journal is a cultural magazine that 'believes in the cultural unity of the Telugu-speaking people of Andhradesa. And it will do all in its power to provide opportunities for the nascent talent and genius of the Andhras, wherever situated, to fulfil itself in the various walks of Life'.[61] The creation of a separate province was to fulfil one of the goals of the AMS from its founding in the 1910s, which was to nurture Telugu culture and unity amongst the Telugu speakers who were spread across borders in different princely states and British Indian provinces. He stated that the aims of the ADL were not only to bring the Telugu-speaking peoples from neighbouring provinces to the Madras Presidency, but also to agitate for the inclusion of those from the native princely states such as Hyderabad. In addition, he stated that the ADL had to advocate for Telugus abroad.[62] For Rao, the bonds of language were strong enough to bring these disparate populations together.

The goal, Rao admitted, was to privilege Andhras over other ethnic groups within the province—even to eliminate all cultural signs and symbols that did not belong to the Andhras. This is not atypical for forms of ethnic nationalism—a nationalism that does not hesitate to elevate one language, ethnicity, or race over others. In this sense, Rao advocated a narrow nationalism rather than an expansive and inclusive one. His nationalism was 'expansive' only in the sense of including Telugu-speaking populations from all neighbouring states, including the princely state of Hyderabad. On 29 October 1937, Rao (while serving as the secretary for the ASP based in Bezwada) wrote in *The Mahratta* on the need to reach out to Telugu speakers in princely Hyderabad whom he called 'Andhras'. He, in fact, referred to all Telugu speakers with the term 'Andhras', which in the contemporary period refers primarily to northern coastal (of the Madras Presidency) speakers of Telugu. Rao said that the British Andhras and the Nizam's Andhras should 'awaken' a closer relationship in order to better advocate for the Andhra movement; towards this end, a delegation of British Andhras should be sent to Telangana to foster this relationship. He also wrote that this delegation should first pay respects to the Nizam and Akbar Hydari because after all the 'Nizam is not only the richest man of the world, but he is our first and most distinguished fellow Andhra kinsman'.[63] By suggesting this familial connection between the Nizam and the Telugu people who lived within the boundaries of the princely state, Rao was in a sense pointing to the Nizam's position as the monarch and sovereign who has been for over two centuries in charge of the well-being of the Telugus residing in the Telangana region. In the late 1930s, Rao was still interested in creating links with princely Hyderabad knowing full well that their political situation and conditions were radically different from the Madras Presidency. The map in Figure 2.1, drawn by Venkatasubba Rao, indicates his territorial ambitions for an Andhra province.

In 1937, Venkatasubba Rao wrote a letter published in *The Hindu*, addressing John Erksine, who had told the Rajahmundry Municipal Council that their request for a separate Andhra province was not in his hands, but rather that 'the formation of Provinces is, under the Government of India Act, a matter that [was] in the hands of Parliament and of the Secretary of State'.[64] Invoking the political language of the times, Rao responded in his letter to *The Hindu* that in this climate of 'self-determination' and *swaraj*, the Andhras were due a direct response from the administration for their demands. However, he departed from earlier activists who pointed to the problem of other ethnic groups advancing in the Madras Presidency over and above the Telugus. In an article, 'Andhra Conference Threatens Direct Action', in the *Madras Mail* on 3 April 1939, these Andhra activists pointed to a growing feeling that Tamil speakers were draining the resources of Andhra—a problem they attributed to the unwieldy province of Madras.[65] Because of its size and the dominance of Tamil speakers, the activists argued that the Andhras would not get their fair share of resources. This particular rhetoric foreshadowed contemporary arguments concerning the agitation for Telangana to be formed as a separate state because the region was not receiving due attention in developing its own resources.

As reported in *The Hindu* on 3 April 1939, in the article 'An Ultimatum to India Secretary: Andhra Province in Six Months', the representatives of the Andhra movement met in Bezwada in April 1939. Rao outlined how the movement was going to move forward, with the main proposal being that some sort of direct action should be taken. He then stated that the idea behind a boycott

Figure 2.1 Map of Andhra, 1937

Source: G. V. Subba Rao collection, vol. 31 (1937), Telangana State Archives (TSA), Hyderabad.

Figure 2.2 The Andhra national flag from the *Madras Mail*, 1939

Source: Constitutional Affairs Secretariat, Creation of a Separate Andhra Province (Linguistic Provinces), Telangana State Archives (TSA), Hyderabad.

was for 'the elimination of the underlying causes of British, Tamil, Gujarati, Arabi, Hindustani, Bengalee and other domination over Andhra life'.[66] This was a rather bold stance for the ASP and the ADL, as articulated by Rao; it employed the idea of cultural purity and preference as a way to organize a new province—sharply in contrast with the political goals of many of the Andhra activists who were active in the INC. The ASP was formed by Venkatasubba Rao in 1933 when they demanded immediate council entry and wanted Gandhi to call off the Civil Disobedience movement and his programme to end untouchability. The ADL and the ASP, led by Rao, quite clearly represented the conservative faction of the Andhra movement. They, along with many conservative INC members, were not enthusiastic about the call for the eradication of untouchability and argued that the movement should focus exclusively on political agitation rather than a social reform agenda.[67] His stance against including caste reform within the movement recalls J. Gurunatham's position on Kandukuri Viresalingam and what Gurunatham identified as the apparent lack of political critique in social reformism. One of the forefathers of and inspiration for Rao's ASP was Duggirala Gopalakrishnayya, who participated in the Gandhian anti-tax *satyagraha* in Chirala in 1921 but then, dissatisfied with Gandhi, subsequently joined Das's Swarajya Party in 1925.[68] Gopalakrishnayya became Rao's mentor, and he subsequently declared that his 1950s journal, *Goshti*, was the realization of his mentor's wishes. Rao's criticism of the INC and Gandhian politics in general stems from his alignment with and sympathies with Gopalakrishnayya's politics and break with Gandhi. In an article published in his journal on the 'heroism' of Alluri Sitaramaraju in the 1920s, Rao mockingly referred to Gandhi as 'experimenting with his truths' while 'real' heroes were out on the ground fighting for freedom. Rao represented himself as a conservative aligned with the political ideology of V. D. Sarvarkar as well as Radhakumud Mookherji, who wrote a preface to *Goshti* in 1954 praising Rao's efforts as a true nationalist.[69] In 1955, Rao also received good wishes from Sarvarkar on the success of his journal and his fight for the Hindu cause.

Rao's conservative agenda notwithstanding, the Andhra activists broadly speaking were working in conjunction with INC leaders such as Sitaramayya towards a workable resolution to the question of separating an Andhra province (in a federal arrangement) while safeguarding the fundamental rights of mobility and access for all Indians across provincial boundaries. The INC's position emphasized the liberal safeguarding of minority rights before deciding on creating new provinces. The Andhra demand for a separate province was seen as legitimate, but it was felt that giving into the demand might be dangerous at the current political moment. These concerns largely undergirded the INC policies of separating provinces.

Provincial Politics and Federation

On 6 April 1939, in the *Madras Mail*, Sitaramayya wrote that he had full confidence in the Madras ministry and if they were delaying the process of the formation of the state, it was not because there are any constitutional hurdles. Rather, he pointed out a strong reason for waiting, noting that

> it is good that the conference has not passed any specific resolutions regarding the proportions of the Andhras to the Tamils in the Services. The matter was left to be dealt with at a public meeting. When a province is composed of different communities and the Provincial Government has to deal with more than one territorial unit, it is difficult to blame it for not balancing the interests and the numbers of each territorial unit with those of the other units of the province. For one thing, the separate consciousness is of a recent origin.[70]

Sitaramayya drew attention to the problem of pitting one linguistic group against another within a given province. Regional territorial consciousness was of recent origin, according to Sitaramayya. The fear, he pointed out, was that a problem of numbers would arise concerning the constitution of majorities and minorities with the creation of new provinces.

In fact, the Bardoli Resolution of the INC Working Committee on Public Services, included in Pantulu's *Memorandum on Andhra Province*, stated that a provincial or regional nationality should be encouraged so as to instil in Indians a sense of unity and purpose; in other words, cultivating provincial nationalism was an important project that should be encouraged as it is tied to the larger goal of anti-colonial nationalism. The Bardoli Resolution cautioned, however, that with regards to services, no person of Indian origin should be barred from employment in any part. This resolution with regards to the mobility of Indians across provincial boundaries was clearly important for the INC, and one can see how the cultivation of a national identity over and above the provincial one was a priority and a necessity. Regional autonomy and 'self-determination' at the provincial level meant the balancing of the national and the regional. The Bardoli Resolution went on to say that certain considerations should be taken into account:

> These considerations are—(A) a fair representation of the various communities in the province; (B) encouragement as far as possible of backward classes and

groups, so that they might develop and play their full part in the national life; (C) preferential treatment to the people of their province. It is desirable that this preferential treatment should be governed by certain rules and regulations framed by the provincial governments in order to prevent individual officers from applying different standards. Further it is desirable that similar rules should be applicable in all the provinces.[71]

The INC attempted to safeguard minority groups within provinces so that dominant linguistic groups or castes were not automatically given preferential treatment or unfair advantage at the provincial levels. The INC also wanted to ensure that all Indians had the right to move between states and not be excluded from services in a given state. Beyond the INC's attempt to balance the provinces' demands and to assure minority groups of their rights, there was the additional problem of boundary-making: 'The difficulty about the Andhras' settling their boundaries is that they must get the Tamils on the one side the Kanarese on the second, and the Oriyas on the third, to sit by them and think out the problem together.'[72] Furthermore, the Andhra movement did not have the same momentum in the other regions as it did in the northern coastal districts of the Madras Presidency. The Telugu-speaking regions of Rayalseema and Telangana were not unequivocally committed to the formation of an Andhra province. Telangana, of course, was not even part of British India in order for it to be a part of these political debates. Despite that, some Andhra activists such as Venkatasubba Rao included the princely Hyderabad districts in mapping the Andhra province.

Ultimately, for the INC, the debate came down to whether provinces should be redrawn from their colonial boundaries before federating or they should be redrawn afterwards with the formation of an Indian union of states. The argument against carving out a new province was put forward and debated in the MLA. What they ultimately debated in the assembly was with regards to whether the Government of India Act of 1935 clearly outlined that provinces could be formed only after a federation was agreed upon. The Round Table Conferences and later the Government of India Act of 1935 proposed federation as a path for British Indian provinces and native states to work together towards a common political future. However, the MLA debated the procedure and timeline for constituting separate provinces. For the two decades since the Montagu–Chelmsford reforms, provincial politics had turned to crafting more rationally demarcated provinces that would enable democratic institutions to easily take root and to flourish. In 1938, K. P. Mallikarjunudu moved a resolution in the MLA on 31 March for steps to be taken to constitute separate provinces with autonomous provincial administrations corresponding to languages spoken in the region.[73] The main point he raised was that language—the vernacular or regional language—should be taken into consideration when demarcating new provinces as India gradually moved towards representative democratic institutions. Naturally, the idea that the use of the language of the region in further entrenching democratic institutions occurred to those arguing for the redrawing of provinces. However, they went even further by arguing that language was not simply a natural marker of a group but something constitutive of and inseparable from the group. Specifically, Mallikarjunudu states:

> States are organisations invented by man for the purpose of fulfilling, what I may call, national personality. Students of political science are familiar with the idea that language and race are some of the most important factors in the formation of States…. Language is not a mere symbol of thought, as some people imagine. But, it is its own manifestation. Language and thought are one and the same and they are indivisible, as the greatest of poets, Kalidas, described in his famous work 'Raghuvamsa'….[74]

Mallikarjunudu pontificates that language and thought are inseparable; in other words, language determines or shapes the formation of ideas and concepts. And for a new political imaginary to take root, it must be disseminated in the language itself. Political ideas need to be taught in the vernacular language for the community to understand, embrace, and appropriate for their own benefit. Mallikarjunudu goes on to state, 'Adoption of vernacular language helps us to democratise representative institutions and opens up the fertile field for the growth of real responsible Government.' This is precisely what the early founders of the AMS also argued when they said that representative institutions and government depend upon people grasping the ideas first—that the process of democratization of the people depends upon diffusion of ideas through the use of the vernacular language, as well as debating those ideas freely in the public sphere. Language does not automatically constitute a culture or a group, but it is the ground upon which democracy would need to take root. Furthermore, he goes on to say, 'It helps to pass leadership into the hands of enlightened rural population. Political consciousness of the masses will be aroused, and people will begin to take due place in the formulation of national policies.'[75] For Indians to truly take on responsible government based on popular sovereignty, the people need to be 'enlightened' and awakened to their democratic and civic duties. In order for a linguistic community—one that was democratically constituted—to flourish, a province had to be carved out.

Mallikarjunudu's argument for the redrawing of provincial boundaries was a compelling one—the argument being essentially that administrative units or provinces in British India were originally drawn for administrative convenience and not on the basis of race, nation, or language: 'Sir Thomas Holderness, once Under-Secretary of State for India said, "With the exception of Burma, no province represents a natural unit; that is to say, the provinces do not stand for differences of race or language or geographical distribution".'[76] Mallikarjunudu points out that the Nehru report also asserted the importance of redrawing provincial units on a rational basis. He quotes from the report: 'It is merely due to accident and the circumstances attending the growth of British power in India. As a whole it has little to do with geographical or historical or economic or linguistic reasons. Even from the purely administrative point of view, it is not a success.'[77] The accident of empire was quite obviously not a rational basis for retaining the administrative units as they were. Sitaramayya made a similar argument in his article, 'India on a Federal Basis', in the *Madras Mail* in April 1939, in which he argued that historical accidents should not determine the provinces and that, in fact, language provided a logical marker for any future provincial division.[78]

Mallikarjunudu goes on to quote from a series of reports over the years to argue that linguistically organized provinces were necessary for the development of self-government institutions at the local and regional level. In fact, only this arrangement was the realization of the principle of self-determination and the proper constitution of the people. In particular references to the formation of linguistic provinces in southern India, he spoke of their specific individuality as regional cultures. In reference to Andhra, for instance, he argues: 'The Telugu-speaking area, including the Agency tracts, consists of 82,000 square miles and the population is 19 millions odd. One the question of territory, there is no case against the formation of an Andhra Province.'[79] He went on to argue that there was no doubt that Andhra should be made a separate province because of its size, language, and culture. Furthermore, he states that it was an urgent matter because 'there is now the peoples' Government in power, and people are desirous that this question must be settled when there is a popular Government in power'.[80] Finally, he proposes that the provinces be constituted before the formation of a federation. Here he states the urgency for forming a new province, and just like the AMS activists he argues that the nationalist goal of achieving self-government would not be compromised in forming a new Andhra province. In Mallikarjunudu's proposals, we can see how the idea of federation, the principle of nationality, and the right of self-determination were being knitted together in the argument for linguistically demarcated provincial boundaries.

The debate referenced earlier resolutions on forming an Andhra province ever since the establishment of the AMS in 1913. This was a consequence of the INC itself coming to the conclusion in 1903 that provinces should be formed on the basis of language. In 1917, the INC created a separate Congress unit for the Andhra districts and formed the Andhra Provincial Congress Committee (APCC) in 1920. There were many resolutions previous to the current debate, from the 1921 general resolution for the redistribution of provinces on a linguistic basis in the legislative assembly in Delhi to 1927 when Pantulu moved a resolution in the Council of State, and P. Anjaneyulu moved a resolution in the Madras Legislative Council that passed with a majority.[81] The Government of India did not act on any of these earlier resolutions, which left the Andhra activists to believe that the INC had not been taking their demands seriously and instead putting them on the back burner. As for the INC, they pointed to fears that regional aspirations for reorganizing provinces would potentially lead to disunity with the precarious alliance between the Tamil and the Telugu Congress workers in the Madras Presidency and threaten the momentum of the anti-colonial nationalist movement in the 1920s and the 1930s.

Even in 1938, the debates were tense and a resolution on an Andhra province was set aside in the MLA and ultimately rejected by prominent figures such as T. S. S. Rajan, who argued that a federation at that time was a recipe for disorder and chaos after the considerable gains achieved by the INC and the nationalist movement.

> This Council recommends to the Madras Government that the opinion of this House be communicated to His Majesty's Government of Great Britain that it is politically and morally impossible for the people and Government of this province to tolerate the imposition of the scheme of Federation as laid down in the Government of India Act of 1935, and that the said scheme would, far from bringing about all-India unity, provoke forces of conflict in the provinces and the Indian States, and that this Council hopes that the Government of Great Britain will respect the wishes of the people of India and immediately devise means, even for transitional purposes, to set up a Central Government free from the objectionable features of the Federal scheme of the Government of India Act to be evolved in consultation with the responsible Provincial Governments and national leaders.[82]

The fear of disunity that the reorganization of provinces would potentially provoke laid the basis for the those who opposed the resolution. The INC's official line was to defer the question of creating new provinces (or reorganizing provinces) for fear of 'Balkanization' of South Asia after British withdrawal.

The 1935 Government of India Act employed the discourse of self-determination to promote a federation of states, but the federation that was proposed was eventually rejected by both the INC and the AIML. What unfolded in the MLA debates in 1938 on federation and over the possibility of constituting an Andhra province revealed the fault lines and complications in separating out linguistically homogenous districts and forming a new province. The primary concern was that divisions at the provincial level would lead to disagreements at the national level—specifically in terms of reaching consensus with regards to making political demands on the colonial government. Divisions at the provincial level, it was feared, would diminish the power held by the INC—though, as we have seen in this chapter, since the second decade of the twentieth century, several new political organizations had emerged, representing different constituencies in the Madras Presidency and effectively checking the dominance of the INC. These were the Justice Party, the Self-Respect movement, and the AMS, as well as increasingly vocal Dalit organizations in the Madras Presidency. The Andhra movement faced challenges even as it gained ground with INC supporters working in the AMS and lobbying for separating out Telugu districts from the Madras Presidency. What emerged in the MLA debates were contentious issues concerning which districts were to be included and, of course, how Madras as a thriving colonial city would figure into the process. Lastly, another important point of contention in the debates over the Andhra movement was how the movement and the INC positioned themselves with regards to the Telangana region (Telugu-speaking region) in princely Hyderabad.

Self-Determination, the Principle of Nationality, and the Fate of Federation

In 1942, the CPI published a tract on Pakistan, explaining the idea of self-determination and nationalities. In the tract, G. Adhikari argues that the principle of nationality would not be contradicted by the language of federation, thus making a case for linguistic basis for provinces:

> The grant of the right of self-determination to all the nationalities of our land will in fact lead to a greater and more glorious unity of India than we have ever had till now. National unity that is forged on this basis will let loose such a flood of popular energy and initiative that our land has never seen since the glorious days of Congress–Khilafat unity. The Free India that will emerge as the result of this will be an India where all disruptive feudal–imperialist influences are destroyed, where the utmost democracy prevails, where the people have come

into their own in every national state. Under such conditions, the interests of the people in every national state, that make up the Indian Union, are identical; they have everything in common, nothing in conflict. They gain everything by sticking to each other; they only stand to lose by breaking away.[83]

If the INC opposed the right of self-determination to a 'nationality', Adhikari argues, it 'means supporting the domination of weaker nationalities by stronger ones'.[84] Adhikari attempted to elucidate the growing split between the INC and the AIML in the 1930s, especially after the results of the 1937 elections produced a stronger INC as a national political force. He also disputed the INC argument that the AIML was a feudal party with interests at odds with the progressive turn of the nationalist movement. Rather, he argued that the AIML was transforming into a true anti-imperialist party that represented the growing progressivism of the Muslim masses (both urban and rural) as the AIML was expanding its base.[85] He stated that both the INC and the AIML opposed the 'imperialist federation' proposed by the 1935 constitution, which indicated that both parties were anti-imperialist and democratic in nature. Adhikari's radical interpretation of self-determination is indicative of how deep the discourse penetrated in shaping political imaginaries in British India.

Adhikari's tract illustrates the shift of the CPI from a strategy of working with the left bloc of the INC in the 1930s to that of breaking with it and charting their own path of revolutionary politics.[86] The CPI reconsidered the AIML in this new light, arguing that it was indeed anti-imperialist and that a federated arrangement would resolve the nationality question with the recognition of Hindu–Muslim majorities in regional states and give weight to regional linguistic identities. The right of self-determination proposed by Adhikari was not only a call for democratization and representative government but also a vision of how federated units could potentially work together. The regions should develop their 'nationality', wrote Adhikari, as a federation would allow for the flourishing of nationalities. Adhikari's political vision was an ideal conception of a federation, in which the right of self-determination gave each nationality the right to exist, develop, and secede if necessary. The last freedom of secession is important particularly because it would guarantee that no one dominant nationality imposes its political interests over those of others. But it was this possibility of those nationalities breaking away that the INC saw as potentially leading to a politically powerless and weak set of small states after British departure.

In the midst of these discussions and cleavages arising between political associations in British India, the princely states had to position themselves to protect their interests rather than be absorbed into whatever solutions resulted from discussions between the Indian nationalists and the British government. The rhetoric that emerged for a separate province, particularly for the Andhra activists in the northern coastal districts of the Madras Presidency, argued for the development of not only the region's resources and economy but also its people, through language and education. It was both representational and pedagogical in its aims. As Pandian argued with regards to the Justice Party, there was a shift from culture to politics. The AMS as a cultural organization—an organization to develop the region with respect to social reform issues and the economy— worked to organize on a linguistic basis the need for representation specially addressing Telugu speakers in the Madras Presidency but clearly also meant for cross-border constituencies. As we saw illustrated in the debates in the MLA, the discussion surrounding a federation for British Indian provinces fostered a radically different set of political concerns than what we see in the princely states such as Hyderabad (discussed in detail in the next chapter, Chapter 3). The federation debates pointed to very different discussions regarding sovereignty, autonomy, and political reforms moving the native states toward representative democracy.

Sitaramayya's 1939 article 'India on a Federal Basis' in the *Madras Mail* was clipped and kept in the news briefings in the confidential reports of the Nizam's political department, along with other Andhra movement material in the media.[87] This particular piece was singled out because it proposed a 'a trilingual sub-federation' for Hyderabad, arguing that the state should be divided up into three linguistic units: Kannada-, Telugu-, and Marathi-speaking regions. Sitaramayya was a prominent leader knowledgeable about and deeply immersed in south Indian politics and part of the All-India States Peoples' Conference (AISPC)—organized by the INC to oversee peoples' movements in the princely states. His article sought to balance the desires and demands of the Andhra activists in the Madras Presidency, as illustrated in the MLA debates from the late 1930s, with the AISPC's discussions with the civil societal organizations in the princely state of Hyderabad. The Hyderabad administration kept watch over developments in the Andhra movement, especially when they made claims on princely territory. However, rather than quell some of the criticisms with open dialogue, the administration pushed Telugu activists further away towards the INC (and eventually the CPI) and their resolution for the numerous princely states to join a democratically constituted Indian Union.

Notes

1. Cemil Aydin, 'The Two Faces of the West: Imperialism versus Enlightenment (1882–1905)', in *The Politics of Anti-Westernism in Asia: Visions of World Order in Pan-Islamic and Pan-Asian Thought*, 93–125 (New York: Columbia University Press, 2007).
2. Chittaranjan Das, *Freedom through Disobedience* (Madras: Arka Publishing House, 1922), 37.
3. G. Adhikari, *Pakistan and National Unity: The Communist Solution* (Bombay: People's Publishing House, 1944).
4. See Christopher John Baker, *The Politics of South India 1920–1937* (Cambridge, UK: Cambridge University Press, 1976).
5. Bhogaraju Pattabhi Sitaramayya, *History of the Indian National Congress*, vol. 1: *1885–1935* (New Delhi: S. Chand Publishing, 1969), 56–57. The ACC was given permission to form in 1917, which was opposed by Annie Besant and Tamil Congress members.
6. See David Washbrook, *The Emergence of Provincial Politics: The Madras Presidency 1870–1920* (Cambridge, UK: Cambridge University Press, 1976), 9.
7. 'On the Duty of Candidates', *Krishna Patrika* (1920), in *The Freedom Struggle in Andhra Pradesh (Andhra)*, vol. 2: *1906–1920 A.D.*, edited by M. Venkatarangaiya, 525–526 (Hyderabad: Andhra Pradesh State Archives [APSA] and Research Institute, 1969), (emphasis added).
8. This is markedly different from C. R. Reddy's dismissal of the provincial politician unschooled in liberal democratic practice. See C. R. Reddy, 'Dyarchy and After', *Indian Review* 23, no. 5 (May 1922): 294–304.
9. Venkatarangaiya, *The Freedom Struggle in Andhra Pradesh*, vol. 1, 285–286.
10. 'The Hindu', 3 November 1905, in Venkatarangaiya, *The Freedom Struggle in Andhra Pradesh*, vol. 1, 286.
11. 'A Swadeshi Meeting', *Madras Mail*, 5 October 1905, in Venkatarangaiya, *The Freedom Struggle in Andhra Pradesh*, vol. 1, 287.
12. Venkatarangaiya, *The Freedom Struggle in Andhra Pradesh*, vol. 2, 9.
13. Venkatarangaiya, *The Freedom Struggle in Andhra Pradesh*, vol. 2, 10.
14. 'A Vande Mataram Procession in Rajahmundry', *The Hindu*, 14 February 1907, in Venkatarangaiya, *The Freedom Struggle in Andhra Pradesh*, vol. 2, 177.
15. Sitaramayya, *History of the Indian National Congress*, 69.
16. Nazmul Sultan examines the problem of peoplehood as conceptualized by anti-colonial thinkers in their attempts to grapple with ideas of self-rule, or *swaraj*. See Nazmul Sultan, 'Self-Rule and the Problem of Peoplehood in Colonial India', *American Political Science Review* 114, no. 1 (2020): 81–94.

17. V. P. Menon, *The Transfer of Power in India* (Calcutta: Orient Longman, 1957), 12–13.
18. Menon, *The Transfer of Power*, 13.
19. Menon, *The Transfer of Power*, 13.
20. Venkatarangaiya, *The Freedom Struggle in Andhra Pradesh*, vol. 2, 101.
21. See Erez Manela, 'Imagining Woodrow Wilson in Asia: Dreams of East–West Harmony and the Revolt against Empire in 1919', *American Historical Review* 111, no. 5 (December 2006): 1327–1351.
22. *Report on India's Constitutional Reforms* (Calcutta: Superintendent if Government Printing, India, 1918), 14.
23. Menon, *Transfer of Power*, 16.
24. *Deshabhimani*, quoted in Venkatarangaiya, *The Freedom Struggle in Andhra Pradesh*, vol. 2, 68–69.
25. Baker, *The Politics of South India*, 26–27.
26. A joint conference of the districts of Godavari, Krishna, and Guntur was held at Nidadavolu in May 1912, where V. Ramadas Pantulu called for a separate province for the Andhras. See Venkatarangaiya, *The Freedom Struggle in Andhra Pradesh*, vol. 2, 79.
27. Konda Venkatappayya, *The Andhra Movement* (The Andhra Maha Sabha Publication, series no. 1) (Madras: Andhra Maha Sabha Publication, 1938), 40.
28. Gadicherla Harisarvottamaravu, *Votu* (Bezwada: Andhra Parishad, 1923).
29. See Nazmul Sultan, 'Between the Many and the One: Anticolonial Federalism and Popular Sovereignty', *Political Theory* 50, no. 2 (2021): 247–274, DOI: 10.1177/00905917211018534.
30. Digavalli Venkatasivaravu, *Adinivesya Swarajyamu* (Dominion Status) (Bezwada: Andhra Grandhalayam Mudraksharasalayam, 1933).
31. Digavalli Venkatasivaravu, *Vyavaharakosamu: English–Telugu Dictionary of Technical Terms; Telugu Synonyms, Meanings, Explanations and Definitions of English Words and Phrases Relating to Politics, Economics and Law; Public Finance, Stock Exchange, Business and Cooperation; with a Glossary of Hindustani Words* (Bezwada, 1934).
32. See Kalluri Chandramouli, *Nanadesa Rajyanga Niranyanamulu* (An Account of Constitutions of Various Countries) (Nidubrolu: Tatamudraksharasalayandu, 1933).
33. Konda Venkatappayya, *Adhunika Rajyanga Samasthalu* (1932).
34. Suravaram Pratapa Reddy, *Prajaadhikaaramulu* (People's Rights) (1953 [1938]), 20–21.
35. See Baker, *The Politics of South India*; Eugene F. Irschick, *Politics and Social Conflict in South India, 1916–1929* (Berkeley: University of California Press, 1969).

36. See Pritipuspa Amarnath Mishra, 'Divided Loyalties: Citizenship, Regional Identity and Nationalism in Eastern India (1866-1931)', PhD dissertation, University of Minnesota, 2008.
37. K.V. Narayana Rao, *The Emergence of Andhra Pradesh* (Bombay: Popular Prakashan, 1976), 48, note 88.
38. See Nicholas Dirks, *Castes of Mind: Colonialism and the Making of Modern India* (Princeton: Princeton University Press, 2001); Bernard Cohn, *Colonialism and Its Forms of Knowledge: The British in India* (Princeton, NJ: Princeton University Press, 1996).
39. The Adi-Andhra Mahasabha was established in 1917 by Dalit activists in the coastal Andhra districts of the Madras Presidency. See Gundimeda Sambaiah, 'Mapping Dalit Politics in Contemporary India: A Study of UP and AP from an Ambedkarite Perspective', PhD thesis, Department of Politics, SOAS, University of London, 2013, 217.
40. Irschick, *Politics and Social Conflict*.
41. On linguistic nationalism, see Lisa Mitchell, *Language, Emotion, and Politics in South India: The Making of a Mother Tongue* (Bloomington: Indiana University Press, 2009), specifically on the changes that Telugu underwent in the nineteenth-century Madras Presidency. For other languages and regions, see Sumathi Ramaswamy, *Passions of the Tongue: Language Devotion in Tamil India, 1891–1970* (Berkeley: University of California Press, 1997) and Veena Naregal, *Language Politics, Elites, and the Public Sphere: Western India under Colonialism* (New Delhi: Permanent Black, 2001).
42. Venkatappayya, *The Andhra Movement*, 13.
43. Venkatappayya, *The Andhra Movement*, 13.
44. Venkatappayya, *The Andhra Movement*, 11.
45. Venkatappayya, *The Andhra Movement*, 12.
46. See Mrinalini Sinha, 'Premonitions of the Past', *Journal of Asian Studies* 74, no. 4 (2015): 821–884.
47. See Rama Sundari Mantena, 'Vernacular Publics: Language and Progress in Colonial South India', *Modern Asian Studies* 47, no. 5 (2013): 1678–1705.
48. The meeting was held in Bapatla. There were 2,000 visitors at the meeting, including 800 delegates from Telugu districts of the Madras Presidency, as well as from Nagpur in the Central Provinces and from Warangal and Hyderabad in the Nizam's territories.
49. 'Vande Mataram' is a nationalist song and slogan, which can be translated as 'Hail to the Motherland', and has its origins in the Swadeshi movement in Bengal.
50. See Bernard Bate, '"To Persuade Them into Speech and Action": Oratory and the Tamil Political, Madras, 1905–1919', *Comparative Studies in Society and History* 55, no. 1 (2013): 142–166.

51. K. V. N. Rao, *The Emergence of Andhra Pradesh*, 49.
52. G. Venkatasubba Rao, an ardent advocate of a separate Telugu province and state, wrote in 1954 that Telugu activists since J. Gurunatham from the first decade of the twentieth century had been aspiring for linguistic states and created a model for the formation of new states (Maharashtra, Gujarat, and Karnataka, for instance) in independent India. See G. Venkatasubba Rao, 'From 1947–1954', *Goshti* 10, no. 1 (October 1954): 3–4.
53. Venkatappayya, *The Andhra Movement*, 20.
54. Venkatappayya, *The Andhra Movement*, 20.
55. V. Ramdas Pantulu, *Memorandum on Andhra Province*, part 1: *A General View of the Problems Arising from the Formation of the Andhra Districts of the Madras Presidency into a Separate Province*, with foreword by B. Pattabhi Sitaramayya and published by the Andhra Provincial Congress Committee (Madras: GS Press, 1939), 33.
56. *The Hindu*, 26 May 1913.
57. K. V. N. Rao, *The Emergence of Andhra Pradesh*, 51.
58. Venkatappayya, *The Andhra Movement*, 9–10.
59. Pantulu, *Memorandum on Andhra Province*, part 1, 37.
60. 'Separate Andhra Province: Madras Premier's View', *Times of India*, 4 December 1937, in G. V. Subba Rao collection, Telangana State Archives (TSA), Hyderabad.
61. *Goshti*, in G. V. Subba Rao collection.
62. 'Andhra Defense League, Its Aims and Objects', *The Mahratta*, 11 March 1938, in G. V. Subba Rao collection, vol. 31.
63. G. Venkatasubba Rao, 'Andhra Province: A Programme. A Boycott Movement Foreshadowed', *The Mahratta*, 29 October 1937, in G. V. Subba Rao collection, vol. 31, newspaper clippings from 1937.
64. G.V. Subba Rao collection, vol. 31, newspaper clippings from 1937.
65. G. V. Subba Rao papers, vol. 33, APSA, Hyderabad.
66. G. V. Subba Rao papers, vol. 33.
67. *The Hindu*, March 1937, in G. V. Subba Rao collection, vol. 31, newspaper clippings from 1937.
68. See Andhraratna D. Gopalakrishnayya, *Life and Message* (Goshti Book House, 1928).
69. *Goshti*, October 1954, 1.
70. Sitaramayya, in *Madras Mail*, 6 April 1939.
71. Pantulu, *Memorandum on Andhra Province*, part 1, 57.
72. Sitaramayya, in *Madras Mail*, 6 April 1939.

Self-Determination, Federation, and the Provinces 103

73. Center for Research Libraries (CRL), 'Constitution of Separate Provinces on Linguistic Basis' (Microfilm), Madras legislative assembly debates, Madras, March 1938.
74. CRL, 'Constitution of Separate Provinces on Linguistic Basis', 656.
75. CRL, 'Constitution of Separate Provinces on Linguistic Basis', 656.
76. CRL, 'Constitution of Separate Provinces on Linguistic Basis', 656.
77. CRL, 'Constitution of Separate Provinces on Linguistic Basis', 659.
78. Inst 47 (S. No. 918) List 10 (1939), Constitutional Affairs Secretariat, Creation of a Separate Andhra Province (Linguistic Provinces), in *Madras Mail*, 15 April 1939, TSA, Hyderabad.
79. CRL, 'Constitution of Separate Provinces on Linguistic Basis', 660.
80. CRL, 'Constitution of Separate Provinces on Linguistic Basis', 661.
81. 'Resolution Re: Constitution of Separate Provinces on Linguistic Basis', Madras legislative assembly debates, March 1938, 661.
82. 'Resolution on Federation', Madras legislative assembly debates, March 1938, 108.
83. Adhikari, *Pakistan and National Unity*, 42.
84. Adhikari, *Pakistan and National Unity*, 42.
85. Adhikari, *Pakistan and National Unity*, 28–29.
86. Gene D. Overstreet and Marshall Windmiller, *Communism in India* (Bombay: Perennial Press, 1960), 189.
87. Bhogaraju Pattabhi Sitaramayya, 'India on a Federal Basis', *Madras Mail*, 15 April 1939.

3
Princely Hyderabad, Anti-Colonialism, and Federation

> By far the worst part of the Constitution is the proposed Federal structure, for it makes the feudal Indian States permanent and, in addition, given them some power to interfere in the affairs of the rest of India. The whole conception of the union of Imperialism, Feudalism and Democracy is incapable of realization, and can only mean entrenchment of all reactionary elements.
>
> —Jawaharlal Nehru, *Foreign Affairs*, 1938

Anti-Colonialism, Federation, and the Nation State

Jawaharlal Nehru, the charismatic leader of the anti-colonial nationalist movement in British India, published an essay entitled 'The Unity of India', in *Foreign Affairs* in 1938, to explain to Americans and other international observers what he found objectionable in the constitutional arrangement for the Government of India put forward by the British.[1] In the essay, he argues that it was indisputable that India is diverse in its peoples, cultures, religions, class, and castes and that this diversity posed a great challenge for the nationalist movement. This, in itself, was not surprising, he acknowledges to a global audience. He further suggests that the INC was aware that they would need to manage that diversity in making a case for self-government and independence to be accepted into a world of nations. However, what was worth noting, he writes, is that the socio-economic conditions of British India, as well as the political divisions, were created by the British over a century of colonial rule. The problems facing India were not due to Indian particularities but rather a 'monstrous imposition' as the *Bombay Chronicle* reported in January 1938 on Nehru and Edward J. Thompson's[2] views. The article documents Nehru's opposition to federation and his decrying that it was an impossible solution if a constitutional arrangement is meant to bring out a union of 'Imperialism, Feudalism and Democracy'.[3] While the British proclaimed that they brought a kind of political unity to India, Nehru was clearly seeking to highlight how colonial rule actually brought about stagnation, especially so in the uneven political geography of early-twentieth-century South Asia.

Even the political 'unity' the British proclaimed they brought to the subcontinent had an uneven history, as Kavita Datla has recently argued. She writes:

> The parceling of sovereign rights was not an accidental outcome of the Company's military endeavors, nor was it simply a reflection of the way things had to be. Rather, it was a consequence of British attempts to spread their power, cut their costs and avoid political controversy; attempts that were a foundational element of the expansion of the British Empire in South Asia.[4]

Datla's argument illustrates the unevenness produced by imperial treaties with the numerous native states in the subcontinent that the English East India Company signed onto and the conquest of territories that they had to directly administer. British India and the native states combined to produce a fragmented sovereignty in the subcontinent.[5] For Nehru, the artificial political terrain was clearly a product of colonial rule and imperial policies and a product of uneven forms of rule. This was not an uncommon view and was widely held in the INC, as we saw earlier with Bhogaraju Pattabhi Sitaramayya, who made similar remarks about the creation of provincial borders of British India as a result of 'pure chronological growth' of the British Empire in South Asia and not on the basis of historical or linguistic considerations.[6] Nehru put the blame squarely on the British: 'The feudal Indian State system, the gilded Maharajas and Nabobs, and the big landlord system were essentially British creations in India.'[7] However, he goes further and argues that the native states system was not only over 100 years old, but also that over the course of the century 'Europe and the world have altered past recognition' while the princely states remained the same as 'feudal relics which prevent all growth'.[8] One can discern that embedded in Nehru's remarks was a theory of history in which British colonial rule thwarted Indian political conditions in such a way that the uneven political terrain of the colonies remained relics of the past while Europe marched ahead in its progress towards democracy and popular sovereignty.

Thompson, in the English weekly *Time and Tide* published in January 1938, agreed with Nehru's overall assessment of British rule in India and the challenges that the uneven political terrain posed for India's political future. He called the attitude of the Indian princes the most urgent political problem confronting India.[9] In the 1930s, the native princes participated in the Round

Table Conferences held in London which divided many of the princely states between those that supported the idea of federation (specifically, federating with British Indian provinces) and those that saw the idea of federation as threatening their autonomy and sovereignty. Nehru and Thompson believed that by the late 1930s, the princes' call for political autonomy through a federation of states was a retrograde proposition that was no longer acceptable to liberal nationalists in the INC.

The system of princely states in British India originated through treaties with the East India company starting in the mid-eighteenth century.[10] These states and their alliances with the East India Company were critical in the expansion of the British Empire in the Indian subcontinent starting in the eighteenth century, as Datla explains:

> India's native states, or "country powers," as the British referred to them in the eighteenth century, underwrote the expansion of the East India Company in the East. The tribute paid by these states became an important financial resource at the company's disposal, as it attempted to balance its books in the late eighteenth century. Additionally, the troops maintained to protect these states were significant in Britain's late eighteenth century military calculations. These states, in other words, were absolutely central to the forging of the British imperial order, and generative of the very practices that came to characterize colonial expansion and governance.[11]

The British negotiated treaties with native princes and allowed them a degree of autonomy over their internal affairs, in sharp contrast with the directly ruled territories of British India.[12] At the time of independence, the largest of the princely states were Kashmir, Hyderabad, Mysore, and Baroda. Because of their distinct status as native states, they were separated from the political and social transformations taking place in the directly ruled territories of British India.

It should not therefore be surprising that the emergence of civic and political institutions within princely state territories differed considerably from British India.[13] While a dynamic and confident nationalist movement in British India arose from the growth of civic institutions that fostered associational life in the nineteenth century, princely states underwent different trajectories.[14] While there were no overtly anti-monarchical political movements in the princely states,[15] there was a push towards responsible government from social and political movements therein based on the principle of popular sovereignty. What I show in this chapter is that the emergence of political movements within the princely state of Hyderabad were in practice anti-monarchical. My argument is twofold.

First, I examine how, in the interwar period, a dynamic anti-colonial nationalist movement led by Nehru and Mohandas K. Gandhi confronted and negotiated with what they clearly saw as alternative (and possibly conflicting) political imaginaries arising from uneven forms of rule instituted by British colonial rule—imaginaries that had to be disciplined by the INC's own version of a sophisticated anti-colonial nationalism. Second, in exploring the multiplicity of political imaginaries at the end of empire, I ask, how can we understand the contributions of the princely states, which gave rise to different politics and modes of political expression than those in the directly ruled territories of British India?

From the very beginnings of the INC, the aim of liberal nationalists was political reform in order to make colonial government amenable to native interests by bringing in a larger number of Indians into the governing structure. INC nationalism began with liberal nationalists demanding inclusion into representative institutions and then shifted rather quickly to militant nationalism that sought, as Partha Chatterjee has cogently argued, 'the collective right of a nation to freedom and equality with other nations, grounded in popular sovereignty'.[16] This was the radical democratic turn in nationalist thought that invested sovereignty in the people and in the national form. The movement shifted gradually from the goals of self-government, representative government, and dominion status within a commonwealth to calls, eventually, for the formation of an independent nation state.

During these shifts in political discourse and goals, the INC had to contend with other groups with stakes in the progress towards self-government. To be sure, the INC was not the sole voice or party in negotiating political reforms within British India, but they did have to address the concerns of the people they purported to represent. Those challenges have been addressed especially in the historiography on the rise of the AIML under the leadership of Muhammad Ali Jinnah in the 1930s and the 1940s and its dialogue with the INC on the question of the minority status of Muslims in any independent state, and in B. R. Ambedkar's critique of INC politics and Gandhian tactics from the standpoint of Dalits who would gain a minority status in a new Indian republic.[17] Nonetheless, the INC envisioned a clear trajectory where their movement would propel them from an imperial territory governed by the British to an independent nation state. In other words, their commitment to popular sovereignty and the national form was indisputable. While this goal of an independent nation state was not officially declared until 1929, the goal of self-government pervaded the discourse of nationalism and took root in the interwar period.

Why was there a push for the nation state (with its tendency towards forces of homogenization with respect to the disparate territories and constituencies) rather than support for a federation of states made up of an uneven political terrain of South Asia? Furthermore, why did the INC so wholeheartedly embrace the national form of the modern state? In order to understand this trajectory of the INC, let us first consider the historical context in which the international arena had just seen the formation of the League of Nations. Erez Manela, in *The Wilsonian Moment: Self-Determination and the Origins of Anticolonial Nationalism* (2007), has suggested that the idea of self-determination took root during the interwar period and fuelled anti-colonial nationalism. By placing anti-colonial struggles in an international political context, Manela compels us to consider discourses of self-determination and self-government on a global scale. Chatterjee, in thinking through liberal internationalism at this time, argues that the 'recognition by the League of Nations of national sovereignty as the goal of what was in effect colonial trusteeship was a major step in the global normalization of the nation-state'.[18] This goal was not unusual within the larger international context. For instance, Anthony Anghie suggests that the Mandates System, developed in the interwar period to manage territories no longer under the rule of the German and Ottoman empires, laid out a developmental model of helping former colonial territories to achieve self-government and ultimately an independent nation state. Anghie writes:

> The broad, primary goal of the Mandate System was to prevent the exploitation of the native peoples; its secondary goal was to promote their well-being and development. The term 'not yet able to stand by themselves' suggested that the system was a temporary arrangement until such time as the peoples were capable of becoming independent. As a result, Article 22 was described as meaning 'trusteeship with independence as the goal of the trust'.[19]

While Woodrow Wilson enshrined these political goals in the League of Nations to ease the transition from empire to nation primarily in the aftermath of the dissolution of the Ottoman Empire, the League also aimed to 'protect' native peoples from further exploitation. What is noteworthy is that the League of Nations and the Mandate System promoted the nation state as the ultimate goal for colonial peoples at the end of empire. Michael Collins, reflecting on this period as the federal moment, cautions us to remember that these international organizations such as the League were ultimately concerned with creating and maintaining an international order after empire—in a way that former imperial powers would still hold considerable influence in post-imperial territories and societies.[20]

One can see at the outset that the nation state offered clear advantages for the INC than the alternative paths through federation proposals. First and foremost of those advantages was for national building and recognition within a new global order after empire. It might be useful to think comparatively in an international context to see why the anti-colonial movement in India shifted wholeheartedly to a commitment to the national form over ideas of federation that were still in circulation in the 1930s, especially with regards to discussions of the political future of the princely states.[21] Even though the INC was moving away from the idea of federation, federation proposals were not completely dismissed in the international arena. Frederick Cooper, in his study of French West Africa entitled *Citizenship between Empire and Nation: Remaking France and French Africa, 1945–1960*, raises the question of alternate political futures that were possible in the interwar period and in the subsequent period of decolonization.[22] A question that lies behind this critical literature is why the nation state won out in the early twentieth century. This was a time when dynamic proposals for federation, or federated states, were being offered up to possibly counter the dangers of majoritarianism of the modern nation state. The nation state was not an inevitable outcome of anti-colonial struggles, argues Cooper, and we should not view alternative proposals as less radical because their aim was not the establishment of an independent nation state. A federation in the aftermath of empire, Cooper argues, was such an alternative. For French West African thinkers such as Leopold Senghor, a federation allowed for extending the relationship between France and its colonies. Cooper calls this 'imperial citizenship':

> The citizenship that French West Africans were claiming in the postwar years was not that of a nation-state, but an imperial citizenship—in a composite political entity, built by conquest, governed in a way that had subordinated and denigrated its subjects, but which was, activists asserted, to be transformed into a structure that would ensure the rights and cultural integrity of all citizens. Such a conception both assumed the history of colonization and transcended it.[23]

Through the continuing connection between the imperial centre of France and the colonies, colonial subjects would be able to achieve greater citizenship rights, such as voting rights, and greater representation in the government without severing ties with the colonial power. The idea behind continuing a relationship with France was to maintain political and economic stability in the colonies.

Gary Wilder, on the other hand, argues that the Martinique anti-colonial thinker Aime Cesaire's ambivalence towards the nation state had to do with the long history of slavery, the Haitian revolution, and the problem of freedom in the Caribbean: 'Given this long-term history of emancipation and foreclosure, Antillean actors after World War II approached the prospect of decolonization mindful that freedom was a problem with no ready-made solution.'[24] There was a great deal of hesitation on the part of Senghor and Cesaire to embrace the nation state as the end goal of anti-colonial struggle. Adom Getachew writes that the high imperial moment within which Senghor and Cesaire argued their positions was bound to end in failure—mainly because the French were unwilling to form a federation with their former colonies, giving equal rights or proposing an equivalence between the French and native peoples. In other words, race played an enormous role in shaping post-imperial imaginaries. Getachew argues that the important post-imperial moment occurred when more creative and strong proposals for federation circulated in relation to the idea of the African Union.[25] The Western African example as elucidated by Cooper, Wilder, and Getachew affirms that even in proposals of federation, or a federated state, anti-colonialism encompassed an emancipatory politics inclusive of the extension of rights and protections connected to full citizenship and of representative institutions broadly.

However, when we turn to British India, it becomes clear that the princely states in India had altogether different political motives when debating federation proposals towards an all-India federation of states. These unique principalities viewed the federation debates as a way to weigh alternative political futures and also, on a practical level, a way to assert their own sovereignty and independence from the increasingly dominant and threatening popular nationalism of the INC. Crucially, as I will argue, the proposals for federation offered by the Indian princes lacked a real alternative path from either federating with or merging with whatever states would result from independence from British rule—particularly because, as we will see in the case of princely Hyderabad, there was no real critique of monarchical rule and thus whatever political solution the Hyderabad administration offered in the 1930s and the 1940s was far from a politics of emancipation that was at the heart of conceptions of popular sovereignty and of British Indian politics.

Princely States, Federation, and Political Futures

What were the particular political problems posed by the native states in British India? In 1938, after the important Round Table Conferences in British India discussing the fate of the Indian dominions, Thompson called out what he viewed as the dubious position of the Indian princes. Specifically, Thompson argued that the princes did not possess sovereignty and could not hold the British government and the government of India to a settlement dating to the early nineteenth century. He declared, 'Whatever the treaties say—this is 1938, and India is a country of 400 million—the dead hand of 1819 cannot fetter 1938 to feudal conditions.'[26] As Nehru himself noted, the native states were, according to him, a relic of an earlier era and their proposals were a reflection of stagnant ideas. Both Thompson and Nehru were reacting to the conflicting set of positions taken by the native states in the late 1930s.

Yet the princes' discussions with the British government and the government of India had started much earlier. On 20 August 1917, Edwin Montagu, the secretary of state for India, announced in the House of Commons that Indians would gain power in every branch of the government, with the ultimate goal being the 'gradual development of self-governing institutions with a view to the progressive realisation of responsible government in India as an integral part of the British Empire'.[27] This also gave way to imploring the native states into constitutional discussions. In line with this goal, a Chamber of Princes was established by a Royal Proclamation on 8 February 1921. This carefully worded proclamation stated that the Chamber of Princes would be a consultative body, but the internal matters of the native states would be left alone:

> My Viceroy will take its counsel freely in matters relating to the territories of Indian States generally and in matters that affect these territories jointly with British India or with the rest of my Empire. It will have no concern with the internal affairs of individual States or their Rulers or with the relations of individual States with my Government, while the existing rights of these States and their freedom of action will in no way be prejudiced or impaired.[28]

Along with the Simon Commission's review of the Government of India Act of 1919, the Butler Committee was appointed to address the role of the native states in the political reforms in British India and the movement towards its dominion status. Harcourt Butler came to India in January 1928, and though he met with the princes, he did not make an effort to meet with the representatives of the peoples and communities of the native states. At this stage, the dialogue was between the British government and the princes and did not include the demands of the masses.

The AISPC, which took place in Bombay in December 1927, sent a deputation to the Butler Committee to London in 1928 to make a case for the inclusion of representatives of the people in the federation discussions.[29] The *Manchester Guardian* interviewed the leaders of the deputation and reported, in the 23 October 1928 issue, that the deputation had organized the trip in order to make their voices heard and their interests taken seriously. In particular, three prominent figures—G. R. Abhyankar from Law College in Poona, Paputlal Chudgar, and Dewan Bahadur M. Ramachandra Rao—arrived in London to make their case for why it was important for the states' people to be considered in the discussions between the princes and the Butler Committee. The AISPC corresponded with the Butler Committee and asked to be included in the discussions. The princes did not agree to this and did not allow the deputation to be included in the Butler Committee as they argued that the committee was established to determine the relationship between the paramount power and the native states as defined by the treaties. The princes argued that the Butler Committee therefore could not inquire into the investigation of the relations between the rulers and their subjects.[30]

Abhyankar published a piece titled 'Self-Determination for the States People', arguing that the princes had neglected the fundamental rights of their people—namely civil rights and constitutional liberties that should be guaranteed to all states' subjects.[31] Instead, the princes, Abhyankar argued, had misled the British and falsely claimed that the people in the native states had basic freedoms, a say in the government, and the right to air their grievances and to rise up against the government if and when necessary. In other words, they had painted a picture in which the princes abided by what the people wanted and recognized that their own princely power was derived from the people. Abhyankar denied that this was the case. In fact, he asserted that the people of the native states had greater powers before the arrival of the British because they at least had the right to depose a corrupt monarch or administration. With the assertion of the paramount power, the British had deprived the people of these rights.[32] Because the native princes were backed by the British as the paramount power, the native peoples were deprived of previously held rights of dissent. In the new political climate in the interwar period with the growing strength of the INC in British India, Abhyankar argued that the right of self-determination was due to the people of the native states and that they had a right to participate in any discussion on the political future of those states. He asked, 'When the princes are talking of federation are they alive to the fact that it is the people of every States [sic] who must have a voice in any scheme of federation?' Furthermore, he argued:

> The Indian States people, therefore, demand the right of self-determination along with the subjects of British India, not only in matters of common interest, but also in matters of their internal administration. They do not want the Indian Princes to rule in an autocratic manner. They further claim that responsible governments must be established in the States and the Indian Rulers must be made to rule as constitutional monarchs.[33]

Princely Hyderabad, Anti-Colonialism, and Federation

The deputation led by Abhyankar to London for the Butler Commission made clear to the British public that the states' people demanded the right of participation to put pressure on the native princely states and to move them toward responsible government in conjunction with British Indian subjects. They reasoned that the political goals of the British Indian subjects were inseparable from the states' peoples.

In the 1930s, at the beginning of the decade, the INC was keen on including the princes in the Round Table Conferences (1930–1932) towards the goal of introducing responsible government and representative institutions. The 1928 Nehru report explicitly stated:

> Indeed if there ever was a case for a round table conference at which perfect understanding could easily be reached it was this. With the representatives of the princes, of their people, of the British government and of the people of British India assembled at such a conference all difficulties would have been solved with mutual goodwill.[34]

The main contention going forward was about who would have the power to shape the 'internal affairs' of the native states. There were indeed divisions within the Chamber of Princes. One faction supported political reforms that would bring subjects of the native states closer to subjects of British India in terms of what rights and liberties they possessed. Participating in the conferences was seen as a way to assure the native states that they were not excluded from discussions shaping the political agenda of British India.

What soon became clear is that the princely states and provinces were thought of as equal partners in the discussions and negotiations of political reforms. An internal report produced by the Hyderabad administration stated, 'Hyderabad had no direct interest in the political problems which were then agitating British India and indeed would have liked nothing better than to have been left alone to fashion her own destiny in her own way.'[35] Hyderabad's administration entered discussions at the Round Table Conferences only reluctantly through pressure to do so and because they were left with no real choice. In a speech to *Paramount News* in November of 1932, Akbar Hydari presented Hyderabad, to a British audience, as one of the most important states in India that is larger than England and Scotland combined. He goes on to say that the reason the Nizam's government cooperated at the Round Table Conference was to work towards 'giving India a constitution which will satisfy the legitimate aspirations of Indians and preserve those links with the British Empire to which Hyderabad attaches the greatest importance'.[36] What is implied in this statement is that because Hyderabad was an important state in the region, it should have had been involved in helping Indians (British India) and their aspirations for self-government. Hyderabad already had autonomy, so they did not need to negotiate a political arrangement for self-government. The Hyderabad administration argued that though their relations were with the British Crown, the Crown was acting through the government of India. Therefore, they could not be indifferent to these political discussions that could impact their status. They went on to state that there were two courses open to them. One was for Hyderabad to stay out of the constitutional debates concerning the relations of the Crown with British India—the logic being that Hyderabad had formed an independent relationship with the Crown through treaties and had no direct legal relationship with the government of India. The other course would be to enter into discussions to support India's aspirations and efforts towards political reforms in British India towards the goal of self-government. If Hyderabad entered into discussions, it could act in its own self-interest and best assure its 'effective sovereignty' over Hyderabad's dominions. After the first Round Table Conference, it was decided that Hyderabad would take the second course and work towards an 'All-India Federation'. The Hyderabad administration was intent on protecting Hyderabad's sovereignty as an autonomous state and preventing the Government of India from gaining any authority over the internal affairs of the princely states. As Datla has argued, the question of sovereignty of the princely states was deliberately left ambiguous by the British.[37] Nehru outright argued that the British were using the princes and their so-called treaties to sow fissures and weaken the bargaining power of the INC.[38] The princes proclaimed that the treaties between the native states and the British Crown gave them sovereignty over their territories. The INC, on the other hand, made arguments that the Crown had never determined the policies defining the relations between the Government of India and the princely states. In fact, in practice, the Government of India had been managing the affairs while staying out of the 'internal' affairs of the native states. These two sets of agendas clashed when it came time to defining the parameters and powers of an All-India Federation.

The Federal Structure Committee (FSC) met starting in September 1931 after the first Round Table Conference. A federation was suggested with a centre flanked by units of federation comprising states and provinces. The Hyderabad delegation took a leadership role in the discussions in order to assure 'the progress of the Federal Structure Committee to the goal of an All-India Federation of a type which by vesting effective power in the Units of the Federation and the Crown provided the best institutional safeguards for the preservation of Hyderabad's internal autonomy'.[39] The Hyderabad delegation seemed to accept that within the federal structure, the British Parliament acting through His Majesty's government would control defence, relations between Indian states, and finance; only with that guarantee would they proceed with the discussions. They wanted to be assured that they were equal to British Indian parties at the table, if not seen endowed with even greater powers. There was much distrust with the INC and its representatives such as Gandhi. One primary discussion was to chart out the 'strength, composition and powers of the Federal Legislature, the proportion of States' representatives in it as compared with the representatives from British India'.[40] The Hyderabad delegation reported that the balance of opinions was towards a small legislature. The opposition to a small legislature came from the smaller Indian states and from British India. The former felt they would be able to increase the representation of Indian states with a larger legislature by arguing for individual representation of each state, as it was the smaller Indian states that would have a combined representative while the larger states such as Hyderabad would have individual representation. The British Indian side, on the other hand, opposed a small legislature because they believed it to be undemocratic and that a larger legislature would diminish the weight and power of the Indian states. Considering most British Indian parties felt that the Indian states were feudal relics, the INC aimed to increase the power of the British Indian provinces.

In fact, the INC deliberately muted its discussion of the changes that the native states would have to undergo if they agreed to be part of the federation at the Round Table Conference, so as not to confirm the princes' fears that the INC sought to fully integrate the princely states into a federal structure, leaving very little room for autonomy. Sitaramayya argued in the *Madras Mail* on 15 April 1939 that one of the INC's goals was

> the realignment of boundaries, the division of India into handy provincial units must be based not on accident but on design. The provinces to-day [sic] are the result neither of logical nor of ethnological considerations. Historic accidents have determined their boundaries and a foreign nation could not easily grasp the significance of such a pell mell mixture of communities.[41]

He further suggested that Hyderabad be broken into a sub-federation of three units: Maharashtras, Karnatakas, and Andhras. This was in line with his previous remarks on why redrawing provincial boundaries was necessary as they too were an accident of empire. In reference to Malayalam speakers in Cochin, Travancore, and Malabar in British India, he wrote that they all 'have a common culture, and common historic traditions, a common biological descent and common civic institutions and social laws, common systems of marriage, and inheritance, common manners and customs, common religion and common forms of worship'.[42] Sitaramayya's remarks here foreshadowed what would eventually become of Hyderabad after the forced political merger in 1948 by an independent India. In the late 1930s, the INC's position was that the native states were an integral part of their conception of India: 'The Congress stands for the same political, social and economic freedom in the States as the rest of India and considers the States as an integral part of India, which cannot be separated.'[43] It is clear from these statements coming from the INC that the princes were confirmed in their belief that their political interests were in conflict with the interests of the INC.

Native States as 'Conservative Islands'

Hydari led the Hyderabad delegation at the Round Table Conferences and worked to build a consensus for an acceptable All-India Federation that would ease the fears of the native states and check the power and desires of the British Indian delegates. Hydari's and the Hyderabad delegation's goal was to work towards a federal structure that would give the greatest amount of internal autonomy to Hyderabad. The work towards a federation was based on the assumption that the new government that would come about with the withdrawal of the British in India would not be a continuation of the Government of India. Rather, the new government would be an All-India Federation where

> the centre of power will be with the Provinces and the States who will have mutually agreed that certain subjects where co-ordination in the interests of India as a whole is necessary should be administered through a central agency—the Federal Government. Invested by its constituent units with the necessary powers the Federal Government unlike the present Government of India will not be the master but the agent of the several federating units, be they Provinces or States.[44]

It is clear from this statement that the reason the Hyderabad delegation was committed to talks towards a federation was to shape the future of India after Britain's withdrawal. As Hydari expressed earlier in the report, staying out the discussions would be detrimental to Hyderabad in that decisions would be made without their input. Therefore, being at the centre of the Round Table discussions was critical in their eyes with Hydari's leadership in shaping a viable political future for Hyderabad. In the 'very confidential' enclosure of the secret report on the Round Table Conference, Hyderabad saw itself alongside other princely states as 'conservative islands in the ocean of democratic British India' and as stabilizing elements in the future legislature where British Indian interests constantly threatened to undermine these elements with their calls for a more democratic polity. In effect, the Round Table Conferences garnered the support of the princes precisely because the latter believed they would be able to forge a bastion of conservatism and maybe even align with conservative forces within British India. Hydari knew that if he positioned Hyderabad as a princely state alongside moderate nationalists in British India, along with minority communities, the 'extremists' would be isolated in their calls for direct action.

By characterizing the INC as being driven by extremists, the princes sought to portray themselves as conservatives. However, it is not clear what exactly their conservatism consisted of. Howard Erdman's 1967 study on the rise of the Swatantra Party as a conservative alternative to the 'socialist' INC gives us the following definition of conservatism: 'Conservatism is primarily ... associated with the aristocratic defense of the feudal-agrarian *ancien regime*. Secondly, conservatism has also come to refer to middle-class resistance to more radical, lower-class demands.'[45] In India, conservatism took on its own nuances when the princes sought to characterize themselves as the defenders of tradition and legacy. During the constitutional discussions of the 1930s, Liaquat Hyat Khan expressed the general sentiment of the princes at the second Round Table Conference on 30 November 1931:

> It would be perfectly fair on the part of the British-Indian representatives to ask the Indian States to make sacrifices in the common interests of a greater India; it would be perfectly legitimate on their part to expect that the Princes should willingly and gladly cede a certain amount of their power and authority to the newly constituted Federal Government, in order to create one, united, and undivided India, for the benefit of the three hundred and fifty millions of India's sons and daughters; but, certainly, it cannot be legitimately argued that the Princes should, in course of time, sacrifice all their sacred heritage and legacy, in order that British India may realise its political ambition.[46]

Khan pointed to the problems arising from the perspective of the princes. He stated that while it was understandable that the princely states would have to give up a few things in federating with the British Indian provinces, he brought attention to the fact that the native states could not possibly give up their 'sacred heritage and legacy'. The princes expressed their conservatism through the language of 'heritage and legacy' by which they aimed to protect themselves against what they saw as the extremists in the INC and their desire to radically transform Indian society and culture. So rather than a middle-class response to lower-class radicalism, the conservatism of the princes was based on the idea of heritage and tradition. The native states as culturally autonomous regions without direct colonial rule were distinct spaces from the colonized territories of British India. They represented historical continuity that needed to be protected against British Indian politics. British India lacked historical continuity because of it being a product of colonial conquest. The conservative faction of the princes viewed these transformations that the INC extremists were demanding as harmful to their conception of historical continuity.

This faction of princes also represented conservatism in more ways than one. The attempt to retain control and authority over internal 'sovereignty' indicated their resistance to new political ideologies circulating in the British Indian provinces. Ultimately there were two divergent paths taken by British Indian movements and the Indian states. The native states, as Khan clearly articulated, attempted to maintain control of their territories and rights as well as hold onto their heritage and legacy. The princes did this by revisiting treaties between the native states and the British Crown, broaching discussion of the meaning of sovereignty and paramountcy, and finally turning to international law to resolve the unique position they found themselves in—namely between the British government and the Government of India. The INC and other political parties in British India, by contrast, were not able to rely on international law to make their case for political independence. Rather than appeal to international law, they were led to mass politics and forged more radicalized political movements that not only called for political freedom but also transforming their societies anew. These latter ideologies were what the conservative princes saw as threatening and their representatives repeatedly tried to dismiss as 'extremist'.

Disputing that the two 'parties' of the native states and the British provinces were of equal status, Khan went on to declare that

> … any constitutional scheme which it is intended that the States should accept must necessarily recognise the incontrovertible fact that, whereas the Indian States enjoy and exercise sovereign power and authority, the other federating units of the proposed federation are neither sovereign nor autonomous; hence, the constitution must necessarily provide adequate and substantial safeguards for the maintenance and preservation of the internal sovereignty of the States'[47]

Khan argued that there is a fundamental difference between the Indian native states and the British Indian provinces and that while the princes might have had to sacrifice a few things when entering into negotiations, the provinces were in an altogether different position. The provinces sought to gain authority and control over internal administration (through federation and dominion status); however, the native states only stood to lose what they already possessed—namely internal sovereignty. Clearly Khan understood that participating in the Round Table talks with an equal footing with the representatives of the British Indian provinces and political associations such as the INC and the AIML erased the status of the princely states as independent and sovereign. It was with this apprehension that the native states entered into the Round Table discussions on the structure of an All-India Federation with what they saw as a weakened position. The subsequent protective stance the princes took on holding onto what fragmented shards of imperial sovereignty they had, however, was interpreted by the INC leadership as their stubborn unwillingness to introduce necessary political reforms within their territories and to expand citizenship rights and representative government.

It became clear that the federation proposals from the princes and their administrators were not animated by any semblance of emancipatory politics, as might have been the case with the Western African proposals. The INC while negotiating at the Round Table Conferences with the princes simultaneously decided to undertake more radical politics by turning directly to the native states' peoples and appealing to them. In effect, the INC after the long-drawn-out discussions with the Indian princes decided to give up on the federation idea and rather pursued a radical democratic agenda to support peoples' movements within the native states towards a representative government (and parliamentary democracy), thus firmly committing themselves to popular sovereignty. Overall, the movement against federation orchestrated by the INC leadership—ultimately taking a liberal nationalist position—was that a loose federation proposal threatened the furthering of democratic reforms.

Lloyd Rudolph and Susanne Rudolph argue that India's commitment to federalism was a way to 'share and negotiate divided sovereignty'.[48] Louise Tillin posits that the quasi-federalism adopted by India in 1947 was critical in 'democratic consolidation'.[49] What we see from the discussions from the 1930s is that the INC was able to forge together conservatives and socialists behind its proposals for independence. This lasting coalition of potentially divergent political goals allowed Nehru and Gandhi, along with the INC, to push towards the goal of an independent nation state—as seen in an INC narrative triumphant in the Constituent Assembly.[50] For Nehru, however, political and economic stability would depend on an Indian union with a strong centre and not a loose federation of states and provinces. This was the critical point of contention between the parties representing the political interests of minority communities such as the AIML and Ambedkar's representation of Dalits. The AIML, in particular, proposed a loose federation of states and provinces in order to accommodate the political interests of the Muslim minority in British India.

Under the leadership of Nehru, the idea of a nation state with a strong centre took hold. As a consequence, the INC shifted political discussion and negotiations from a federation (the All-India Federation as proposed in 1935) to an Indian union which required that all people in the former Indian states and the British provinces would have equal protections and rights. For Nehru, this would be the realization of a radical democratic project in India. The INC began to shift its strategy with the native states after the Round Table conferences (1930–1932) that resulted in the Government of India Act of 1935 and the victory of INC representatives in the 1937 elections.

The States' People and Popular Sovereignty

The global movement towards the nation state as the legitimate state form rested on the idea of popular sovereignty—a popular sovereignty based on constitutions, minority rights, and the accommodation of cultural diversity. The AISPC established in 1927 signalled a shift for the INC towards the goal of demanding greater rights within native states for their subjects—mainly the expansion of civil liberties, citizenship rights, and representative government. At the Calcutta session of the INC in 1928, Nehru moved to remove the clause that stated that the INC would not interfere with the internal affairs of the native states. At the session, it was declared:

> This Congress urges on the Ruling Princes of the Indian States to Introduce responsible Government based on representative institutions in the States and to immediately issue proclamations or enact laws guaranteeing elementary and fundamental rights of citizenship such as rights of association, free speech, free press, and security of person and property. This Congress further assures the people of the Indian States of its sympathy with and support to their legitimate and peaceful struggle for the attainment of full responsible Government in the States.[51]

Nehru argued that the political task in the princely states was different from that within the British Indian territories. In the princely states, Nehru argued, the political goal was the attainment of 'full responsible government' inclusive of representative institutions and based on popular sovereignty. Understandably, this posed a significant threat to many princely states whose respective monarchs had not entertained the thought of giving up power, especially in such a radical manner as turning that power over to representative institutions. This is not to imply that there were no progressive monarchs who pushed for radical political reforms within their states.[52] From the perspective of those monarchs who

Princely Hyderabad, Anti-Colonialism, and Federation

resisted these reforms, joining a federation with an independent India would mean essentially surrendering their power.

Gandhi, too, was a strong critic of the arbitrary power of the Indian princely states, having himself come from the small princely state of Rajkot in the modern-day region of Gujarat. Gandhi's political philosophy was based on an idea and commitment to self-rule. In his 1909 classic *Hind Swaraj* (Indian Home Rule), Gandhi addressed his interlocutor within the text on the idea of freedom and self-rule and asserted:

> I believe that you want the millions of India to be happy, not that you want the reins of Government in your hands. If that be so, we have to consider only one thing: how can the millions obtain self-rule? You will admit that people under several Indian princes are being ground down. The latter mercilessly crush them. This tyranny is greater than that of the English; and, if you want such tyranny in India, then we shall never agree. My patriotism does not teach me that I am to allow people to be crushed under the heel of Indian princes.[53]

For Gandhi, the idea of self-rule was not simply the replacement of British rulers with Indian ones. When Gandhi entered the nationalist movement and joined the INC-led agitation against colonial rule in India, one of the tenets of Indian nationalism as articulated by early nationalists such as Dadabhai Naoroji and Gopal Krishna Gokhale was that Indian representatives in the government were better positioned to govern over their own people because they had an ear for the concerns and interests of their own community. Gandhi, on the other hand, argued early on that it was not simply the replacement of European bodies with Indian ones that would alter colonial rule; rather, Gandhi argued the necessity of a radical politics based on popular sovereignty. For the idea of self-rule to take root in princely states, the people would have had to do constructive work to prepare themselves to then chart out a political programme.[54] Gandhi, even as late as 1938, was hesitant about the INC providing aid to people's movements within the princely states. He felt that both the princes and the people need to come around to trust the INC and their work. However, in *Harijan*, on 20 April 1940, Gandhi wrote that though in international law princely states might be recognized as independent, it was not worth much because that independence was defended (or provided) by a stronger party—the British Empire. Gandhi argued that the princes would have had to eventually come around and join the Indian Union as it would be in the best interests of the states' people as well as in their own interests. He wrote:

I can, therefore, only conceive a settlement in which the big States will retain their status. In one way, this will be far superior to what it is today; but in another, it will be limited so as to give the people of the States the same right of self-government within their States as the people of the other parts of India will enjoy. They will have freedom of speech, a free Press and pure justice guaranteed to them.[55]

Furthermore, by 1942 Gandhi explicitly contended that the arbitrary power of the princes must go, that their autocracy must go, and that the liberty of the peoples should not rest on the will of a single individual—the autocratic monarch.[56] While Gandhi undercut the idea of an uneven Indian union—that peoples of the princely states must enjoy the same rights as the people of the provinces when India achieves independence—he rightly pointed out that the princes' autocracy rested on British protection and that their power did not derive from within. After British departure, the princes could retain their states when joining the union as they would join as stronger than ever before having achieved independence. However, Gandhi ultimately argued that the autonomy and strength must derive from the people and not the monarch.

Ambedkar approached the question of the princely states' sovereignty with scepticism and put the blame on the British for their shirking of responsibility and encouraging the princes to seek autonomy from an Indian union rather than working with Indian nationalists towards a common goal.[57] Ultimately, Ambedkar argued, it was in the interest of the princes to join the Indian Union as it would guarantee that they can remain constitutional monarchs and retain their rights of dynastic succession. Unlike Gandhi, Ambedkar saw the monarchs as self-interested political actors who could be convinced to join the union because it would benefit them. Gandhi, adhering to his political philosophy, saw the princes as good ethical actors just as the regular people of the native states were acting in good faith about their common political future. As ethical actors, the princes, too, in Gandhi's eyes, should have desired what was overall good for their states and their peoples. Gandhi and Ambedkar, along with Nehru, were in essence all committed to popular sovereignty—the idea that political power rested with the people and not with old-world monarchs. Even if the monarch represented 'heritage and tradition', as Khan outlined on the position of the native princes at the Round Table Conferences, both Gandhi and Nehru believed their political commitment to independence, and freedom was necessarily tied to the native states' people gaining political power. The INC made an additional commitment to the will of the people of India when they declared a constituent assembly as an integral part of official policy in 1934. In 1933, the Congress Working Committee stated:

The only satisfactory alternative to the White Paper is a constitution drawn up by a Constituent Assembly elected on the basis of adult franchise or as near it as possible, with the power, if necessary, to the important minorities to have their representatives elected exclusively by the electors belonging to such minorities.[58]

This shift opened up floodgates of opinion regarding not only the All-India Federation but also the appropriate nature of that union—especially with regards to how the federation would impact the peoples of the native states. At the Bombay conference of the AISPC, on 17 December 1927, Ramachandra Rao declared, 'It is obvious, however, that in our struggle for national emancipation and for the development of India as whole into a self-Governing world State the people of British India and the Indian States have to act in concert till the goal is reached.'[59] He went on to say that reforming the internal administration in the Indian states was of the utmost importance, possibly even more so than the federal union between the Indian states and British India.[60] The immediate problem to tackle was the position of the prince who ruled personally with control over legislation and administration. Rao argued that the princes' rule was essentially feudal and patriarchal in nature. No matter how enlightened a prince was, there was no guarantee that the successor would be equally enlightened. Therefore, Rao declared, 'A settled constitution which recognizes the responsibility of the administration to the people and containing all the essential elements of a popular government is the only safeguard for the protection of the people.'[61]

At the 26 December meeting that same year in Madras, Srinivas Iyengar gave the presidential address and pointed out what he perceived as a fundamental misunderstanding about the princely states. There was an assumption, he stated, that because there were no racial barriers between the people and the government in the states, they were less burdened with taxes and had greater access to the ruling class. Iyenger argued this was not the case. In fact, the states' peoples enjoyed less freedom of the press and basic civil liberties than their counterparts in British India. This particular set of observations by Iyenger made it clear that the AISPC had to come up with alternative strategies, distinct from the tactics of anti-colonial nationalism directed at the British as foreign rulers. If we recall from the earliest nationalists, Naoroji suggested that the racial divide between the ruler and the ruled was one of the prominent obstacles for the flourishing of democratic institutions under colonialism. This set into motion the formulation of anti-colonial nationalism, a set of critiques addressing the inequalities perpetuated by the British in their attempt to govern an 'alien' culture and society that defined and shaped the INC in the latter's quest for self-government. In the case of the princely states, however, because the princes were of the same race and culture as the 'subject peoples' in fact, Iyengar argued, there was an assumption that without the racial divide, the ruler and the ruled should be able to work towards a common goal of self-government. However, the problem was deeper. The princes became a symbol of the old-world, outdated political arrangements: feudalism and monarchy. Political movements in the princely states had to address the conditions that perpetuated unequal sets of rights and liberties for their subject peoples.

At the southern AISPC at Trivandrum on 12 January 1929, M. Visveswaraya gave a presidential address focusing on the pressing needs of the states' peoples. Visveswaraya wrote that the Butler Commission, which was created to discuss the future of the Indian states and their role in the constitutional discussions, seemed exclusively concerned with the treaties between the native states and the British Crown and the finances of the states rather than showing any concern about the condition of the peoples or their demands for their political future. In other words, Visveswaraya wrote that the Butler Commission was exclusionary towards the peoples of the states. If the commission was concerned with the princes and their political futures, who was looking out for the states' peoples? He went on to then outline that there were indeed four interested parties in these discussions on the political future of the Indian subcontinent: '(*a*) The British Government and the British people; (*b*) The Indians residing in British India; (*c*) The Princes ruling the Indian States; and (*d*) The Subjects People of these States.'[62] Identifying the four interested parties made clear that these parties did not share the same political goals and, in fact, held rather different stakes in the Round Table Conferences.

This was an important point for Visveswaraya to raise as it was critical to distinguish between the interested parties in the march towards independence based on ideas of political freedom. The AISPC being held in various parts of India attempted to bring together the interests of the Indians residing in British India and those of the people of the native states and to argue that they were one and the same. This was a shift from the earlier decades when the INC explicitly stayed out of 'internal affairs' of the princely states, implying that the political problems of the states' peoples and the subjects of British India were fundamentally different because they had different governments. However, after the Nehru report, it became clear that in working towards dominion status and representative government, the INC had to have a firmer vision of how the princely states would fit into a federal union. After the passing of the Government of India Act of 1935, the INC became bold in its efforts to provide support for the groups representing the states' peoples. Ultimately, AISPC argued that the states' peoples and the 'Indians residing in British India' shared common political goals of working towards a representative government based on popular sovereignty. With this goal of political reforms in mind, the conferences of the AISPC were held with the objective of achieving full responsible government in the native states.

In July 1931, a confidential memo from the Information Bureau was addressed to Hydari, who at that time was consumed by the deliberations at the Round Table Conferences in London, on the 'extremism' of the Hyderabad Political Conference (HPC) and its members, especially their demands from the Hyderabad government.[63] The memo also pointed to a new group that would organize Muslims in the princely state and offer a counter set of opinions on how best to proceed in terms of political reforms within the state—the idea being that one political party could not possibly aim to represent the political interests of all constituencies in princely Hyderabad. However, the HPC did have Muslim and Hindu leaders and representatives of the major linguistic groups with the state: Telugu, Marathi, Kannada, and Urdu. Despite the political organizing in the state, the Hyderabad administration was reluctant in pushing forward political reforms. The HPC's president of the Working Committee wrote a letter on 19 November 1935 addressed to Kishen Persad Bahadur, the president of the Nizam government's Executive Council. The letter drew attention to some of the political reforms introduced in Hyderabad by the late Salar Jung I in the 1890s. At the Darbar on 17 November 1919, the letter stated that the late Nizam gave a memorable speech in which he acknowledged the need for reforms and that the changing times and the 'complexities of modern life' led him to decide

> ... after much reflection to give my Government a new constitution which would secure greater efficiency and progressive force. Experiments elsewhere have proved that the Council form of Government has many and varied advantages over Government vested in a single official however eminent. It is my earnest desire therefore to secure these advantages for the well-being of my people.[64]

However, the political reforms designed to bring into princely Hyderabad the principle of representative government were repeatedly deferred.

The letter states that the Hyderabad State Reform Association (HSRA) was formed to 'create and enlighten public opinion and interest the people in the public affairs of the country'.[65] The HPC were repeatedly censored and not allowed to hold meetings. They were finally able to hold a meeting in Berar in October 1931 at which a number of resolutions were passed. The HSRA demanded that political reforms be taken seriously in the Hyderabad state as they were in other smaller native states:

We need not repeat here that the principle of representation has been admitted by H.H. the late Nizam in the year 1892 and the same was admitted in its fuller sense by the present Ruler H.E.H. the Nizam in his Farman dated 14th. Jamadiul Awwal 1338 Hijri. It is high time the Government should actively think of introducing a wide elective principle in the Government of the country when the people are fast developing a political consciousness. The democratic spirit is felt throughout India. All the British Indian Provinces will soon be in possession of autonomy. Most of the major and even some smaller Indian states have already got representative institutions advancing gradually towards responsible Government. Extension of the elective principle in the Councils is the aim of every progressive Government now.[66]

As the movement towards autonomy was progressing for the British Indian provinces with the federal principle outlined in the Government of India Act of 1935, the demands of the HPC become more vocal. As we can see in the confidential memos, the political activity was not falling on deaf ears. The Nizam's administration was working to appease all parties by assuring them that the administration was serious in designing political reforms to accommodate the diversity of opinion within the state.

This momentum led to a series of meetings bringing together the Nizam's administration directly with the leaders of HPC and the Majlis-e-Ittehadul Muslimeen (Majlis).[67] A meeting in July 1937 of Nawab Bahadur Yar Jung, Kashinathrao Vaidya, and Akbar Ali Khan produced a set of agreements on political reforms in Hyderabad, one of which included the integrity of the state unit: 'The first question was about maintaining the political integrity of the State intact. It was decided that Hyderabad should continue to remain a political unit in the Commonwealth of India.' The commitment to the integrity of the political boundaries of the Hyderabad state is noteworthy as it often gets lost in the aftermath of the linguistic reorganization of the states in post-independence India. The agreement further stated, 'Institutions which tended to weaken political integrity or which let loose centrifugal forces should be abolished.' This was in reference to the various regional and language-based organizations in Hyderabad state—namely the Andhra, Maharashtra and Karnatak conferences. They went to say that an all-Hyderabad organization should instead be started with common political principles and a common language, although district branches of the organization could function in the local vernaculars. The primary resolution at this early stage of talks between political organizations was that all parties agreed to the integrity of Hyderabad as a political unit. The regional 'cultural' organizations that were divided by language were seen as a potential threat to envisioning Hyderabad as a single political unit, though they did resolve that district branches of an all-Hyderabad organization could function using regional languages. The 'unity talks' of July 1937 also included a discussion of what kind of federation Hyderabad as a state, along with consultation with its peoples, would agree on. Three principles were outlined with regards to the question of federation: '(*a*) That Hyderabad's entry into Federation should not jeopardise the political and administrative power residing within the State; (*b*) That it should not entail financial losses; (*c*) That the potentialities for economic development should be curtailed.'[68] This was, of course, what the princes were advocating for at the Round Table Conferences (1930–1932)—that the native states would be assured of their administrative and economic control over their territories and their integrity as a single political unit. The federation discussions primarily revolved around these assurances. It was around the nature of the union, however, that most of the disagreements arose between Indian leaders from British India and the princes. And ultimately it was with regards to these issues that the INC leaders distrusted the princes, especially because they did not consider the princes to represent the 'peoples' and their political interests within the native states.

Many of the political leaders from organizations within the Hyderabad state—most prominently the HPC—worked with the idea of the Hyderabad state remaining a single political unit in a federated union of states. However, they were more concerned with the reluctance of the Nizam's administration in outlining concrete political reforms that would expand citizenship rights, representative institutions, and basic civil liberties such as freedom of the press and the formation of political organizations to create and disseminate public opinion. A letter from Azhar Hassan, the home secretary to the Nizam, indicates the hesitation that accompanied political reforms:

> Since your organization aims at a form of Government deriving authority from the majority in the Legislature, it is directed against the principle, recently made the subject of an official pronouncement, that the needs of the people must continue to be determined by the undevided [*sic*] responsibility of the Ruler for the welfare of the subjects. Lest Government's attitude in the matter should require further clarification, I am desired to say that the terms of the resolution sent with your letter are not satisfactory that the existing ban still continues and that, therefore, the activities of the organization are unlawful.[69]

While there were clear commitments to formulating essential political reforms from the Nizam himself—that is, to move towards a representative legislature—Hassan's response was certainly disheartening for Vaidya. On 14 March 1940, Vaidya wrote to Hassan to challenge the ban on the Hyderabad State Congress (HSC) due to it calling itself a 'National' conference. He wrote:

But you further object to a Government deriving its authority from the majority of the Legislature. I suppose it means objection to Responsible Government even under the aegis of the Asaf Jahi Dynasty. If so the objection cuts at the root of civil liberty and freedom of expression of opinion. We claim that the permanence of the Dynasty can best be secured by the free co-operation of the people of the State.[70]

Vaidya pointed out that the permanence of the Asaf Jahi dynasty could be assured with the 'free cooperation of the state', that the demands for a representative government should not be seen as threatening to the very existence of the Asaf Jahi dynasty, and that the restriction of the Hyderabad state's peoples' rights and liberties should not be the avenue through which the dynasty attempts to survive the political upheaval of Indian independence. Vaidya further explained that the activities of the HPC were not organized to disrupt public peace but rather to foster public opinion through constructive work: 'I should also tell you that the activities of the association were purely constructive such as Khaddar, Hindu–Muslim Unity, drive against illiteracy and Harijan Uplift. As to Responsible Government the object was only to formulate public opinion in the matter.'[71] Vaidya slipped in that the object of the HPC was not to demand responsible government but rather to shape public opinion.

Vaidya and his associates employed creative tactics to engage in dialogue with the Nizam's administration. Ultimately, the Nizam's administration entered into talks only to defer any resolutions on how best to incorporate the opinions of public organizations that claimed to speak for the people and their interests in the future of political reforms in Hyderabad state. The administration seemed more interested in dragging the political reforms while engaging in dialogue with various parties within the state. One tactic was simply to create hurdles for members of the HPC as well as other language-based organizations such as the AMS to carry on conducting business. In the confidential reports of the Nizam's 'Information Bureau' are documented attempts to restrict meetings from being held as well as politics, the Nizam, and his policies from being discussed. The back and forth between various organizations and the Information Bureau illustrates starkly the fear with which the Nizam's administration was adapting to new political conditions in British India in the 1930s and the 1940s.

In 1938, at the 'unity talks' conducted between the Nizam's administration and members of the HPC with Bahadur Yar Jung of the Majlis, the administration wanted assurances that the members at the talks were indeed representative of various interested groups within Hyderabad. Meanwhile, the HSC worked tirelessly to produce a consensus amongst its various constituents that would represent people across the political spectrum. Not only were the HSC taking cues from the INC in British India to coordinate their agitational politics because they shared the same political goals, but the HSC also pursued direct dialogue with the British. The following extract comes from a memorandum prepared for the British Parliamentary Delegation at Hyderabad Deccan on 25 January 1946:

> India is one undivided whole and the people in Indian States cannot be differentiated from those in British India. They belong to the same race and they have inherited the same culture. They speak the same languages and they have their places of pilgrimage in every part of India. No political arbitrary divisions can separate them and if there appear some differences, they are merely artificial. The Indian States, therefore, should be integral parts of a free India. In such a Free India, there must be some common back-ground of free Institutions and standards of social and economic welfare. India cannot be free in British and unfree in Indian India.[72]

The HSC appealed to the delegation that, in fact, the peoples of Hyderabad (like the people of all princely states) were of the same race and culture as the peoples of British India and thus the princely states should be part of a free India with democratic institutions. It was a desperate attempt to speak directly to the British. While the states' peoples were not invited to the Round Table Conferences as were British Indian leaders, they nevertheless sent a memorandum expressing their concerns. The princes and their administrators remained the mediators between the native states and the British without any representatives such as prominent political leaders from within the communities. Therefore, on the model of the INC, the AISPC's aim was to create a forum for all states' peoples' organizations to meet and discuss common political goals and to build on the commonalities between British India and the native states.

Nonetheless, they differed in one important political strategy. As opposed to the INC, the Hyderabad political leaders from the HSC argued that Hyderabad should remain a single political unit—a state within the Indian Union. This presented a potential problem in the long run in that it ran counter to the linguistic policies of the INC that organized the regional units along linguistic lines. The HSC adhered closely to an idea of a federation of states as conceived after the Round Table Conferences. In 1937, the HSC clearly stated its objective in agreement with the administrations—that Hyderabad the princely state should remain a territorial unit within the Commonwealth of India so as to preserve the historical identity of the state and its cultures. What they envisioned was a federalism of the Indian Union in which princely states would be equivalent to British Indian provinces.

What becomes clear in sorting through the federalism discussions in the princely state of Hyderabad is that the different parties entered into discussions on federating with a union (of states and provinces) for very different reasons, leading to radically different political goals. In the Hyderabad state, there were distinct political interests that divided the goals of the Nizam's administration against the states' peoples' movements. The latter were working towards a federated Indian Union—not simply in order to protect the Hyderabad state as a sovereign political unit but rather to ensure the extension of fundamental rights to its peoples and the building up of institutions for a robust representative government. This trajectory towards a representative government became the real point of contention between the administration's position and the majority of political movements within the state, with the exception of the Majlis.[73] The political groups were in essence anti-monarchical and shared the political goals of the anti-colonial nationalists in British India. However, the Hyderabad state's administration, working to thwart these political movements, saw the march towards a representative democracy as a direct threat to the historical identity of the Hyderabad state as an inheritor of Mughal legacy in South Asia and, on a global scale, as the last Muslim polity after the dismantling of the Ottoman Empire. Hence, for the administration, a federation of states, if conceived appropriately, would have allowed the historical identity—its monarchical status—to hold together after Indian independence. The princely states' peoples' movements aligned their political goals with those of the anti-colonial nationalists prominent in British India. While crafting a political future for the Hyderabad state, they envisioned a withering away of the monarchical state, all the while retaining the historical borders of the state.

Notes

1. Jawaharlal Nehru, 'The Unity of India', *Foreign Affairs*, January 1938.
2. Thompson was a historian and translator who was sympathetic to Indian nationalism and also the father of the historian E.P. Thompson.
3. 'Edward Thompson Also Speaks Out: Jawahar Explains Indian Opposition to Federation to American Readers', *Bombay Chronicle*, 30 January 1938.
4. Kavita Datla, 'The Origins of Indirect Rule in India: Hyderabad and the British Imperial Order', *Law and History Review* 33, no. 2 (May 2015): 321–350, 347.
5. See Lauren Benton, *The Search for Sovereignty and Law and Colonial Cultures* (Studies in Comparative World History) (Cambridge, UK: Cambridge University Press, 2001).

6. Konda Venkatappayya, *The Andhra Movement* (The Andhra Maya Sabha Publication, series no. 1) (Madras: Andhra Maha Sabha Publication, 1938), 12.
7. Nehru, 'The Unity of India', 237.
8. Nehru, 'The Unity of India', 240–241.
9. Nizam's Political Department, Installment 47, List 10, Serial 743, newspaper clipping of 'Monstrous Imposition of Feudal Relics: Edward Thompson Also Speaks Out', *Bombay Chronicle*, 30 January 1938, Telangana State Archives (TSA), Hyderabad.
10. Ian Copland, *The Princes of India in the Endgame of Empire 1917–1947* (Cambridge, UK: Cambridge University Press, 1997), 1. Copland writes that at the time of Indian independence there were 600-odd princes who were all pensioned off and that their ancestral domains were integrated into the Indian Union.
11. Datla, 'The Origins of Indirect Rule', 322–323.
12. Datla, 'The Origins of Indirect Rule', 322–323.
13. On the particularities of the princely states and specifically Hyderabad, see John Roosa, 'The Quandary in the Qaum: Indian Nationalism in a Muslim State, Hyderabad, 1850–1948', PhD dissertation, University of Wisconsin–Madison, 1998; Barbara Ramusack, *The Indian Princes and Their States* (The New Cambridge History of India) (Cambridge, UK: Cambridge University Press, 2007); Copland, *The Princes of India*; and Lucien Benichou, *From Autocracy to Integration: Political Developments in Hyderabad State (1938–1948)* (Chennai: Orient Longman, 2000).
14. See C. A. Bayly, *Recovering Liberties: Indian Thought in the Age of Liberalism and Empire* (Cambridge, UK: Cambridge University Press, 2012) on how associational life transformed and shaped nineteenth century social and political movements.
15. See Sarath Pillai, 'Fragmenting the Nation: Divisible Sovereignty and Travancore's Quest for Federal Independence', *Law and History Review* 34, no. 3 (August 2016): 743–782, 744.
16. Partha Chatterjee, 'Nationalism, Internationalism and Cosmopolitanism', *Comparative Study of South Asia, Africa and the Middle East* (2016): 320–334, 322.
17. See Faisal Devji, *Muslim Zion: Pakistan as a Political Idea* (Cambridge, MA: Harvard University Press, 2013).
18. Chatterjee, 'Nationalism, Internationalism', 324.
19. Anthony Anghie, *Imperialism, Sovereignty, and the Making of International Law* (Cambridge, UK: Cambridge University Press, 2005), 121.

20. See Michael Collins, 'Decolonisation and the "Federal Moment"', *Diplomacy and Statecraft* 24, no. 1 (2013): 21–40.
21. Nazmul Sultan examines Indian theorists of pluralist federalism who were critical of national self-determination (and its basis in monist conceptions of sovereignty) as the only inevitable outcome of anti-colonial nationalism. See Nazmul S. Sultan, 'Between the Many and the One: Anticolonial Federalism and Popular Sovereignty', *Political Theory* 50, no. 2 (June 2021): 247–274, DOI: 10.1177/00905917211018534.
22. Frederick Cooper, *Citizenship between Empire and Nation: Remaking France and French Africa, 1945–1960* (Princeton, NJ: Princeton University Press), Kindle edition.
23. Cooper, *Citizenship between Empire and Nation*, 9.
24. Gary Wilder, *Freedom Time: Negritude, Decolonization, and the Future of the World* (Durham, NC: Duke University Press, 2015), 20.
25. Adom Getachew, 'Securing Postcolonial Independence: Kwame Nkrumah and the Federal Idea in the Age of Decolonization', *Ab Imperio* 3 (2018): 89–113.
26. Nizam's Political Department, Installment 47, List 10, Serial 743, newspaper clipping of 'Monstrous Imposition of Feudal Relics: Edward Thompson Also Speaks Out', *Bombay Chronicle*, 30 January 1938, TSA, Hyderabad.
27. *Report on India's Constitutional Reforms* (Calcutta: Superintendent of Government Printing, India, 1918), 1.
28. V. P. Menon, *Integration of the Indian States* (Madras: Orient Longman, 1995 [1956]), 17.
29. Center for Research Libraries (CRL), *Work in England of the Deputation of the Indian States People's Conference* (Poona: Aryabhushan Press, 1929).
30. CRL, 'Princes or People? Problem of the Indian States', in *Work in England*, 48.
31. CRL, 'Self-Determination for the States People', in *Work in England*, 75.
32. CRL, 'Self-Determination for the States People', in *Work in England*, 75–76.
33. CRL, 'Self-Determination for the States People', in *Work in England*, 77.
34. All-India States Peoples' Conference, *Mr. Bhulabhai J. Desai and the Peoples of the States* (Bombay: All-India States Peoples' Conference, 1947), 22.
35. Nizam's Political Department, Installment 45, List 10, Serial 202, 'Secret Report on Roundtable Conference', TSA, Hyderabad.
36. Nizam's Political Department, Installment 45, List 10, Serial 192, 'Sir Akbar Hydari's speech', November 1932, TSA, Hyderabad.
37. See Kavita Datla, 'Sovereignty and the End of Empire: The Transition to Independence in Colonial Hyderabad', *Ab Imperio* 3 (2018): 63–88.
38. Jawaharlal Nehru, 'Address by Jawaharlal Nehru to the All-India States People's Conference', in *Documents and Speeches on the Indian Princely States*, vol. 2, ed. Adrian Sever, 576–578 (New Delhi: B. R. Publishing Corporation, 1985), 576.

39. Nizam's Political Department, Installment 45, List 10, Serial 202, 'Secret Report on Roundtable Conference', TSA, Hyderabad, 4.
40. Nizam's Political Department, Installment 45, List 10, Serial 202, 'Secret Report on Roundtable Conference', TSA, Hyderabad, 5–6.
41. Constitutional Affairs Secretariat, Installment 47, List 10, Serial 918. Newspaper clipping of 'India on a Federal Basis: A Study of Its Pyramidal Structure', *Madras Mail*, 15 April 1939, TSA, Hyderabad.
42. Constitutional Affairs Secretariat, Installment 47, List 10, Serial 918, 'Creation of a Separate Andhra Province', TSA, Hyderabad.
43. Constitutional Affairs Secretariat, Installment 47, List 10, Serial No. 702, 'Resolutions Passed by the All India States' Workers' Convention Held at Navsari', 15 February 1938, TSA, Hyderabad.
44. Nizam's Political Department, Installment 45 List 10 Serial 202, 'Secret Report on Roundtable Conference', TSA, Hyderabad, 7.
45. Howard Erdman, *The Swatantra Party and Indian Conservatism* (Cambridge, UK: Cambridge University Press, 1967), 3.
46. Adrian Sever (ed.), *Documents and Speeches on the Indian Princely States*, vol. 2 (Delhi: B. R. Publishing Corporation, 1985), 495.
47. Sever (ed.), *Documents and Speeches*.
48. Lloyd I. Rudolph, and Susanne Hoeber Rudolph. 'Federalism as State Formation in India: A Theory of Shared and Negotiated Sovereignty'. *International Political Science Review (Revue Internationale de Science Politique)* 31, no. 5 (2010): 553–572.
49. See Louise Tillin, 'India's Democracy at 70: The Federalist Compromise', *Journal of Democracy* 28, no. 3 (July 2017): 64–75.
50. See Sandipto Dasgupta, '"A Language Which Is Foreign to Us": Continuities and Anxieties in the Making of the Indian Constitution', *Comparative Studies of South Asia, Africa and the Middle East* 34, no. 2 (2014): 228–242.
51. *Mr. Bhulabhai J. Desai and the Peoples of the States*, 17.
52. See Copland, *The Princes of India*.
53. Mohandas K. Gandhi, *'Hind Swaraj' and Other Writings* (Cambridge Texts in Modern Politics), ed. Anthony Parel (Cambridge, UK: Cambridge University Press, 1997), 76–77.
54. Mohandas K. Gandhi, *Harijan*, 1 October 1938, in Sever (ed.), *Documents and Speeches*, 574–575.
55. Mohandas K. Gandhi, *Harijan*, 20 April 1940, in Sever (ed.), *Documents and Speeches*, 583.
56. Mohandas K. Gandhi, *Harijan*, 2 August 1942, in Sever (ed.), *Documents and Speeches*, 591.
57. B. R. Ambedkar, 'Statement by Dr. Ambedkar (17 June 1947)', in Sever (ed.), *Documents and Speeches*, 633.

58. Granville Austin, *The Indian Constitution: Cornerstone of a Nation* (New Delhi: Oxford University Press, 2002 [1966]), 1.
59. *Addresses Delivered at the 7th Session of the Deccan States Subjects' Conference, Bombay, 1927; the Indian States' Peoples' Conference, Bombay, 1927; the Indian States' Subjects' Conference, Madras, 1927; and the Southern States' People's Conference, Trivandrum, 1929* (Bombay, 1929), 2.
60. *Addresses Delivered at the 7th Session*, 19.
61. *Addresses Delivered at the 7th Session*, 19.
62. *Addresses Delivered at the 7th Session*, 4.
63. Constitutional Affairs Secretariat, Installment 47, List 10, Serial No. 548, 'Letter to Sir Akbar Hydari from Aziz Ahmad', 30 July 1931, TSA, Hyderabad.
64. Constitutional Affairs Secretariat, Installment 47, List 10, Serial No. 548, TSA, Hyderabad. The HPC's president of the Working Committee wrote a letter on 19 November 1935, addressed to Persad Bahadur, the president of the Nizam government's Executive Council.
65. Constitutional Affairs Secretariat, Installment 47, List 10, Serial No. 548, TSA, Hyderabad.
66. Constitutional Affairs Secretariat, Installment 47, List 10, Serial No. 548, TSA, Hyderabad.
67. For a history of the party and its politics in the 1930s and the 1940s, see M. A. Moid and A. Suneetha, 'Rethinking Majlis' Politics: Pre-1948 Muslim Concerns in Hyderabad State', *Indian Economic and Social History Review* 55, no. 1 (2018): 29–52.
68. Nizam's Political Department, Installment 47, List 10, Serial 1197, 'Hindu Muslim Unity Talks', TSA, Hyderabad.
69. Nehru Museum and Memorial Library (NMML), 'Letter from 29 May 1939 to Kashinathrao Vaidya from Azhar Hassan (home secretary to the Nizam)', AISPC File 65.
70. NMML, 'Letter from 29 May 1939 to Kashinathrao Vaidya from Azhar Hassan (home secretary to the Nizam)', AISPC File 65.
71. NMML, 'Letter from 29 May 1939 to Kashinathrao Vaidya from Azhar Hassan (home secretary to the Nizam)', AISPC File 65.
72. NMML, 'Memorandum Presented to the British Parliamentary Delegation at Hyderabad Deccan', 25 January 1946, signed by Kashinathrao Vaidya, Syed Siraj-ul-Hasan Tirmizi, M. Narsing Rao, and G. Ramachar, AISPC File 66, parts 1, 27.
73. The Majlis did not explicitly oppose the continuation of the monarchical structure though they welcomed political reforms—however, only if the reforms would perpetuate the historic 'Muslim' dominance of the Hyderabad state. See Moid and Suneetha, 'Rethinking Majlis' Politics'.

Part II

Civil Liberties

4

Publicity, Civil Liberties, and Political Life in Princely Hyderabad

The federation debates carried on by the Nizam's administration led to an impasse between the Government of India and the Hyderabad state, with the majority of the political associations and their representatives within Hyderabad shut out of the negotiations. Meanwhile, it is important to note that princely Hyderabad was all the while the site of a thriving civil society in the early twentieth century with a dynamic political landscape. Discussions on the role of the state, civil rights, publicity, and representative government were common in Hyderabad's public organizations, which represented the views and interests of the state's multiple linguistic and religious communities. Two glaring questions confronted the Nizam's administration in the 1930s: the question of sovereignty—more specifically, the political future of the princely state of Hyderabad—and the demand for civil liberties fuelling peoples' movements at the time. As I have argued in the previous chapter, the Hyderabad state entered into discussions of federation at the Round Table Conferences with a great deal of hesitation, given the lack of real commitments regarding what the state would gain in any federation arrangement. However, it did enter into discussions with the British and the colonial government harbouring ideas about how to regain its sovereignty after the withdrawal of British paramountcy. As Ian Copland has suggested, the Indian princes floated varying sets of political ideologies, and not all agreed on the goal of political reforms within the British Empire. In the second decade of the twentieth century, the princes were simultaneously angling for more influence in managing the relations between the British government and the states while also demanding greater autonomy for the native states to manage their own internal affairs. The latter meant that they would hesitate entering into discussions about internal reforms pertaining to fundamental rights and civil liberties of the states' peoples.

In 1916, the princely state of Bikaner's Ganga Singh, who was sympathetic to the INC's modern wing's desire for dominion status (what the settler colonies such as Canada and Australia already had), requested that the British government should make *self-government* within the British Empire the ultimate goal.[1] This was a progressive goal emerging from the princes, inspired by the INC's anti-colonial nationalism and agitational politics. This set the princes on track towards multiple interpretations of self-government. In a sense, the princes could have potentially asked for more autonomy and to be left to rule within their territories without the interference of the British government. Within these discussions regarding self-government, British India's devolution of power could have been interpreted as making way for greater autonomy for the princely states. Instead, however, the British administrators (along with the progressive contingent of the princes) interpreted the idea of self-government as setting the native states on a track of developing self-governing institutions within the states. During these conversations, the Hyderabad state strongly resisted political reforms that would interfere with anything to do with internal governing.[2] Despite this resistance of Hyderabad's administration to taking on the challenge of introducing representative institutions within the state that would give voice to the interests of the people, the discourse of self-government had a profound impact on civil society discussions and public organizations. It invigorated princely Hyderabad's civil society through the formation of a number of influential organizations that disseminated their views on necessary political reforms as well as their visions for the political future of the princely state.

The 1930s did not give rise to the first voluntary associations in Hyderabad; rather, those civil society organizations that were active at this time put considerable pressure on the political debates of the time. The dramatic debates of the 1930s illustrate the Hyderabad state administration's complicated and often ambiguous response to the end of empire in South Asia. Yet there was a dynamic relationship between the Hyderabad state administration and political leaders and groups articulating political interests for a democratic future for the people. For this reason, the administration pursued two contradictory paths. On the one hand, it adopted a course to reclaim Hyderabad's sovereignty through re-negotiating its prior relationships and treaties established between the British and itself—a path that did not necessarily include voices from the political leaders of emerging constituencies. On the other hand, the monarchical state was under considerable pressure in the early decades of the twentieth century from a burgeoning civil society to expand democratic institutions and extend greater rights to its people. This chapter will take a closer look at the discourse of civil liberties taken up by public associations in princely Hyderabad and how it impacted the state administration's position towards the idea of representative government and the necessary internal political reforms that it entailed. The early decades of the twentieth century in Hyderabad state became a battleground between the state administration and the burgeoning public sphere that the administration could not contain.[3] I argue that civil liberties were taken up by public organizations in princely Hyderabad and, simultaneously, by the INC in an effort to pressure the Hyderabad government to begin charting a path for representative government. The discourse of civil liberties presented a useful rhetorical strategy for both the Hyderabad civil society groups and the INC to enter into dialogue with the Hyderabad administration regarding the reconfiguration of power at the end of empire. I consider the intention and efficacy of this strategy—for example, whether it sought to bypass the intransigence of the Nizam's administration and their constitutional debates and sought to turn its focus to the streets towards mass political mobilization. This may well have been the case considering the many deadlocks princely Hyderabad's constitutional debates faced. Ultimately, the chapter ends with a discussion of why civil society groups were unable to coordinate their efforts and wrest from the administration an inclusive political future for the state of Hyderabad.

Civil Liberties and the British Empire

While the princely states were in the midst of pursuing constitutional questions with the British government in India and in Britain, there were important parallel discussions being conducted by the people of the Indian states, which spoke to their multifaceted political aspirations. The INC began to take interest in native Indian states and political reforms in the late 1920s, deviating from their previous policy of non-interference in states matters.[4] In 1927, associations bringing together representatives from native states in the west and the south formed to increase their involvement in INC activism in British India and bring greater attention to the condition of the states' people. Even before the founding of the AISPC by the INC, which aimed to influence and nurture movements for political change in the princely states, there had already been a considerable increase of political activity on the ground.[5] Barbara Ramusack, in her charting of this history, has suggested a shift from petitions to public demonstrations. We see this in princely Hyderabad with the proliferation of public organizations in the 1930s. As opposed to the explicit communal identities of the Arya Samaj and the Hindu Mahasabha, Hyderabad's lesser-known local organizations were seeking political change through demands for the freedom to congregate and the freedom of speech. The infamous Gasthi 53 that restricted political speech was the source of much grievance for many of these groups. The order was put together in September 1921 to ban social or political meetings that explicitly brought up political issues and to restrict the entry of outsiders from British India stirring up local politics. Gasthi 53 superseded Gasthi 52 in 1929, specifically banning any political meeting without prior permission.[6] Working within these constrained sociopolitical conditions, activists in Hyderabad civil society organizations set their sights on agitating for the expansion of civil liberties and fundamental rights as a way to make inroads towards demands for free political expression and to gradually propose changes that would move the state towards representative institutions.

How did public associations in princely Hyderabad settle on pushing for civil liberties to force the Hyderabad government to take their interventions seriously? The Hyderabad state was a reluctant discussant of political reforms and the idea of federation, as documented by many historians who have written on the mixed attitude of the administration towards negotiations with the British at the height of Indian anti-colonial nationalism. First, in order to understand why the INC decided to put pressure on the Hyderabad state at all, I look at the formation of the Indian Civil Liberties Union (ICLU) and the perspective of one of the organization's prominent founders on the importance of civil liberties in the anti-colonial struggle against the British Empire. It is important to locate and disaggregate the motivations of the ICLU within British India and its relationship to the princely states because it became an important tool used by the INC to put pressure on those states. For both the ICLU and the INC, coordinating the push for greater rights for subjects within both British India and the princely states was central to the broader anti-colonial struggle. It is within this framework that I turn to the formation of the ICLU.

In 1936, Ram Manohar Lohia, famed Indian nationalist and socialist, published a short book on the origins of civil liberties in Europe. At the same time, the ICLU was established in 1936 by Jawaharlal Nehru. ICLU's founding is important in that it created an outfit that could advocate for civil liberties across imperial boundaries to British Indian neighbours. The discourse of civil liberties provided an avenue for British Indian subjects to criticize the domestic policies of their princely neighbours. Nehru decided to meet with the leaders of the American Civil Liberties Union (ACLU) and the National Council for Civil Liberties (NCCL) of Britain, after which he decided that India would benefit from such an organization. In principle, the ICLU was designed to work independently as a check on political parties and institutions within British India. The ICLU believed it was critical to have in place institutional mechanisms to check the power of political organizations (and parties,) especially dominant ones—such as the INC. Nehru wrote:

In America, England and France powerful civil liberties unions, of a purely non-party character, have been established to resist all such encroachments and their activities have borne substantial fruit. In India the necessity for such a joint effort embracing all groups and individuals, who believe in civil liberties, is obviously even more necessary than elsewhere.⁷

Nehru also believed such an organization would serve as an organ to publicize on the international level the curtailment of liberties in British India. This would not only provide an institutional backing of democratic struggles within British India, but it would also establish a firm foundation for protecting democratic institutions in an independent India that would be the eventual outcome of a successful anti-colonial movement. Lohia tracked the emergence of civil liberties globally as a discourse central to democratic politics to nineteenth-century France, Britain, and the United States—and then strategically shifted his attention to the British Empire. Lohia argued that the French League of the Rights of Man, formed in 1898, first articulated an agenda for the protection of civil liberties of individuals and groups within a bounded national territory but that they extended their reach beyond those national boundaries. He wrote, 'The League intervenes on every occasion where injustice, an arbitrary act, an abuse of power or an illegality is done against the individual, the associations and the peoples. Its action consists in appeal to public conscience. Presentations to public authorities, petitions to Parliament, publication of literature, conferences and demonstrations.'⁸ Different modes of publicity, such as petitions, print publications, and public demonstrations, could publicize the act, prick the conscience of the public, and enable political debate. Political activists like Lohia in early-twentieth-century India became increasingly aware of the power of publicity for politics. While print publications and newspaper predate this period, it is clear that newspapers and journals thrived in this new era of publicity.⁹ The ICLU, founded by Nehru and given historical weight and legitimacy by Lohia, benefited from this new era and sought to use publicity to its advantage.

The NCCL in Britain was formed in 1934 to defend 'freedom of speech, freedom of assembly, freedom of association, freedom of thought and expression, full rights for all peoples under the British Parliament, democratic control of government'.¹⁰ Lohia naturally extended the NCCL's declaration to the British colonies where, in Gambia, Nigeria, Trinidad, Sierra Leone, and in India, political parties were banned and leaders arrested and imprisoned without trial for carrying on the normal work of civil society within a democratic government. The idea behind the ICLU being an independent unit outside of an official political party was that it could be the stage for what Lohia called the *eternal struggle waged by the citizen against the state*. As such, the ICLU's aim was to 'throw the searchlight of publicity on legal, judicial, executive, police and private excesses'.[11] Lohia also understood that this 'eternal struggle' of civil liberties in a global order of nation states could traverse across national boundaries to apply to citizens in multiple polities. This would be possible within an international order that recognized a commonly held notion of rights. The interwar period was ripe for this kind of discourse, as Lohia stated that 'colonial peoples and oppressed masses all over the world [were] thinking out an alternative Society and ... propagating and organizing and striking for its acceptance'.[12] In this era of radicalism, Lohia spoke of political futures being shaped by a general climate of anti-colonial politics. The discourse of civil liberties mobilized in anti-colonial movements in India was composed of two elements: (*a*) rights as bounded entities and (*b*) rights that derived moral force as part of a universal discourse that applied to all people regardless of the political imaginary. Of course, what these political movements ultimately sought was a people's government—or popular sovereignty that operated with elections and representative legislatures. Rights were conceptualized as abstract and universal, but only meaningful and enforceable within a polity that guaranteed people's sovereignty. In other words, rights were both bounded entities and universal. These dual qualities of the rhetoric of civil liberties and rights gave anti-colonial activists the language to mobilize against empire and refuse the state of exception that would enable colonies to be ruled differently.[13]

In princely Hyderabad, the discourse of civil liberties was mobilized by a diverse set of British Indian actors, including the INC, the Arya Samaj, the Hindu Mahasabha, and, most importantly in the present context, public associations formed within Hyderabad that spoke to local and regional concerns. On 3 March 1938, Bhogaraju Pattabhi Sitaramayya, a prominent member of the INC and the author of the monumental three-volume *The History of the Indian National Congress* (1935), sent a letter on behalf of the AISPC, a newly formed group, headed by INC members to oversee political and social movements emerging within the princely states, to the Nizam's administration. The letter emphasized the absolute necessity of protecting civil liberties in all forms of government:

> I beg leave to invite your attention to the fact, which is no longer disputed in all civilized Governments, that Civil Liberties of the citizens form the very foundations ... of National Government in any country. While there are democracies under which Civil Liberties are being abridged most unexpectedly there may be personal rule under which such liberties are allowed. The question, therefore, of Civil Liberties has become, more or less, independent

of the forms of Government and is really an idea of the benevolence of the rule that obtains in a land.[14]

Sitaramayya employed the discourse of civil liberties in its universal framework to convey to the native governments of the princely states that while the INC would not negotiate the states' form of government, it would nevertheless call for full civil liberties for the people therein. In the end, however, the AISPC did negotiate the form of government the princely states eventually agreed to as they merged with an Indian Union. Here, what I want to highlight is the use of the discourse of civil liberties as a rhetorical strategy to enter into political negotiations with princely Hyderabad. As outlined by Lohia, the call for civil liberties could traverse political boundaries between British India and princely states. This was a strategic move on the part of the INC and its AISPC wing. Sitaramayya attempted to separate the questions of representative government and civil liberties in order to make the INC's intervention in what were deemed to be the internal affairs of the princely state of Hyderabad less threatening. The same year a petition was submitted to the Nizam through the president of the Executive Council, pleading for the government to honour the integrity of the state by encouraging political life within it. The petition repeatedly called the period under discussion a 'New Era' in cultural and political awakening and argued that if the Hyderabad state would only take the lead, it could demonstrate to the 'backward'-looking Indian princely states the viable political futures they, too, could pursue. The petition declared, 'The development of public consciousness, which is the corner stone of the success and progress of the "New Era", is a work which no progressive Government can well afford to check or be indifferent to.'[15]

On 27 July 1937, Sitaramayya published a piece in the *Indian Express* titled 'Self-Surrender Is Self-Realization: Concede Fundamental Rights to States' People', a message sent to the Deccan State Subjects' Conference that was to celebrate the Fundamental Rights Declaration Day on 1 August. That day was deliberately chosen and fitting, he wrote, as it marked the death anniversary of Bal Gangadhar Tilak, an anti-colonial nationalist who emphasized the necessity of individual rights and duties in a democratic polity. Sitaramayya wrote:

> The Princes are as much an integral part of the structure of Indian Democracy as the people over whom they hold sway, and it is as much to their interests as to the interests of their people that the latter should be admitted to their fundamental rights in order that the Princes and People may alike fit themselves into the structure of a well-ordered Federation.[16]

Sitaramayya collapsed the difference between the people and the princes in that there was no racial or nationality barrier as in British India where the ruling power, the British, belonged to a nationality different from that of the subject people. The princes, the peoples of the native states, and the peoples of British India, in the INC's political imaginary, were all of one and the same nationality. In that case, it was in the interests of all to allow all people, whether in British India or in the native states, to hold fundamental democratic rights. The discourse of civil liberties was not only at the centre of debates in the INC as it contemplated its role in shaping politics in the princely states, but it also became critical to the political strategies taken up by public organizations in Hyderabad.

Civil Liberties and Publicity in Hyderabad

Just as a new politics emerged in the Madras Presidency with the rollout of devolution schemes put forward by the colonial government in the first two decades of the twentieth century, princely Hyderabad, too, was undergoing some radical changes. To chart the centrality of public life shaping a new politics in Hyderabad, I turn to a dynamic figure there in the 1930s: Mandumula Narsing Rao. As the founder of the *Raiyat*, an Urdu-language newspaper, Narsing Rao fostered a vibrant public and contributed to political discussion in the years leading up to princely Hyderabad's forced merger with the Indian Union in 1948. Hyderabad, the city, was home to roughly 48 per cent Telugu speakers—though most, especially those educated in the city, were multilingual, versed not only in Telugu but also in Urdu and Persian. Narsing Rao was one of those intellectual figures in Hyderabad who was able to navigate between the language worlds of Telugu and Urdu. In his memoir, Narsing Rao introduces himself as hailing from a small village just outside of Hyderabad city (Talakondapalli), where he was taught Urdu and Persian by a tutor with rigour.[17] While Telugu was the medium of the local school he attended, Narsing Rao's father wanted him to have good future prospects for work. Learning Urdu and Persian made good sense to his family since they were the languages of administration in princely Hyderabad. While Urdu was not a mandatory primary language in local village schools, higher educational opportunities in Hyderabad required literacy in Urdu.[18] His father encouraged him to pursue higher studies in Urdu, which seemed to Narsing Rao quite unusual in retrospect, leading him to enrol at the Dar ul Ulum High School, near Charminar in the city centre. In contrast, his peers such as Burgula Ramakrishna Rao and Suravaram Pratapa Reddy, both prominent Telugu intellectuals in Hyderabad, were encouraged by their families to attend English medium and/or British Indian colleges for gaining useful skills and job prospects. Having achieved high levels of proficiency in both Urdu and Persian,

Narsing Rao felt confident to lead an Urdu daily in the city of Hyderabad, a city that he moved to as a student. Urdu was not his mother tongue, and his friends often questioned why he was so loyal to it rather than Telugu. The fact that Narsing Rao was a prominent member of the AMS, an organization devoted to preserving Telugu in princely Hyderabad, speaks to the vibrant cosmopolitan culture that shaped his politics and his commitment to both Telugu and Urdu cultures.

When the *Raiyat* was founded in 1927, another prominent newspaper, the *Golkonda Patrika*, was already in circulation, which was founded by Suravaram Pratapa Reddy. Another English daily, the *New Era*, was edited by Sayyad Asadullah. Both of these prominent figures were close friends of Narsing Rao. Newspapers from British India were also available in Hyderabad, such as *The Hindu* from Madras, the *Mahratta* from Pune, and the *Amrutha Bazaar Patrika* from Calcutta. While the *Hyderabad Bulletin* was in circulation in Hyderabad, there were Telugu newspapers coming out of places such as Nalgonda (the *Nilgiri*) and Warangal (the *Telugu Patrika*) in Telangana. From the secret political files of the Nizam's government, it is clear that the emergence of these newspapers was indeed threatening to the Hyderabad state, as Narsing Rao suggested, given their role in disseminating the political debates and languages streaming in through Hyderabad's borders with British India. According to Narsing Rao, in the second half of the 1920s, Hyderabad saw a general cultural and political awakening with the establishment of newspapers and journals conducive for political debate. There were a number of critical elements that came together at this time for Narsing Rao to be able to carry out the task of producing a newspaper in a climate where the Nizam's administration was suspicious of any activity that could be construed as political. The prominently placed *kotwal* (police commissioner), Raja Bahadur Venkata Rama Reddy, was able to help Narsing Rao publish the *Raiyat* at his own printing press.[19] To work for the newspaper, Narsing Rao recruited Pandit Narendraji, who later became a prominent leader of the Arya Samaj in Hyderabad, and Osmania University graduate Basheer Ahmad Taheer.

In his recollection of those years, Narsing Rao speculated that newspapers ought to serve as watchdogs monitoring government activities and policies, but just as importantly, he felt they should also facilitate the awakening of the people to their own interests: 'In a state without political parties—in order to influence opinion—to confront people's problems—to bring into view the hardships and happiness of its people to the government—that is the purview of newspapers.'[20] For Narsing Rao, newspapers such as the *Raiyat* as well as the *Golkonda Patrika* contributed to a vibrant public political life and simultaneously informed the public by scrutinizing government policies. The expansion of the public sphere could then provide the essential intermediate space for interaction between the state and its subjects. Ideally, the liberal public sphere envisioned by Narsing Rao would work not only to articulate the political interests of the people but also to shape political reforms. There was nothing new per se in this understanding of a free press, but newspapers carried a particularly heavy burden at the time, given the absence of formal and legitimate political parties as well as continuing press censorship. Despite these limitations, newspapers and print media with limited circulation shaped the terms of political debate, as seen through the proliferation of Telugu- and Urdu-language newspapers during this period. At the same time, it is important to acknowledge the limited nature of the liberal public sphere in a society with low levels of literacy and where public oratory still played a large role in disseminating information and framing political discussion.[21] Along with the circulation and exchange of ideas through print, the era of mass politics and organization gave rise to public political oratory, as Bernard Bate persuasively argues in the case of British India. Bate suggests that in the years 1918–1919, mass politics arrived in the Madras Presidency when speakers of Telugu and Tamil shifted away from using English in conducting public meetings and toward the use of vernacular languages. This turn was momentous in that it signalled the shift to the era of mass mobilization toward democratic politics.[22]

Narsing Rao identified a key turning point in the late 1920s, just at the time when he was starting his newspaper, that of Hyderabad youth—Osmania University graduates and others returning from European universities—expressing new political desires and sentiments. Ali Yavar Jung (Ali Yar Khan), Baqar Ali Mirza, and Fazlur Rahman were such figures.[23] This generation that was university-educated, as well as some who returned from schooling in Europe, formed a new association called the Anjuman-i Taraqqi-i Hyderabad—which also included prominent figures in Hyderabad such as Padmaja Naidu, Latif Sayyad, and Burgula Ramakrishna Rao. Yavar Jung was appointed the president of the Anjuman. However, after his return from Oxford University, Yavar Jung was soon also appointed a lecturer of History at Osmania University.[24] Unfortunately the Anjuman did not last longer than three years, disbanding when Yavar Jung was asked to join the Nizam's administration as the Constitutional Affairs advisor by Akbar Hydari during the Round Table Conferences. Broad social issues that the Anjuman took on were classic social reform concerns such as child marriage. Narsing Rao wrote that because child marriage was still prevalent in Hyderabad, a movement was started to address this. A group gathered at the Reddy Hostel, established in 1917 by Venkata Rama Reddy at Osmania University. In attendance was Abdul Haq, a professor of Urdu there; Yavar Jung; Burgula Ramakrishna Rao,

later the chief minister of Hyderabad from 1952 to 1956; and Narsing Rao—
all of whom gave speeches on this occasion. Disappointed with the Anjuman's
quick demise, Baqar Ali Mirza left Hyderabad and made his way to Allahabad
in north India to work alongside Nehru. The two had met in Brussels when
they both attended the International Congress against Colonial Oppression and
Imperialism in 1927.[25] Mirza was part of the communists' circle in Germany that
gathered around the charismatic figure of Virendranath Chattopadhyay, who had
long-standing links with Hyderabad. Chattopadhyay also happened to be the
brother of Sarojini Naidu and son of Aghornath Chattopadhyay, a prominent
figure in the city of Hyderabad who was also the head of Nizam College.[26]

Another organization that shared membership with the aforementioned
associations emerged as politically significant in the 1930s. Pratapa Reddy, the
founder of the *Golkonda Patrika*, was one of the leaders of the AMS, which
was emerging as a central organ for Telugu intellectuals in the Hyderabad state.
Narsing Rao attended the first meeting. The AMS met in 1930 with Pratapa
Reddy's chairmanship in Jogipeta, Medak. Some of the social issues discussed
there included child marriage, the status of widows, and the education of Dalits.[27]
Narsing Rao wrote that one of the stipulations that the Hyderabad government
made on the AMS was that it should not be led by non-*mulki*s (outsiders or non-
residents of the princely state of Hyderabad),[28] presumably fearing that British
Indian elements would infiltrate Hyderabad public associations and influence
politics within the princely state. There is a long history to the politics of *mulki*s
in princely Hyderabad, where Hyderabadi Muslims felt they were overlooked
for recruitment into the Nizam's administration in the previous decades. They
decried that the administration often turned to the recruitment of north Indian
Muslims. In this instance, however, the administration itself was using the charge
of non-*mulkli* elements threatening the political stability of the regime. This
was a legitimate concern as there was an AMS in the Madras Presidency at the
time agitating for a separate province to be carved out of the region for Telugu
speakers. However, Narsing Rao commented that this request to keep non-*mulki*s
out of the AMS was ironic considering the presence of non-*mulki*s in the upper
levels of the Nizam's administration. The most prominently placed non-*mulki*
in Hyderabad at the time was Hydari, who led the constitutional discussions
on Hyderabad's behalf at the Round Table Conferences in London in the early
1930s. Soon after, we see a proliferation of associations emerging in the 1930s
from the Swadeshi League (1930), whose members shared previous association
with the Anjuman, and then later Padmaja Naidu joined to form the Nizam's
Subjects League (NSL) in 1935. The HSC did not appear officially until 1938.

Its public absence until then likely contributed to the vitality of the regional groups in Hyderabad representing the three significant linguistic groups besides Urdu: the AMS, the Mahratta Parishad, and the Karnataka Parishad.[29]

Narsing Rao, whose membership spanned the Anjuman, the AMS, the NSL, and, finally, the HSC, represented himself as a balanced liberal who was critical of the policies of the Nizam's administration. Activists who founded the AMS, on the other hand, harboured a diversity of political ideologies and critiques of the Hyderabad state and the Nizam's administration. The Hyderabad government itself became extremely suspicious of Pratapa Reddy's *Golkonda Patrika*, and that suspicion carried over to the AMS as well. The suspicion was due to Reddy's connections with Telugu intellectuals in the Madras Presidency and the AMS operating there. The Information Bureau in Hyderabad took exceptional interest in the *Golkonda Patrika*'s articles and political commentary and kept track of political critiques made of the Hyderabad administration. Largely due to this kind of monitoring, the AMS in the 1930s tried to present itself as a purely cultural and social organization—involved only in supporting libraries, calling for the teaching of Telugu, and pushing an agenda of cultural revival of sorts—as well as a social reform organization discussing issues of child marriage and caste discrimination.

The second AMS meeting was held in Devarakonda and attended by students from the Reddy Hostel; the most prominent of those students in attendance was Ravi Narayana Reddy, the future AMS leader and communist leader of the Telangana Revolt. The social and cultural issues they discussed were considered to border on the political, making the Hyderabad government reluctant to grant permission for the next meeting for nearly three years. The Information Bureau seemed to be particularly sensitive to any insinuation that judged the administration as being inadequate. In a confidential memo to Yavar Jung, the director of the Information Bureau, dated 28 April 1936, regarding Pratapa Reddy and his *Golkonda Patrika*, Aziz Ahmad wrote:

> Mr. Reddy does not show much sense of responsibility…It is gratifying to learn that Mr Reddy is trying his best to see that the paper is neither anti-Government nor communal. But he considers the article under reference as pro-Government. If this is his conception of Pro-Government attitude, then one can only wish that he was anti-Government.[30]

It was clear that the Information Bureau felt that the *Golkonda Patrika* had been printing controversial articles on the Nizam's administration and state policies. In the 1930s, a series of letters between Pratapa Reddy and the Bureau saw the former repeatedly called upon to defend the opinions and articles published in his newspaper. The contentious issues included opinions expressed by the newspaper on the migration of Andhras from British India who were taking over Telangana land; the paper argued that the Hyderabad government should try to protect the Telangana peasants from these property transfers. Pratapa Reddy defended the article to the Bureau by pointing out that this was a question of protecting *mulki* interests, something that the Hyderabad administration purportedly tried to protect. He wrote to the director of the Bureau, in a letter dated 25 April 1936, insisting that far from expressing anti-government opinion, the article was relatively pro-government: 'The whole trend of the article which will strike one who reads it as a whole was to point out that lacs of nonmulkies are ousting mulkis and such migrations should be stopped.'[31] He repeatedly managed to dissuade the Bureau from revoking the circulation of the *Golkonda Patrika* in the Hyderabad state.

The Information Bureau was also concerned by the *Golkonda Patrika*'s articles on the place of Telugu in Hyderabad. While the AMS and the *Golkonda Patrika* attempted to promote Telugu within the Hyderabad state, language issues were seen as increasingly political from the administration's perspective. A longish article by M. Hanumantha Rao[32] sparked the attention of the Bureau by calling for the use of vernacular languages in the local courts. The article compared British Indian practices with those of Hyderabad, arousing suspicion that the *Golkonda Patrika* harboured an anti-government stance and was straying dangerously close to political territory. Accusations and anxieties that the newspaper was becoming 'too political' could lead to calls for its dismissal. The Bureau had a policy of approving a list of newspapers that were given permission to be published as well as circulated within the Hyderabad state—this was called the 'White List'. The Bureau also translated another article for governmental scrutiny published in the *Golkonda Patrika* that was defending the Andhra movement. The newspaper then published an article in January 1936 by Sayed Mohamad Abbas titled 'Unity or Disintegration' in which the author questioned the goals of the Andhra Conference. Abbas implied that an assertion of regional affiliation by the Andhra Conference could potentially lead to the disintegration of Hyderabad and furthermore that the Andhra Conference was recklessly toying with political problems.

An article refuting Abbas's criticisms was published immediately in the next issue in February. Pratapa Reddy, the author of this article, wrote of Abbas:

> Even though he is a graduate, the writer could not adequately define politics. Every atom in this world he had described as 'politics.' He has, obviously, not

taken into account the Government's view of politics. He has not understood the conduct of the Andhra Conference.... All economic problems, he says, are political problems. The Government has given us the idea that to be non-political means to be loyal, to be mild in criticizing the acts of Government, and to obey law. Is there any meaning in saying that there is politics in asking Government to mitigate taxes in an area, or to ask it to begin early the Tungabhadra Project, or to repair a tank here and a canal there?[33]

Pratapa Reddy drew attention to the contradictions in the Nizam's administration's policies concerning freedom of speech and civil liberties. He rightly asked whether the administration considered that for a Hyderabad subject to be loyal, they must be 'non-political'? Clearly, these were the boundaries of speech that journalists such as Narsing Rao and Pratapa Reddy had to learn to navigate. Still, Pratapa Reddy argued that the people of Hyderabad did possess the right to question governmental policies concerning taxes and other issues that were of an economic nature. He declared the right to question governmental policy an inalienable right and insisted that such matters were not, as the administration argued, 'political'. Clearly, the idea of the political understood by Hyderabad activists in public associations was to question the form of government that Hyderabad should take and the problem of political representation—both freedoms that were not unrestrictedly permitted. In questioning the parameters of the political, the *Golkonda Patrika* pushed the limits of permissible public speech within Hyderabad.

Just before the Round Table Conferences, the *Raiyat* was asked to cease its publication. This was in response to its publication of articles critical of the Nizam's administration's handling of the railway strikers in 1928.[34] While newspapers were taking up political and social matters of the day in order to publicize the gradual progress of political reforms in Hyderabad, the administration was simultaneously keeping track and monitoring them to see what debates were taking place in the public sphere and whether they would threaten the public peace. The Nizam's Political Department (also known as the Constitutional Affairs Secretariat) kept a close eye on the *Golkonda Patrika*, which was seen as sensational journalism needlessly stirring the political passions of the people. According to one Political Department report, on 23 May 1938, the AMS was printing pamphlets on *vetti* (a form of bonded labour prevalent in the Telangana countryside) to teach *harijan*s (a term used by Mohandas K. Gandhi to refer to untouchables) to reform caste practices.[35] The Department further stated:

> Untouchability is gradually disappearing from this village owing to the efforts of some public-spirited caste-Hindus. Every day a caste-Hindu leads a Bhajana

party in the local Harijan School for Children. The *Golconda Patrika* is also being read out to the Harijans. The pamphlets published by the Andhra Maha Sabha on Vetti and other subjects are being read out to the Harijans. Owing to these efforts of the caste Hindus the Vetti has almost disappeared from this village.[36]

Here, the Political Department was seemingly interested in monitoring these activities but not necessarily putting a stop to them as long as they remained purely 'social', and not 'political', issues. However, there was concern that radical reform efforts might upset existing social forces—this is where the charge of communalism was used to limit the scope of political critique of the *Golkonda Patrika*. From the articles gathered by the Information Bureau, the *Golkonda Patrika* seemed very much engaged in political critique and, as such, was accused not of being 'communal' but of expressing 'anti-government' sentiment. Both the *Golkonda Patrika* and its association with the AMS were seen as expressing 'regional' interests. While promoting culture was deemed appropriate, even the discussion of language instruction in schools became a political issue. The regionalism expressed by the Hyderabad branch of the AMS and the *Golkonda Patrika* was ultimately seen as threatening to the political future of princely Hyderabad, prompting the administration to keep a steady eye on the AMS in the Madras Presidency and its demands for a separate province.

The limits placed on the formation of political groups and the monitoring of political speech were enabled by Gasthi 53, a circular put into place on 21 November 1929. It was not a coincidence that at the very moment when the AISPC was being organized to encourage democratic reforms within native states and just before the Round Table Conferences on a federal structure inclusive of British Indian provinces and the native states, the Hyderabad state issued Gasthi 53, clamping down on political speech. If anything, however, the circular contributed to the rise of the rhetoric of civil liberties and made it even more central to the public organizations that emerged in the 1930s. On 21 September 1937, the *Hyderabad Bulletin*, which was put out by the Information Bureau of Hyderabad, published the address to the Executive Council made by Hanumantha Rao, the honorary secretary of the Gasthi 53 Committee:

> We are on the threshold of great expectations.... Your excellency's fame as the maker of modern Hyderabad was never so clearly understood as it is at this moment. The fatherhood of a new and popular constitution for the State is to be yours. At such a juncture I request your Excellency, on behalf of 53 Gasthi Committee, to rescind the Gasthi and give the proposed reform a happy start.... The Government was pleased to issue a communiqué after that,

but the Gasthi has not been altered. In the districts it is becoming increasingly difficult for the people to be vocal. I implore your Excellency to rise to the golden occasion and like the perfect statesman that your Excellency is, fulfill the popular expectations by rescinding the above Gasthi.[37]

Clearly the purpose of Gasthi 53 was to restrict public life and political debate, particularly debate conducted without government oversight. Numerous members of the HSC appealed directly to the Hyderabad government to expand and nurture public life and political education by lifting the ban on public meetings and political discussions deemed 'anti-government'. The charge of being anti-government when engaging in political critique of governmental policies seemed especially egregious in that these journalists and activists who formed public associations were committed to the integrity of Hyderabad as a political unit and its political future. Sirajul Hassan Tirmiji, the president of the HSC, wrote a letter to the Hyderabad Executive Council with concerns over the Gasthi and its uses to suppress free speech and association. He congratulated the Nizam's administration for initiating much needed constitutional, educational, and administrative reforms in the previous decades, 'such as the Legislative Council, the vernacularization of education and the separation of the Judiciary and Executive'.[38] He urged the Executive Council to remove this remaining civil 'disability' because the restrictions associated with Gasthi 53 deprived people of their fundamental rights of speech. He wrote, furthermore, that the Gasthi was contrary to the reforms the Nizam's government itself has initiated. The unease with which political reforms were carried out by the Nizam's administration was directly related to its censorship and surveillance of political associations that would necessarily begin to represent particular constituencies. The Gasthi's existence and the Nizam's administration's indecision as to how to allow for 'political education' through the formation of political associations revealed the state's underlying fear regarding the formation of political constituencies. Tirmiji contended that with the impending constitutional reforms announced by the Nizam's government, the Gasthi had to be cancelled because political culture needed to be encouraged in the state. In fact, he argued that it was the duty of the government to give people a political education and train them to take up administrative posts.

To further rub salt into the wounds of the Hyderabad administration's indecision concerning the state's political future, the ICLU, whose president at the time was Rabindranath Tagore with Sarojini Naidu as the chairman, sent a letter to Hydari, the president of the Executive Council, on 13 December 1937, addressing the issue of lifting the ban on political processions:

> Meetings and processions and such other public demonstrations have become a necessary part of the life of every society that wishes today to preserve and promote the various institutions within it which help its growth. Politics is a dominant part of life and liberty of lawful demonstration must be granted by the State to all political creeds. Toleration, on which political and civil liberty depends, must be extended to all irrespective of likes and dislikes. An order of the kin you have issued will not only be an encroachment on the freedom of public demonstration but will chock social progress at its very source.[39]

The ICLU used its position from within British India to push for civil liberties across the border in Hyderabad—precisely what Gasthi 52 and 53 had been enacted to prevent. It is important to note that the ICLU was addressing the situation in Hyderabad precisely before the planned 1938 *satyagraha*. Meanwhile, the INC lent its support to the planned public demonstrations through the HSC.

Those who supported the AISPC and its role in federation discussions early on insisted on guarantees to the 'fundamental' rights of the people in the native states.[40] Dewan Bahadur M. Ramachandra Rao published a paper, 'The Position of the Subjects', in the *Federated India* in February 1932, drawing attention to the necessity of considering the people or the subjects of the native states and their rights in the Round Table Conference discussions. Ramachandra Rao insisted that the FSC, established in 1931, should not simply allow the princes and their representatives to steer the discussion of how to include the native states in a federated union without taking the voices of the subjects into consideration. He argued:

> ... a Federal Constitution for the whole of India must materially affect the status and position of the people of the Indian States. I also suggested that the rights and obligations of the citizens of the Federating States and of British Indian Provinces to the new Federal Government of United India should be carefully examined and clearly defined, and that certain fundamental rights should be embodied in the constitution, and also that the necessary judicial machinery for enforcing these rights should be set up.[41]

For Ramachandra Rao, it was clear that in any federated arrangements being discussed at the Round Table Conferences, fundamental rights and civil liberties were essential for the betterment of the states' peoples and their political future. He stated that the states' peoples had been congregating and organizing discussions at a series of conferences to come to an agreement on what specific fundamental rights were critical for them in any federal constitution. Ramachandra Rao argued that fundamental rights guaranteed by a structure of federal citizenship were essential, as were three other elements: a federal judiciary, representation of the people in a federal legislature, and finally linking the federal judiciary of the native states with the federal Supreme Court.[42] In his visit to London in 1929 to address the Butler Committee, which was to discuss the paramount power of the princes, Ramachandra Rao published a series of heated exchanges in the *Clarion* with Rushbrook Williams, the foreign minister of the princely state of Patiala. Ramachandra Rao took the side of the states' subjects by promoting their interests, arguing that the distinct idea of self-determination for the peoples was as important as anything the princes might be willing to bring to the table.[43] The AISPC, which collectively represented the peoples of the native states, sought to have the peoples' interests considered equal to as well as distinct from those of the princes.

However, the Nizam's administration was reluctant to make that commitment to political reforms, especially civil liberties, even as it participated in the Round Table Conference discussions and the FSC. Rather, it was at great pains to chart out its position that it was dangerous to allow abstract rights and liberties when faced with communal discord erupting in the city and state of Hyderabad, which, the administration insisted, enjoyed relative calm in distinct contrast to the prevalence of communal conflicts in neighbouring British India. Hydari, in a speech to the Legislative Council of Hyderabad in 1938, answered his critics by arguing for the necessity of the policies enacted by the Hyderabad state to restrict civil liberties of the states' subjects. The reason for restrictions, he insisted, was to limit the spread of communalism, which he considered the greatest threat to the integrity of Hyderabad's spiritual and physical frontiers. As he put it:

> It is in defense of these that a ban has now been imposed on certain outside newspapers found guilty of spreading communal ill-feeling in the State and not stopping even at telling the most glaring falsehoods. Statements like the one that Hindus in the State were not allowed to ride or to wear white and had to pay jizya—a statement corrected later as having been made due to 'a strange mistake of the typist'—or that women and children were assaulted, tortured or killed during the disturbances in the City when not a single woman or child was so much as touched, are typical of the lies circulated by them.[44]

Lending proof to his argument, both the Arya Samaj and the Hindu Mahasabha did not desist from using the rhetoric of civil liberties to publicize what they characterized in communal terms as the oppression of 'Hindu' subjects in a 'Muslim' polity. One can understand why Hydari drew attention to and criticized the sensationalism of Arya Samaji and Hindu Mahasabha propaganda outlets.

For these reasons, the restrictions placed on Hyderabad organizations and political meetings were to defend the integrity of Hyderabad from separatist and communal sentiments seeping in from neighbouring British India. He further specified that civil liberties should not be parochial in reference to 'Hindu' civil liberties or 'Muslim' civil liberties. With the Arya Samaj and the Hindu Mahasabha seeking to overturn Hyderabad's controversial and fragile efforts to keep communal violence from erupting within its borders, even explicitly non-communalist associations such as the AMS (based on language affiliation) were held in check by the Hyderabad state's administration. The Nizam's administration's scrutiny of the AMS and the newspaper of one of its leading intellectuals and activists, Pratapa Reddy's *Golkonda Patrika*, brings into focus the inherent contradictions of the Hyderabad state's policy of placing restrictions on the civil liberties. For instance, Narsing Rao, who was part of the HSC and the AMS and entered into talks with the Hyderabad state's administration, steered clear from communalist organizations and represented the liberal gradualist position with regards to political reforms. However, he along with his organizations, too, were subject to these very same restrictions on civil liberties and what the civil societal organizations were calling fundamental rights. Fear that the disease of communalism would enter into the state from British India was expressed repeatedly by the Nizam's administration and used to suppress what the states' peoples identified as fundamental rights and civil liberties.

Meanwhile, the Majlis, founded in 1928, began to organize Muslims in the princely state of Hyderabad into one single association and attempted to represent their political interests as a whole. The organization was established by Nawab Bahadur Yar Jung to counter the influence of Hindu groups in the princely state, such as the Hindu Mahasabha and the Arya Samaj, both of which had become vocal religious groups purporting to represent 'Hindu' interests in 'Muslim' Hyderabad. The Majlis felt that in the communalized atmosphere that the Hindu Mahasabha had cultivated, Muslims in Hyderabad had no choice but to organize. In the course of the 1930s, the Majlis began to function like the AMS in addressing issues of literacy, working to establish reading rooms for its constituents, and continuing its programmes of eradicating 'un-Islamic' customs.[45] In other words, at the start of its formation, it functioned more like a socio-religious reform group for Muslims in Hyderabad. By the end of the 1930s, when discussions of constitutional reforms were initiated by the Hyderabad state's administration and the NSL, the Majlis began to shift its focus to politics and articulate a specific political agenda. The Majlis started to proclaim itself as representing the political interests of Muslims and defending the Nizam's state and Muslims in general. Furthermore, it declared that it would also uphold parity between Muslims and Hindus in any constitutional arrangement. In particular, the Majlis argued for a majority representation for Hyderabad's Muslims in any legislative body acknowledging the state's 'Muslim' character. When it shifted to a public organization devoted to the political interests of Hyderabad Muslims, it saw the HSC as its rival. The Majlis became representative of Muslim interests parallel to the HSC and in a sense also questioned its representativeness. As representative of Muslim interests, the Majlis was prepared to enter into discussions with the liberal leaders of the HSC on political reforms. Just as the HSC leaders were working with the INC through the AISPC, so too were the Majlis working and in dialogue with the All India States' Muslim League and their representatives in native states.[46] In an article in the *Bombay Chronicle*, dated 25 March 1940, on the states' Muslims demands at their first meeting in Lahore, Yar Jung spoke about how the AISPC got a head start in organizing in the native states, while the AIML remained apathetic to the native states' Muslims.[47] The Maljis only came to represent a significant political force by the late 1930s when constitutional reforms were being discussed on the political future of the Hyderabad state. Unlike the other civil societal organizations such as the HSC or the AMS, the Majlis was not particularly concerned with the civil liberties or fundamental rights of Hyderabad's subjects. Rather, it set its sights on tempering what it saw as the threat of Hindu majoritarianism undermining the integrity of Hyderabad as a historically Muslim state. With the growing tide of political dissent and louder calls for greater fundamental rights and civil liberties for Hyderabad's people, the Nizam's administration responded to these internal pressures for political reform and the political participation of Hyderabad subjects by inviting the leaders of the HSC and the Majlis's Yar Jung for talks.

Reforms and the Question of Political Representation

The Nizam's administration initiated discussions on political reforms starting as early as the 1920s, with the appointment of Ali Imam as the president of the newly constituted Executive Council. Imam was a British Indian Muslim from a prominent family in Bihar as well as a member of the AIML.[48] Within the larger context of pan-Islamism and the Khilafat movement in British India, Imam felt it was a privilege to work for a Muslim sovereign and took up the work of reform enthusiastically. The post-World War I rhetoric of self-determination that had been popularized by both the League of Nations and Gandhi's Non-Cooperation movement brought new goals of representative government to British India and the princely states of India. Imam was charged with investigating a system of direct elections for the Hyderabad state. The idea was to bring the principle of election and representative government to the princely states more generally. While Imam was favoured by the British to bring in much needed reforms after the establishment of the Executive Council, it is unclear how he was received by the Nizam and his administration. The Aiyangar report on constitutional reforms in Hyderabad, released in 1938, quoted Imam at length on education, civic mindedness, and political representation that needed to be cultivated in princely Hyderabad in order for reforms to be successfully instituted. He argued for the necessity of a vibrant public giving rise to informed political opinion central to any representative government:

> Now although the education of the citizens of a State is indispensable to the efficient working of its representative institutions, the extent to which a merely elementary instruction fits them to work such institutions has been, in my opinion, overestimated. 'Knowledge is one only among the factors which go to the making of a good citizen. Public spirit and honesty are even more needful.' It has been well said that 'attainment in learning and science do little to make men wise in politics.' This incapacity need not therefore frighten us. One important factor of fitness to work representative institutions is to be associated with them in practice. No nation is unfit for free institutions.... It cannot be that the Hyderabad people are so ignorant as not to know their wants, or that they are so poor that they have no proprietary or possessory interests, for the perfection of which they are solicitous.[49]

Thus, Imam pursued broad political reforms with the hope that the Hyderabad state, too, would join the general movement of political transformations in South Asia. He argued that the nurturing of public spirit and public life was as important as education to the development of representative government in Hyderabad. Hyderabad not only needed to go in this direction but the people of Hyderabad were also capable of, and ought to start, articulating their own political agenda. By encouraging and nurturing public life, much needed constitutional reforms would follow, accommodating the interests of politically aware people. However, Imam soon resigned in 1921, thanks to machinations on the part of Hydari, the future president of the Executive Council who had become a close confident of the Nizam.[50] Hydari came to Hyderabad from Bombay as a chief accountant in 1905. The reforms of the 1920s were important in that they set the stage for the more radical proposals in the 1930s.

On 2 September 1937, responding to the growing influence of the HSC and the Majlis through their political activism throughout the 1930s, Hydari, by then the president of the Executive Council, read out a *firman* appointing a reforms committee with Dewan Bahadur Aravamudu Aiyangar as the chairman.

There was a great deal of reporting of what the reforms contained and trepidation on the part of the administration about releasing the information to the public, who were by this time eager to hear the administration's political proposals. The Reforms Committee members consisted of Ghulam Mahmood Qureishi, Qadir Husain Khan, Kashinathrao Vaidya, and Mir Akbar Ali Khan. Ali Khan had been advocating for these internal discussions to come to some agreement on the fundamentals of political reforms in the state. Even before the forming of the Reforms Committee by Hydari, informal talks had taken place in July 1937 between Yar Jung, Hanumantha Rao, Vaidya, and Ali Khan,[51] in an effort to move towards a common platform for the subjects of the Hyderabad state. The report prepared by the Reforms Committee was finally submitted on 31 August 1938. The committee, headed by Aiyangar, had decided to offer functional representation as a resolution for the difference of opinion between the HSC and the Majlis—as opposed to straightforward territorial representation that was being considered in British India—as the best way forward for Hyderabad within its current political climate. Functional representation allowed for the representation of group interests as opposed to territorial representation, which used the principle of electing a representative for constituents of a demarcated territory. The report made the case for functional representation in the following passage:

> It has been contended that functional representation will intensify the tendency already existing of dividing the people into groups and classes. The fact is that from the standpoint of interests, the constituencies will be so wide that the question of divisions would scarcely arise. In fact, the division by interests will not be so pernicious or disruptive as the division of a people on the basis of language, religion or race. The system, in so far as it will develop a country-wide outlook, or a common State consciousness, has everything in its favour.[52]

Functional representation provided an alternative to what the committee saw as the dangers of majoritarianism and regionalism (referring to the dangers of the division of people on the basis of language, religion, or race). Vaidya, an influential member of the HSC, was asked to take part in the Reforms Committee discussions. However, he offered a dissenting opinion opposing functional representation. Vaidya's dissent was reported by the Reforms Committee in its report along with the reactions of the Committee to the dissent. Vaidya's dissent, which came late in the process, was in line with the dominant opinion of the HSC and the INC on the question of functional representation—namely that they favoured territorial representation. This was clear in the communication between the HSC and the INC. When it was clear that the Reforms Committee was not able to achieve the goals that it set out to achieve, further talks were held again informally, as was the case in July 1937, with representatives of the two major groups from the HSC and the Majlis. These talks were held in August 1938 to settle differences after the release of the Reforms Committee's recommendations.

Meanwhile, the AISPC through Sitaramayya communicated with the Hyderabad administration that a 'federation' scheme would only be possible if the Indian princely states organized a form of responsible government within their borders and guaranteed their people fundamental rights and civil liberties.[53] Sitaramayya accused the Reforms Committee of turning back the conversation to the days of the 1909 Morley–Minto reforms. He argued that their proposals, especially those regarding functional representation, did not reflect the current state of political reforms as being discussed by the INC and the Government of India. After the Government of India Act of 1935 and the elections of 1937, the INC began to address the princely states with much more confidence than before. This was reflected in Sitaramayya's views of federating with the princely states. Earlier, when the British began discussions on the idea of an Indian federation in the 1920s leading to the Simon Commission report (published in 1930), the British maintained that the princely states were constitutionally linked to the British Crown, not to the Government of India. All the while the INC, through the Nehru report of 1928, began to propose that the treaties and obligations of the princely states should be passed on to the Government of India from the British Crown.[54] This was resisted by the princes, especially Hyderabad, at the Round Table discussions in the early 1930s. However, by the late 1930s, the INC felt emboldened to demand that the princes make fundamental changes in order to join the Indian federation.

The All-India States' Workers' Convention, held in February 1938, also referred to a federation and what the princely states had to do in order to become equal and dynamic partners in the union. A federation scheme for the states would not be accepted, Sitaramayya warned, if it was not based on (*a*) a 'responsible government', (*b*) a popularly elected legislature to represent the government, (*c*) a guarantee of the fundamental rights of citizenship and the protection of those in the federal constitution, and (*d*) the rights of federal citizenship.[55] The INC firmly pushed forward a federation scheme but with stipulations that there were certain fundamental changes that had to take place within the princely states such as Hyderabad if they were to become part of any future federation schemes. The Reforms Committee's proposals arguing for functional representation were dismissed by the INC. The Hyderabad government began announcing the reforms in 1939 and into the 1940s, prompting criticism from all sides of the political spectrum. The INC's criticism was that the Hyderabad government was fundamentally misguided to propose functional representation as its own commitment had been to territorial representation for the future Government of India. In September 1946, Nehru wrote to Swami Ramananda Tirtha, a prominent Marathi-speaking leader in the HSC, and explained that the INC opposed the reforms. He asked Tirtha and the HSC to postpone the implementation of the reforms and voice their opposition through peaceful boycotts (not a full civil disobedience movement). Nehru clearly wanted to keep negotiating with the Nizam's administration without the threat of a full civil disobedience movement disrupting the negotiations. He also suggested to Tirtha that the Nizam seemed open to changing his opinion, which gave Nehru hope that negotiations might lead to necessary political reforms in Hyderabad and a fully responsible government. After meeting with Aiyangar, however, Tirtha decided to reject the reforms scheme entirely.[56]

The spokesperson for the Majlis, Yar Jung, found the constitutional reforms inadequate in that they did not address one of the organization's key concerns: separate electorates for Hindus and Muslims. When the discussions of the Reforms Committee were taking place, Yar Jung and Narsing Rao were brought together for what were referred to as 'unity talks', with the former presenting 'Muslim' interests and the latter presenting 'Hindu' or Congress interests. Prior to this, and even prior to Hydari's announcement of the Reforms Committee in September 1937, a meeting took place in June 1937 between public leaders, both Hindu and Muslim, orchestrated by the Nizam's administration. The public men included Yar Jung, Hanumantha Rao, Vaidya, and Ali Khan.[57] The discussion addressed existing points of difference between Hindus and Muslims to see whether they could come to any resolutions. The seven major points of discussion were (a) *tabligh* and *shuddhi*,[58] (b) policies of the Ecclesiastical Department, (c) local vernaculars in the school curricula, (d) religious instruction in schools, (e) public services, (f) demand for the cancellation of circulars relating to public meetings, private schools, music in front of mosques, religious processions and ceremonies, and physical culture centres, and (g) expansion of the Legislative Council. These issues would continue to dominate the political reforms discussions, especially in the unofficial committees of Hyderabad public intellectuals and leaders. After a report was produced from these meetings (sixteen in total), the Aiyangar Committee was formed later that year along with the Hyderabad People's Convention (hereafter, Convention) to further the agenda put forward by Yar Jung and Narsing Rao. The points of concerns do not explicitly cover the issues of federation and paramountcy, both of which were seen as concerning the external relations of Hyderabad. The matters concerning religion were primarily related to showing equal treatment to other religious matters as the Hyderabad state had taken in regards to Islam. For vernacular schools and language policy, the idea was to ensure that the mother tongue was used at the primary level and that it was extended to the secondary level as well, with Urdu as a compulsory second language. There seemed to be no objection for Urdu to be the medium at the university level at Osmania University and other universities. In addition, it was agreed upon that Muslim students would be compelled to learn a local language as a second language up to the lower-secondary stage. Despite having settled the cultural matters fairly easily, the murkier discussions of political reforms still remained on the table.

This meeting informed the aforementioned and well-publicized 'unity talks' between Nawab Yar Jung and Narsing Rao in 1938. From the earlier talks, there were many points of convergence except for some exceptional political questions. The press at the time represented these talks as a direct result of the HSC's participation in the 1938 *satyagraha*, in which many INC members were jailed along with the students at Osmania University who participated in the 'Vande Mataram' controversy when 600 students were expelled for singing the song in December 1938 (later readmitted in August 1939). The INC high command became intimately involved in the talks between Yar Jung and Narsing Rao. In order for both to proceed, they had to receive consent from community leaders that they were, in fact, representative of their respective communities. INC leaders Nehru and Abul Kalam Azad consulted with both of these men to broker a compromise between the two communities. The *Bombay Chronicle* ran an article that declared that the INC high command was being consulted for the Hyderabad 'unity talks'. Yar Jung also, according to the *Bombay Chronicle*, met with Nehru and Azad in Allahabad in December 1938.[59] Immediately afterwards, Narsing Rao left for Wardha to consult with INC leaders, including Gandhi. The *Bombay Chronicle*, in the 16 November 1938 issue, printed an article saying that the 'unity talks' were to 'appease popular unrest' in Hyderabad and prepare Hyderabad leaders to receive the report of the Reforms Committee.[60] In other words, the talks might have been primarily ceremonial for the Nizam's administration to appear open to dialogue. In December 1938, the *Hyderabad Bulletin* reported that the Nizam's government was prepared to accept any agreed upon formula put forward by the two communities.[61]

Before the 'unity talks' of August 1938, the Convention brought leaders together to discuss the constitutional future of Hyderabad. The *Bombay Chronicle* reported that this group 'was a thoroughly representative body and did much useful work in devising a scheme of Constitutional Reform'.[62]

Nonetheless, the talks broke down, with Muslim members severing their ties with the Convention when a conflict over the reservation of seats for Muslims could not be settled in a satisfactory manner.[63] Muslim members also cited the Convention's unwillingness to consider reservation as a fundamental issue, which led to concerns over the 'franchise and delegation of power to the legislatures'.[64] The main concern, it seemed, was to broker a deal that would take seriously the Muslim community's concerns that the delegation of power to the legislatures could be detrimental to the political power of the Muslim minority in princely Hyderabad. The 'unity talks' were proposed so that the two community leaders would be able to move beyond this political impasse. The talks covered much of the same issues as earlier talks discussed since the summer of 1937. The sessions began with a discussion of what the constitutional goals should be for Hyderabad. Narsing Rao suggested that the idea of 'responsible government' should be the primary goal of constitutional reforms. Even this was contested, however, when Yar Jung declared that the traditions and conditions of the Hyderabad state did not allow for responsible government as an immediate aim.[65] Without a discussion of the minority status of Muslims or the need for reservations of seats to address community representation, Yar Jung was able to revert to suggesting that the traditions of Hyderabad did not allow for responsible government. However, they both agreed that

> ... ministers should be made responsible to HEH [His Exalted Highness] and the constitutional advancement of Hyderabad should be based on such a form of Government which should be evolutionary and which should afford opportunities to the different communities and classes of the State to co-operate effectively with the Government through an elected Legislature.[66]

The cautious wording here reflects the increased tension a year later surrounding the political interests of the 'Muslim' and the 'Hindu' communities. Looking back at the earlier discussions of 1937, the community leaders had a great deal of agreement on much needed reforms within the state. However, the primary issue that dominated the 'unity talks' in late 1938 was the question of responsible government—a question that largely remained unresolved because it could not be made an immediate goal and the idea of transferring powers to the legislature was in itself disputed as much as the composition of the legislature. The question of franchise revealed the need to think through schemes for assuring parity between the religious communities. Ultimately, the 'unity talks' broke down over the unresolved question of the goal of responsible government—a goal that was insisted on by INC members.

The constitutional reforms proposed by the Reforms Committee of 1938 and the subsequent 'unity talks' proved that the problem was even larger than these discussions reveal. There was no resolution to the constitutional questions of what kind of polity the Hyderabad state would adapt to—for instance, whether it would retain its sovereignty without interference from the Indian Union and what shape it would take if incorporated into the Indian Union. The political stakes were high and the Nizam's administration had to speak to its different constituencies through the public organizations, which were making demands on the state to expand their rights and to implement democratic reforms and foster the growth of democratic institutions. Meanwhile, the Nizam's administration also had to contend with the growing strength of the INC, which was preparing to take over the Government of India.

When the reforms regarding the constitutional future of Hyderabad were announced starting in 1938, critics emerged from all sides of the political spectrum. Even the Nizam's administration, throughout the discussion of reforms in 1937–1938, held fast to the idea that elected representatives through a parliament would jeopardize the principle of the Nizam as the head of state and insisted that sovereignty resided in the Nizam. INC leaders opposed the proposed reforms because they were based on functional representation rather than territorial representation. The Majlis opposed the reforms and put forward their own idea of a defence of the history and traditions of the Hyderabad state. The organization issued a strongly worded objection in March 1939, demanding that the government delay proposed reforms, and threatened to begin a massive *satyagraha* against the reforms. Posters spread across the city, decrying the constitutional reforms and pointing to Yavar Jung as the source of the betrayal.[67] The HSC, however, emboldened by the power of the INC in British India, pursued a political strategy to oppose these reforms in totality on the basis that history was on their side. It is clear from the internal correspondence between INC members and the rhetoric they employed in their understanding of the princes that they saw the latter as a feudal relic in desperate need of reform.[68] The INC's confidence that it was on the right side of history, however, made it short-sighted in not foreseeing or outright disregarding the 'minoritization' of Hyderabad Muslims—a problem that Muslim politicians could plainly see. In other words, the HSC did not hesitate in playing majoritarian politics by pushing for representative institutions or responsible government without guaranteeing safeguards for minority communities within a new constitutional arrangement. Granted, the Majlis, seeing that the question of reservation of seats for Muslims was set aside in discussions with HSC representatives, tried to negotiate for Muslim dominance on the basis of the history and heritage of the Nizam's state.[69]

As they continued to build their power bases in Hyderabad, the Majlis and the INC were able to wrest control of the constitutional debates away from the discussions initiated by the NSL, the Convention, and the 'unity talks' between Narsing Rao and Yar Jung—all of which sought to find political solutions for the unique composition and history of Hyderabad. The Majlis and the AMS started off as organizations that defined themselves as solely religious and/or cultural groups supporting community efforts to promote their respective cultural institutions within Hyderabad. However, both organizations began to shift their concerns as they rose to prominence in the 1930s. Their discussions became increasingly and explicitly political, staking political claims for their respective constituencies. The growing politicization of public associations in the 1930s can be linked to the increased use of the rhetoric of civil liberties to criticize the Nizam's administration and its policies—especially policies that placed limits on political association and freedom of speech (in criticizing those very governmental policies). Copland has argued that a growing politicization and proselytization characterized Hyderabad's associational life in the 1930s due primarily to the activism of the Arya Samaj and the Majlis through their *shuddhi* and *tabligh* movements.[70] Not only did this bring more communal strife into Hyderabad, culminating in the 1938 *satyagraha*, but it also clearly politicized the masses, albeit through the language of communalism. At the same time, it is important to keep in mind that the discourse of civil liberties also enabled non-communal public associations in and outside of princely Hyderabad to legitimately challenge and impact Hyderabad governmental discussions on their constitutional future. The curtailment of political discussion and association through the infamous circular, Gasthi 53, opened up an opportunity for civil society associations in Hyderabad to critique the rule of the Nizam and his administration using the language of civil liberties. The framework of civil liberties not only shaped how these groups critiqued politics within a princely state but also how they imagined their political futures. The HSC, the AMS, and the Majlis, along with even the earlier short-lived associations such as the NSL and the Anjuman, participated in a vibrant public sphere through print media and joined 'talks' with the government to address the political impasse the Nizam's administration found itself in the 1930s. Ultimately, the inability of the Nizam's administration to legitimately negotiate with actually existing constituencies in Hyderabad led to a series of political crises at the end of the decade.

Notes

1. Ian Copland, *The Princes of India in the Endgame of Empire, 1917–1947* (Cambridge, UK: Cambridge University Press, 1997), 37. Edwin Montagu went on to make this pledge of self-government in 1917.
2. Copland, *The Princes of India*, 40.
3. The groups that emerged during this crucial period were the Nizam's Subjects League (NSL) (1935), the Comrades Association (1939), the Hyderabad State Congress (HSC) (1939), the Andhra Mahasabha (AMS) (1930), the Majlis-e-Ittehad ul-Muslimin (1928), the Anjuman-i Taraqqi-i Hyderabad (1927), and, lastly, the Swadeshi League (1930), which had the briefest existence (two months) as one of the co-founders, Fazlur Rahman, was dismissed from his post at Nizam's College after the group's inaugural meeting. The Comrades Association and its membership is discussed in a memoir by one of its original members. See S. M. Jawad Razvi, *Political Awakening in Hyderabad* (Hyderabad: Visalandhra Publishing House, 1980). I am explicitly not focusing on the influential groups—the Arya Samaj and the Hindu Mahasabha—because their organizations, while crucial to the politics of the 1930s, have already been discussed in terms of their role in communalizing the Hyderabad political landscape, their dynamic with the Tablighi movement and the Majlis, and, finally, their role in the 1938 *satyagraha*. See John Roosa, 'The Quandary in the Qaum: Indian Nationalism in a Muslim State, Hyderabad, 1850–1948', PhD dissertation, University of Wisconsin–Madison, 1998; Kavita Datla, *The Language of Secular Islam: Urdu Nationalism and Colonial India* (Honolulu: University of Hawaii Press, 2013); and M. A. Moid and A. Suneetha, 'Rethinking Majlis' Politics: Pre-1948 Muslim Concerns in Hyderabad State', *Indian Economic and Social History Review* 55, no. 1 (2018): 29–52.
4. Barbara Ramusack, *The Indian Princes and Their States* (The New Cambridge History of India) (Cambridge, UK: Cambridge University Press, 2007), 216.
5. Ramusack, *The Indian Princes and Their States*, 219. In 1927, the Madras session of the INC declared that it was in the interests of both the rulers and the people of the Indian states to begin to develop representative institutions and to gradually move towards responsible government.
6. Lucien Benichou, *From Autocracy to Integration: Political Developments in Hyderabad State (1938–1948)* (Chennai: Orient Longman, 2000), 35–37. Benichou argues that it was at the height of the Non-Cooperation and Khilafat movements and their impact on Hyderabad that the Nizam felt threatened and proactively sought to curtail the entry of British Indian political movements into Hyderabad.
7. Munmun Jha, 'Nehru and Civil Liberties in India', *International Journal of Human Rights* 7, no. 3 (2003): 103–115, 107.

8. Ram Manohar Lohia, *The Struggle for Civil Liberties* (All India Congress Committee, 1936), with a foreword by Jawaharlal Nehru (Allahabad: Foreign Department, All India Congress Committee, 1936), 5.
9. For scholarship on print publics in British India, see Francesca Orsini, *The Hindi Public Sphere, 1920–1940: Language and Literature in the Age of Nationalism* (New York: Oxford University Press, 2002); Veena Naregal, *Language, Politics, Elites and the Public Sphere: Western India under Colonialism* (New Delhi: Permanent Black, 2001); Bernard Bate, '"To Persuade Them into Speech and Action": Oratory and the Tamil Political, Madras, 1905–1919', *Comparative Studies in Society and History* 55, no. 1 (2013): 142–166.
10. Lohia, *The Struggle for Civil Liberties*, 26.
11. Lohia, *The Struggle for Civil Liberties*, 36.
12. Lohia, *The Struggle for Civil Liberties*, 35.
13. See Samuel Moyn, *The Last Utopia: Human Rights in History* (Cambridge, MA: Harvard University Press, 2010) and Manu Bhagavan, 'Princely States and the Making of Modern India: Internationalism, Constitutionalism and the Postcolonial Moment', *Indian Economic and Social History Review* 46, no. 3 (2009): 427–456. Also see C. A. Bayly, who argues that these rhetorical strategies of appealing to political moralism was essential to the disempowered, especially under colonial conditions. C. A. Bayly, *Recovering Liberties: Indian Thought in the Age of Liberalism and Empire* (Cambridge, UK: Cambridge University Press, 2012), 204.
14. Nizam's Political Department, Installment 47, List 10, Serial No. 702, Telangana State Archives (TSA), Hyderabad.
15. Nizam's Political Department, Installment 47, List 10, Serial No. 702, TSA, Hyderabad.
16. Nizam's Political Department, Installment 47, List 10, Serial No. 702, TSA, Hyderabad; Bhogaraju Pattabhi Sitaramayya, 'Self-Surrender Is Self-Realization: Concede Fundamental Rights to States' People', *Indian Express*, 27 July 1937.
17. Mandumula Narsing Rao, *Yabhai Samvatsaramula Hyderabad* (Hyderabad: Mandumula Narasingaravu Smaraka Samiti, 1977), 10.
18. A report on the curriculum in primary and middle schools in Hyderabad in the 1930s states, 'The medium of instruction in a Primary School shall be the vernacular of the locality. It will be Urdu for those who vernacular is Urdu. Primary schools shall ordinarily have parallel sections in the local vernacular and Urdu.' English would be offered as a second or third language in primary schools but would be compulsory in high schools. However, in secondary schools, instruction in 'information' subjects would be in Urdu. This speaks to the multilinguality of Hyderabad and its educational policies.

See H. E. H. The Nizam's Educational Department, *Curriculum for Primary and Middle Schools* (Hyderabad: Government Central Press, 1931) and Datla, *The Language of Secular Islam*.
19. M. N. Rao, *Yabhai Samvatsaramula Hyderabad*, 94–95 (translation mine).
20. M. N. Rao, *Yabhai Samvatsaramula Hyderabad*, 96.
21. Bate, '"To Persuade Them into Speech and Action"', 146.
22. See Chapter 1 on the turn to the vernacular in political organizations and mass mobilization in south India.
23. M. N. Rao, *Yabhai Samvatsaramula Hyderabad*, 101.
24. Later, in 1942, Yavar Jung was appointed as one of the editors charged with producing the proposed three volumes of 'History of the Dekkan', modelled on the Cambridge History of India series. Yavar Jung was to edit the 'modern' volume.
25. Roosa, 'The Quandary in the Qaum', 412.
26. See Kris Manjapra, *M. N. Roy: Marxism and Colonial Cosmopolitanism* (New Delhi: Routledge, 2010).
27. M. N. Rao, *Yabhai Samvatsaramula Hyderabad*, 112.
28. M. N. Rao, *Yabhai Samvatsaramula Hyderabad*, 114.
29. On the relation between the regional groups and the HSC, see Rama Sundari Mantena, 'The Andhra Movement, Hyderabad State and the Historical Origins of the Telangana Demand', *India Review* 13, no. 4 (2014): 337–357.
30. Nizam's Political Department, Installment 47, List 10, Serial No. 485, TSA, Hyderabad.
31. Nizam's Political Department, Installment 47, List 10, Serial No. 485, TSA, Hyderabad.
32. Nizam's Political Department, Installment 47, List 10, Serial No. 485, TSA, Hyderabad.
33. 'Policy of Golkonda Patrika', Nizam's Political Department, Installment 47, List 10, Serial No. 485, TSA, Hyderabad.
34. Roosa, 'The Quandary in the Qaum', 417–418.
35. Nizam's Political Department, Installment 47, List 10, Serial No. 702, TSA, Hyderabad.
36. Nizam's Political Department, Installment 47, List 10, Serial No. 702, TSA, Hyderabad.
37. *The Hyderabad Bulletin*, 21 September 1937.
38. *The Hyderabad Bulletin*, 20 September 1937.
39. Nizam's Political Department, Installment 47, List 10, Serial No. 702, TSA, Hyderabad.
40. *Work in England of the Deputation of the Indian States People's Conference* (Poona: Aryabhushan Press, 1929).

41. Dewan Bahadur M. Ramachandra Rao, 'The Position of the Subjects', *Federated India* 6, no. 8, 24 February 1932, 7.
42. D. B. M. R. Rao, 'The Position of the Subjects', 8.
43. *Work in England*, 66–81.
44. Akbar Hydari, 'Speech to the Legislative Council by the President H.E.H. the Nizam's Executive Council,' in 'Hindu-Muslim Unity Talks', Nizam's Political Department, Installment 47, List 10, Serial No. 1197, TSA, Hyderabad.
45. Moid and Suneetha, 'Rethinking Majlis' Politics', 4.
46. In fact, it was Yar Jung who founded the All-India States Muslim League and served as its president starting in 1940. It is telling that the organization does not mention 'people' as it figures prominently in the AISPC. The AIML, in contrast to the INC, was not committed to transforming the native states towards self-government or representative government. See Ian Copland, 'The Princely States, the Muslim League, and the Partition of India in 1947', *International History Review* 13, no. 1 (February 1991): 38–69.
47. 'States Muslims' Demands: Separate Electorates & Reservation in Services', *Bombay Chronicle*, 25 March 1940.
48. Margrit Pernau, *The Passing of Patrimonialism: Politics and Political Culture in Hyderabad 1911–1948* (New Delhi: Manohar, 2000), 119.
49. *Report of the Reforms Committee 1938* (Hyderabad-Deccan: Government Central Press), 13–14.
50. Pernau, *The Passing of Patrimonialism*, 119.
51. Nizam's Political Department, Installment 47, List 10, Serial No. 1197, TSA, Hyderabad.
52. *Report of the Reforms Committee*, 53.
53. The AISPC also sent a letter by Sitaramayya on 2 March 1938 to Yavar Jung, Constitutional Affairs Secretariat. See Nizam's Political Department, Installment 47, List 10, Serial No. 702, TSA, Hyderabad.
54. Sunil Purushotham, 'Federating the Raj', *Modern Asian Studies* 54, no. 1 (2020): 157–198.
55. 'Resolutions Passed by The All India States' Workers' Convention, Held at Navsari, 15 February 1938'. Nizam's Political Department, Installment 47, List 10, Serial No. 702, TSA, Hyderabad.
56. Swami Ramananda Tirtha, 'Interview with Raja Bahadur R. S. Aravamudu Iyangar', 28 August 1946, Nehru Memorial Museum and Library (NMML), All-India States Peoples' Conference (AISPC), File No. 66; Letter from Jawaharlal Nehru, 24 September 1946, NMML, AISPC, File No. 66.
57. Nizam's Political Department, Installment 47, List 10, Serial No. 1197, TSA, Hyderabad.

58. *Tabligh* and *shuddhi* were Islamic and Hindu missionary movements during the colonial era.
59. 'Hyderabad Unity Talks: Congress High Command Consulted', *Bombay Chronicle*, 17 December 1938.
60. 'Unity Talks in Hyderabad: Move to Appease Popular Unrest', *Bombay Chronicle*, 16 November 1938.
61. 'A.I.C.C. Member Optimistic: Dr. Hamid on Local Situation', *Hyderabad Bulletin*, 26 December 1938.
62. 'Hyderabad Unity Talks: Their Purpose and Scope', *Bombay Chronicle*, 3 February 1939.
63. 'Hyderabad Unity Talks', *Bombay Chronicle*.
64. 'Hyderabad Unity Talks', *Bombay Chronicle*.
65. 'Hindu–Muslim Unity Talks', Nizam's Political Department, Installment 47, List 10, Serial No. 1197, TSA, Hyderabad.
66. 'Hindu–Muslim Unity Talks', Nizam's Political Department, Installment 47, List 10, Serial No. 1197, TSA, Hyderabad.
67. 'Report on the Anti-Reforms Demonstrations of Shehrewar 12, 1348 Fasli', Nizam's Political Department, Installment 47, List 10, Serial No. 787, TSA, Hyderabad .
68. Jawaharlal Nehru, 'The Unity of India', *Foreign Affairs*, January 1938; 'Monstrous Imposition of Feudal Relics: Edward Thompson also Speaks Out', *Bombay Chronicle*, 30 January 1938.
69. Sunil Purushotham as well as others argue that Mohammad Ali Jinnah, the leader of the AIML, encouraged Hyderabad through direct contact with Jinnah as well as the Majlis to remain separate and sovereign and retain its Muslim heritage and symbolism. See Purushottham, 'Federating the Raj'.
70. See Ian Copland, '"Communalism" in Princely India: The Case of Hyderabad, 1930–1940', *Modern Asian Studies* 22, no. 4 (1988): 783–814.

5

The Break-Up of Hyderabad

The end of the 1930s brought to the fore desperate moves on the part of the HSC (largely in agreement with the tactical strategy of the INC throughout the decade), which began to make greater political demands on the princely state of Hyderabad to bring it in line with constitutional discussions in British India and the Majlis. The Majlis by this time proclaimed that their primary purpose and immediate concern was the preservation of the Hyderabad state. They would do this by opposing the proposals for constitutional reforms drafted in several forums organized by the Nizam's administration. The stand-off between the Majlis and the HSC escalated to the point that it eventually had to be defused in order to stave off a violent encounter.[1] As I have laid out in the previous chapters, the 1940s brought new political forces that disrupted the political impasse established by the end of the previous decade. Furthermore, the two World Wars saw the emergence of the communists as a new political force and another key player in political discussion in British India. The communists increasingly gained power and challenged the liberal stronghold in the INC. In Hyderabad, the AMS as a civil societal organization also gave space for communists, who eventually took the struggle to the Telangana countryside in the mid- and late 1940s. Mandumula Narsing Rao, a key intellectual and political activist (discussed in the previous chapters), made it a point to argue that all parties opposed British rule (thus defining them as anti-colonial)—the Majlis, the INC, the communists, and even the Nizam (the monarchical head). Yet they all expected different things in terms of what would follow after the departure of the British from the Indian subcontinent. For the INC and the communists, the goal was to bring a people's government based on representative institutions to the Hyderabad state; the Majlis sought to establish representative governmental institutions but with the Nizam as the titular head (the most complicated position, for sure—the demand for Muslim sovereignty along with popular government); and for the Nizam, it was most important to reclaim the sovereignty lost over the course of the nineteenth century.² By the end of the 1930s in Hyderabad, after the deliberations of the Reforms Committee, the 'unity talks', the *satyagraha*s of 1938–1939, and the 'Vande Mataram' student movement, it would not be inaccurate to come to the conclusion that public associations in Hyderabad reached a political impasse. The 1940s shattered whatever efforts had been made to foster and build a common political platform across ideological divides and saw the INC, the Majlis, and the growing communist movement in Hyderabad all take contradictory political paths, ultimately leading to a civil war that erupted at the moment of Britain's departure.³

The HSC, which was in theory committed to retaining the integrity of the Hyderabad state and its territorial border (as we will see in detail later), started its overt political struggle against the Hyderabad state on 7 August 1947, ending with police action and the forcible integration of Hyderabad into the Indian Union in 1948.⁴ The working committee of the HSC was given authority to take all necessary steps to secure Hyderabad's accession to the Indian Union and to immediately establish responsible government—these two goals had become the rallying point for the INC in the years 1947 and 1948, when it became clear that the Nizam and his administration were still attempting to prevent Hyderabad from merging with the Indian Union. A committee of action within the HSC prepared a plan with three stages over a period of three to four months. The first stage of the political struggle was to begin with public acts of civil disobedience and *satyagraha*; the second stage was to consist of the non-payment of levy and taxes and the breaking of forest laws to cause economic damage to the Nizam; and the third stage called for 'border incidents' or acts of sabotage that would destroy means of communication, customs, and police *chouki*s. There was also to be a general boycott by students, lawyers, and village officers of the Hyderabad state. The idea was to paralyze the government. Records kept by the AISPC reveal that as suffering increased and the struggle continued longer than expected, people felt they had to turn to violent resistance in order to counter what they described as the atrocities of the Razakars.⁵ Though there were defects, the AISPC nonetheless saw the campaign as a success. This was the violent culmination of a decades-long political effort to shape the future of the Hyderabad state.⁶

As the previous chapters have shown, the future status of Hyderabad as an independent autonomous state was never a clear political goal around which all the actors rallied, especially at the height of Indian nationalism. From the ambiguous negotiations between the Nizam's administration, the British government, and the Government of India to the states' peoples' movements for expansive democratic reforms, no political consensus ever emerged. Instead, negotiations oscillated between political reforms for greater rights for the states' peoples and communities on the one hand and preserving the integrity of the Hyderabad state as autonomous and historically important on the other. The tenuous status of princely Hyderabad was thrown into sharp relief when British prime minister Clement Attlee gave the following instructions to Louis Mountbatten as late as 1947 with regards to what should be done to the native Indian states at the moment of independence and British withdrawal:

> It is, of course, important that the Indian States should adjust their relations with the authorities to whom it is intended to hand over power in British India; but, as was explicitly stated by the Cabinet Mission, His Majesty's Government do not intend to hand over their powers and obligations under paramountcy to any successor Government. It is not intended to bring paramountcy as a system to a conclusion earlier than the date of the transfer of power, but you are authorized, at such time as you think appropriate, to enter into negotiations with individual States for adjusting their relations with the Crown.
>
> You will do your best to persuade the rulers of any Indian States in which political progress has been slow to progress rapidly towards some form of more democratic government in their States. You will also aid and assist the States in coming to fair and just arrangements with the leaders of British India as to their future relationships.[7]

It is clear from this exchange that the British were uncertain as to the fate of the native Indian states at the moment of independence.

Rather than offering a diplomatic history of the events that led to the political impasses of 1947–1948, my aim here is to examine Hyderabad's diverse public civil societal organizations and their political aspirations in the first four decades of the twentieth century. The two previous chapters discussed in detail how the question of federation became central to discussions of Hyderabad's political futures—on the part of the Nizam's administration as well as the states' peoples' groups. The discourse of federation along with that of self-determination shaped how regional movements envisioned their political futures in British India and, in particular, the Madras Presidency. In 1948, the Hyderabad state's precarious position was made clear when it was forced to merge with the independent Indian Union. Federation discussions offered not only the states' peoples' groups but also the Hyderabad administration a way to propose political reforms within the state while still retaining its historical borders.

Historical Borders and the Unity of the Hyderabad State

What were the proposals for unity in Hyderabad? It is useful at this point to revisit what was being proposed in Hyderabad by one of its most prominent civil societal associations in the 1930s, in order to understand how political discussion around the idea of unity unfolded amongst its distinguished intellectuals. The NSL took the lead in building a common political platform for reforms in Hyderabad that would be agreeable to all constituencies—linguistic and religious. The NSL presented itself as a centrist liberal organization that put Hyderabad's political future ahead of all 'communal' or sectarian interests. It put out a circular signed by Padmaja Naidu (Sarojini Naidu's daughter), Abdul Hassan Syed Ali, B. Ramkishen Rao, S. B. Sharma, and Syed Abid Hasan, the latter of whom also authored a short book titled *Whither Hyderabad?*, which outlined and promoted a common political platform for the people of Hyderabad as well as the Nizam and his administration.[8] *Whither Hyderabad?* was an early liberal attempt to imagine Hyderabad as a representative democracy. Hasan set out to persuade both the state's public associations and the Nizam's government that a viable political future was indeed possible for the princely state. He argued that Hyderabad was unique because it not only secured peace in the Deccan after the fall of the Deccan sultanates and the ascension of Mughal power at the turn of the eighteenth century, but also collaborated with the British Empire to stabilize the region for its people. Because princely Hyderabad had not been subjugated by 'foreign' rule, it was able to cultivate what Hasan called a composite culture. The key here was the idea of a composite culture that served to counter the notion that a purely singular nationality would need to ground any political arrangement in the future. This composite culture attached religious diversity and linguistic diversity to a historical legacy going back to the Deccan sultanates in the early modern period. As such, Hasan argued, the people of Hyderabad should be loyal, first and foremost, to the Asaf Jahi house and uphold the sovereignty of the Nizam. He wrote, 'We, the people of Hyderabad with our political consciousness sufficiently developed and with the fullest realisation of the trend of events around us, do hereby resolve that the Dominions of our sovereign shall continue to be a political unit in the Commonwealth of India.'[9] For Hasan, the foundational political unit was the historical Hyderabad state with its important heritage. Retaining the integrity of this princely state was of utmost importance, and it emerged as the primary common platform, second only to then federating with the Commonwealth of India. The idea of working with a federated union with the Government of India was an acceptable outcome for the NSL in the mid-1930s.

There was much to be unpacked in the circular. Loyalty to the Nizam was conceptualized as loyalty to the people of Hyderabad and a commitment to the integrity of Hyderabad as a political unit. As Hasan wrote, 'The Nizam is an institution that embodies the sovereignty of the people of Hyderabad whose national independence will be judged by the extent to which the Nizam himself is free from foreign control."[10] Furthermore, he stated, 'Loyalty to the person and institution of the Nizam, therefore, means peoples' loyalty to their own interests, to their own political integrity; in short, to themselves.'[11] For Hasan, the Nizam and the people were one and the same: the Nizam both embodied the people and represented them as a political unit. Emphasizing the idea of loyalty to the Nizam or the people was Hasan's strategy of framing a new Deccani nationalism. This nationalism, as articulated by Hasan and the NSL, was distinguished by its non-sectarianism and non-communal character. It sought to be non-threatening to both the communities in Hyderabad as well as the ruling administration, but it was also a radically new way of conceptualizing nationalism as emergent from the people of Hyderabad.[12] This was not a cultural nationalism that asserted one language or religion as central but rather a nationalism grounded in Hyderabad's people and their unique history and position in the region.

Importantly, Hasan noted that those 'who have settled down here for good and identified themselves wholly with us and have enrolled themselves as subjects of our Royal Master shall not suffer in any way because of the Mulki movement'. As mobilized by the NSL, the Mulki movement was meant to give priority to Hyderabad residents (born and raised) in the Nizam's administration. Since the days of Salar Jung's reforms in the late nineteenth century, non-*mulkis*, primarily from north India, were employed within the Hyderabad administration. The Mulki movement attempted to draw attention to the necessity of changing this policy and turning to employing Hyderabad subjects within the administration in order for it to truly represent the people's interests. The movement also coincided with calls for democratic legislative reforms for greater representation of the people of Hyderabad and their political interests. The NSL, in other words, was able to transform and shape the Mulki movement (the call for administrative posts to be given to native Hyderabadis) into an incipient nationalist movement with democratic aspirations.

Two groups posed a threat to this emergent nationalism—north Indian Muslims and Hindus from the bordering British presidencies—and both brought with them their own communal and parochial understandings of nationalism from British Indian contexts. According to Hasan, the north Indian Muslims who came to Hyderabad for work had a tendency to tell local Muslims that Hyderabad was a Muslim state with a Muslim ruling class and that it should remain that way even after the British departure from India. The Hindus from British India, on the other hand, provoked local Hindus to assert their numerical power and 'capture the administrative machinery'.[13] Hasan viewed both these political sentiments as problematic and 'foreign' elements, introducing distrust and sewing suspicion within Hyderabad. His book and the NSL circular both sought to thwart any such distrust by awakening the people of the princely state instead to their common political aspirations. As envisioned by the NSL, Hyderabad nationalism was a composite nationalism with a unique culture, history, and territorial integrity. In hindsight, had this vision prevailed there might have been a chance to avoid the eventual 'partitioning' of Hyderabad that followed the Indian state's forcible integration of princely Hyderabad in 1948.

To assure the integrity of the political unit as well as the composite culture of Hyderabad, the NSL formulated a set of political reforms meant to ensure the Nizam's administration's survival. These reforms sought to encourage a federated union between the Hyderabad state and the Government of India, as opposed to looking to the British Crown to grant India independence under international law. Unlike the Hyderabad administration, which seemed to be attempting to federate into a union *and* become an independent state, the constitutional reforms suggested by the NSL put in place a bicameral legislature consisting of an upper chamber and a lower chamber that would include 150 members. In the legislative assembly, or the lower chamber, there would be seats for urban and rural constituencies. The urban seats would include the various corporate interests: Jagirdar's Association, the Hyderabad municipality, the Hyderabad Bar Association, graduates, the Osmania University Senate, banking interests, commercial and industrial interests, pandits, *shastri*s, and the Muslim *ulema*. There was plenty of room for the nomination of candidates by the Executive Council and the Nizam. Dalit interests and women's interests would also be represented through nomination of non-official members into the assembly. These suggestions, in short, were not so different from those considered by the Reforms Committee, which brought out its recommendations in 1938.[14]

The NSL's proposals emerged within political conditions set in place by Diwan Salar Jang's reforms in the late nineteenth century. Karen Leonard offers a nuanced historical picture of the internal dynamics within Hyderabad at the turn of the twentieth century. Instead of dismissing Hyderabad as a political backwater, Leonard traces the roots of the modern bureaucracy to the period of the successful Salar Jang (1853–1883). This period witnessed the successful fostering of non-*mulki* modernization schemes. Leonard argues that in the following years, the non-*mulki*s brought into Hyderabad by Salar Jang dominated political power and continued with their modernization schemes. More interestingly, in the decades leading up to the break-up of Hyderabad, Leonard argues that new cultural–political ideologies emerged which aimed to prevent the disintegration of Hyderabad as an autonomous state—namely *mulki* cultural nationalism or a synthesis of Deccani nationalism and a movement for Muslim sovereignty.[15]

What Leonard does not address, however, are a whole set of other forces such as the linguistically based parties with affiliations with the INC units in British India: the AMS and the Karnatak and Maharashtra Parishads. Leonard nevertheless offers rich insight into how Deccani culture was invoked by *mulki* nationalism in these decades. Similar to what we witness in the Telugu districts in the Madras Presidency, there was a proliferation of Urdu literary societies exploring Deccani Urdu that fed into Deccani nationalism. Societies such as the Osmania Graduates Association, the Hyderabad Political Reform Association of 1919, the Society of Union and Progress of 1926, and the NSL of 1935 were all a product of 'Deccani' nationalism that garnered political loyalty to the Hyderabad state.[16] As we saw earlier, the NSL, in particular, brought together leaders from the AMS and attempted to forge a secular alternative voice to shape the political future of Hyderabad. However, the NSL suffered an early demise because it threatened the delicate balance of power of Muslim elites who were more cautious in aligning with apparent INC supporters expressing Hindu interests in Hyderabad.

The politicized youth of Hyderabad also turned to linguistically-defined regional groups such as the AMS, the Maratha Parishad, and the Karnatak Parishad. John Roosa's work suggests that the regional 'cultural' organizations were popular precisely because they claimed not to be political.[17] Members of these associations, while claiming membership in the regional groups within Hyderabad, also cultivated ties with their counterparts in British India, which were becoming dynamic organs for anti-colonial nationalism. In the framework of anti-colonial nationalism, Hyderabad appeared to be a political 'backwater', as Carolyn Elliot summarizes in her explanation of its gradual political modernization.[18] However, as Roosa points out, the nationalist period not only produced narratives of nationalism and patriotism but also gave rise to the complex story of political democracy and citizenship in India: 'While rarely engaged in overt acts of resistance to the colonial power, there were nationalists in Hyderabad from the late nineteenth century onward endeavoring to build horizontal allegiances and workable alliances between diverse communities.'[19] This observation would extend to British India as well as, in particular, the Madras Presidency. While Hyderabad was hardly a hotbed of anti-colonial nationalism, it did witness radical challenges to the existing monarchical order and proposals for alternate political futures. The groups that proliferated in the 1920s and the 1930s attempted to negotiate constitutional reforms, imagining an alternate political future for Hyderabad after the impending British withdrawal from India. However, in many ways, as I have documented in Chapters 3 and 4, rather than fostering discussion that would shape the political future of Hyderabad, the Nizam and his supporters focused more on simply trying to thwart these discussions, thus setting the stage for the political impasses of the 1940s.

If one were to look at the enduring set of historical forces that shaped these decades before independence, Hyderabad went through some pertinent changes that prepared the way for discussing constitutional reforms by the state as well as shaping the political aspirations of its people. Roosa has argued that the reforms begun by Salar Jang had given a clear advantage to Muslim recruitment.[20] This became more apparent with the introduction of the census in 1881. Salar Jang conceived Hyderabad to be a Muslim state, which contributed to the public perception of Muslim dominance in the Nizam administration.[21] The idea of a Muslim state for Salar Jung certainly did not mean an Islamic state in which religious laws would be implemented to govern the people; nor did the state harbour any plans to encourage the conversion of the Hindu populace. However, it did mean that Muslims—whether *mulki* or non-*mulki*—would be recruited to fill the civil administration and give the state its Muslim character (acknowledging its history, heritage, and so on). Alongside the upholding of the idea of Hyderabad as a Muslim state, the modernization schemes implemented by Salar Jang, with the attendant calls for constitutional reforms starting in the second decade of the twentieth century, nurtured the conditions for the emergence of a thriving public sphere in Hyderabad—a public that would eventually challenge not only the monarchical power of the Nizam but also the dominance of Muslims in the bureaucracy.[22]

Before the founding of the NSL, the Anjuman-i Taraqqi Hyderabad campaigned on economic issues, believing that an economic agenda would bridge the growing rift between the religious communities in Hyderabad. The Anjuman's print organ was the *Raiyat* (1927), the newspaper edited by Narsing Rao, who was also a member of the Anjuman. Aware of the necessity to bridge the growing rift between religious communities, Narsing Rao attempted to stake out the *Raiyat*'s anti-sectarian identity.[23] He wrote powerful editorials in 1935 expressing these sentiments, noting, for example, '… if a few people were injured in religious squabbles; it matters little in a society where thousands are perishing every day because of disease'.[24] In another editorial, Rao wrote, 'These communal organizations (*farqavarana tahrikat*) may have their origins in British India but their poisonous winds reach here too. As soon as people started adopting ideas from British India, an era of evil mindedness and distrust began in the state.'[25] It is interesting to note the perception here that communalism was a disease from British India that threatened to distract from the real political issues in princely Hyderabad. It is also a testament to the differences of political conditions and political discussion in Hyderabad in comparison to those in British India.

In other words, these two organizations, the NSL and the Anjuman, and the discussions they debated were organic to Hyderabad and its peculiar political climate. They both addressed Hyderabad issues, particularly with respect to the integrity and autonomy of Hyderabad as a political unit.

Ultimately, what these various associations and their discussions reveal is a very different political climate in Hyderabad—one that indeed questioned and critiqued the monarchical power of the Nizam, while demanding constitutional reforms and the expansion of representative institutions. While none of them explicitly called for the fall of the monarchy as an institution, the demand for representative government based on territorial representation did not include a place for monarchical authority or the monarchy as heritage/identity. The political imaginaries, as they developed under the conditions of a modernized monarchy upheld by British colonial power, differed considerably from their British Indian counterparts. They shared some similar goals, especially the groups that overlapped and had explicit ties with the INC—namely the goal of greater representational institutions moving towards a popular democracy. However, even the INC groups, liberals, and socialists had to work under conditions of a monarchical power that did not openly engage in dialogue toward greater constitutional reforms. From the 1920s and throughout the 1940s, Hyderabad became a battleground of sorts between the Nizam's administration and a burgeoning public sphere that the state could neither control nor manage. The reforms begun by Salar Jang in the last decades of the nineteenth century transformed the state and its administration into what Janaki Nair has described as 'monarchical modern', simultaneously upholding monarchical power and modernizing the administration.[26] This created the conditions for the emergence of new publics that would eventually contest the monarchical power of the Nizam.

The Nizam himself had been steadily lobbying in the early years of the twentieth century to have the British recognize Hyderabad as a sovereign state. In particular, the Nizam and his supporters tried to have the British agree to adhere to the earlier treaties that said the British would come to its defence when India became independent and Hyderabad was at risk of being engulfed by a larger, potentially hostile state. The Nizam believed that dominion status was a possibility for Hyderabad. This would have appealed to the Hyderabad civil societal associations if there was indeed open dialogue between these groups and the administration over the political future of Hyderabad. But because any discussion of constitutional reforms was seen as threatening the traditional power dynamics of the Hyderabad state, this stalled any innovative thinking through of the possibilities for political autonomy for Hyderabad. On the eve of Indian independence, when the Nizam realized that the Indian Independence Bill did not allow for dominion status to be conferred on Indian states, he protested, 'The way in which my state is being abandoned by its old ally, the British Government, and the ties which have bound me in loyal devotion to the King Emperor are being severed.'[27] This led to tortuous negotiations between the Nizam's Executive Council and the Government of India and ultimately to the standstill agreement that allowed Hyderabad a year of autonomous existence before it would have to decide on either instituting a responsible government or ascending to the Indian Union.[28]

Long before the impasses of the volatile politics of the late 1940s, there was indeed a proliferation of alternative political imaginaries on the future of princely Hyderabad, as we saw with the activities of the NSL and the Anjuman. In 1938, Mohamad Siddeek, who played a pivotal role in the mediation of the 'unity talks' between Bahadur Yar Jung and Narsing Rao, wrote to Jawaharlal Nehru that he has been misled in his understanding of the situation and conditions in Hyderabad. Siddeek was a journalist in Bombay and Delhi and came to Hyderabad in 1933. He witnessed the 'unity talks' and their eventual breakdown when Narsing Rao reportedly visited Wardha to consult with Mohandas K. Gandhi and other INC leaders on the progress of the talks in Hyderabad. In 1938, Siddeek wrote directly to Gandhi to sum up the situation in Hyderabad and to appeal to the INC directly to try to understand the very difficult political conditions that Hyderabad represented. He wrote:

> … sooner or later, Hyderabad will have, more or less, the same type of constitution as the other political units in India, is no longer under dispute between the Hindus and the Muslims of the State. The questions under dispute are: 1. The position of the Muslim Minority under the future regime. 2. The methods of attaining the common goal.[29]

Interestingly, Siddeek framed the problem as being a psychological one between Hindus and Muslims (only the upper classes, he clarified, and not the masses). The elite Hindus felt like second-class citizens in Hyderabad because they did not 'command' prestige and status, and thus they desperately wanted a change in government. The Muslims, on the other hand, felt entitled as the ruling class and had no interest in abandoning the 'traditions of centuries' by changing the government. The Muslim elite, in short, wanted to hold on to their privileged status. Even so, Siddeek wrote that the Muslim elite had come to recognize that change was inevitable. As such, he asked for the following assurances:

1. Hindustani shall continue to remain the official language and the medium of instruction in schools and colleges. 2. Muslims should not be ousted from Government service, which happens to be their only means of livelihood. [Note: a) Muslims have no share, worth the name, in agriculture, trade, industry, banking and other lucrative professions.] b) The percentage of Hindus and Muslims in services of all grades is 65 and 32 respectively. [The Hindu grievance, with regard to services, relates to services of the higher grade only.] 3. In giving representation to the Muslims in the legislature, due regard should be paid to their history and tradition. They ask to be weighed instead of being counted.[30]

This was the clearest expression of the problems, identified by Siddeek, which the Muslim community feared constitutional reforms would produce in Hyderabad—namely the creation of a Muslim minority in what was perceived as a traditionally Muslim state.

Leading up to the 'unity talks', there were also attempts by the Hyderabad Political Conference to address the question of a separate electorate for Muslims. This was rejected initially at their first meeting by the HSC as it did not cohere with their vision of representative government based on territorial constituencies. The lingering question was whether the INC was truly negotiating on behalf of Hyderabad's diverse communities (Hindus and Muslims and Urdu, Telugu, Kannada, and Marathi speakers) or whether it was angling to assert the political agenda of the INC in the princely Hyderabad. This was a genuine concern plaguing the 'unity talks' as well as negotiations between civil societal organizations in Hyderabad throughout the 1930s and the 1940s. Even Narsing Rao, a key player in almost all of these meetings, expressed regret that Hindu leaders in Hyderabad were not paying enough attention to the 'minority' question that Muslims had to contend with in any representative government in Hyderabad and in India in general.[31]

To understand the emerging consciousness of the Muslim population of Hyderabad—a traditionally Muslim state—that they, too, would become a minority community in 'their' own state, it might be useful to turn to Aamir Mufti's work on the construction of the minority in British India. The Muslim community in Hyderabad saw this 'minoritization' of the community as a problem much more dramatically than the political consciousness that Muslims in British India came to in the early decades of the twentieth century, where they feared that they would become a minority community in any constitutional arrangement based on a representative government. On this, Mufti writes, 'Secular nationalism presents a specifically Muslim modernism with the following choice:

The Break-Up of Hyderabad

it can either dissolve itself within that nationalist mainstream, and simultaneously give up any claim to being "representative," or be by definition (and perversely) communalist, retrograde, and effectively in collusion with the feudalizing policies of imperialism.'[32] We see this being played out in princely Hyderabad as the Majlis—representing Muslim interests in Hyderabad—had to oscillate between claiming to be the sole representative of the people and simultaneously speaking for the Hyderabad state and the Nizam as symbols of Muslim heritage.

Mufti goes on to argue that Indian nationalism overall presented to Indian Muslims a 'crisis of representation' where 'the (nationalist) claim for the existence of a singular Indian nation (state) seeks to place "the Muslims" in the place of the national minority'.[33] In Hyderabad, the problem of 'minoritization' of the Muslim community had the added dimension of trying to understand the complicated relationship between monarchical authority and popular sovereignty. The Majlis repeatedly claimed the Nizam as the source of sovereignty, and therefore Hyderabad as a state had to retain its territorial borders. Moreover, at the same time, the Majlis' position, as outlined by Yar Jung, claimed that the power of the king derived from the people. M. A. Moid and A. Suneetha argue that

> the Majlis affected the politics of Hyderabad State in two ways. One, it proclaimed that the sovereignty of the Nizam did not stand alone but needed to be buttressed through support of the Muslim subjects. Two, such support from the Muslim subjects could not be mobilised, unless there was a party such as the Majlis, an explicitly Muslim political party with Muslim interests as its focus.[34]

In his letter to Gandhi, Siddeek identified this particular political problem in princely Hyderabad: the critical question of the 'minoritization' of Muslims who historically held dominant positions within the administration of the Nizam. However, this question did not receive adequate attention from the 'secular' groups attempting to bridge religious communities while also arguing for the integrity of Hyderabad as a historical and political unit. The HSC, the NSL, and the Anjuman, for instance, elected not to address head on the problem of majorities and minorities but to argue instead for constitutional reforms to expand civil liberties for the people and advocate for representative government. These were indeed legitimate and critical issues, to be sure. But by failing to acknowledge the question of a Muslim minority in a historically Muslim state, these organizations lost out on an opportunity to think through constitutional protections for minority communities (both Dalit and Muslim).

Additionally, as we saw earlier, there was a conscious fashioning of a Muslim identity starting in the late nineteenth century that was integral to how the Nizam's administration was representing the identity and heritage of the Hyderabad state. The question of the tenuous position of the Muslim community in princely Hyderabad after political reforms were to be put in place became the focal point for the Majlis (initially formed to address the specific political interests of Muslims in the Hyderabad state) in the late 1930s and the 1940s. In these decades, they began to distinguish their clear political differences with groups such as the HSC in what they envisioned as the future polity for Hyderabad. For instance, the position that the HSC was taking differed considerably from that of the Majlis and the Nizam's administration, both of whom were attempting to articulate the point of view of the Hyderabad state that looked after the interests of all its constituents—the majority and the minority. As Siddeek put it, the psychological issue undergirding political discussions at the time was the fear of the loss of Muslim sovereignty with the decline of the princely state of Hyderabad not only within Hyderabad but also in South Asia as a whole.

For the Majlis, the task was to address the question of 'minoritization' by balancing two prominent goals: first, to consider a constitutional monarchy in order to retain the state's historical territorial boundaries and its composite culture; second, to vest the Nizam's power in the people—thereby, arguably, addressing the concerns of the HSC that the state and its people should be set on a path towards a representative democracy. One of the charges made by the Nizam's government repeatedly since its inception was that the HSC was a communal organization because it tended to enflame communal tensions with its assertion of Hindu majoritarian politics. One could argue that the HSC, by adhering closely to the party line of the INC, did not seriously consider the question of the fate of the Muslim minority—a minority that would result from proposed constitutional reforms within the Hyderabad state. What would be the real safeguards or protections put into place for Muslim representation and the political interests of minority communities? Rather, many of the public political and cultural associations focused their energy on retaining the traditional territorial boundaries of princely Hyderabad, with less concern for the historical and cultural heritage of a princely and Muslim past. At times in the late 1930s and the 1940s, less focus was brought to the latter—the 'composite' culture of Hyderabad that the NSL so assiduously tried to give coherence to in the 1930s. Rather, the idea of unity centred on territorial integrity without giving much thought to the elaboration of its cultural composition.

While the idea of federation offered the administration a path to assert state autonomy and sovereignty after British withdrawal, federation discussions offered something entirely different for civil societal organizations that envisioned a united Hyderabad. For the latter, advocating for Hyderabad to federate with the Indian Union was a way to assure that Hyderabad's future would eventually be that of a democratic polity, not a monarchical and certainly not an autocratic one. These political imaginaries were articulated in a variety of formulations of unity on the part of public associations such as the NSL to the HSC. In 1937, the HSC explicitly declared its opposition to the proposals made by the Reforms Committee of the Hyderabad administration for the future of Hyderabad by declaring them wholly inadequate. The HSC proposed instead that a representative government should be the political goal for a democratic future for Hyderabad's diverse communities. Kashinathrao Vaidya received a letter on 29 May 1939 from Azhar Hassan (home secretary to the Nizam), in which Hassan accused Vaidya and his organization of undermining the Nizam's government and the state of Hyderabad:

> Since your organization aims at a form of Government deriving authority from the majority in the Legislature, it is directed against the principle, recently made the subject of an official pronouncement, that the needs of the people must continue to be determined by the undevided [sic] responsibility of the Ruler for the welfare of the subjects.[35]

In this instance, the administration was reasserting monarchical authority, belying its claims of intention to shift the current government towards a representative government as demanded by public associations throughout the 1930s. From the 1920s onwards, the Hyderabad administration agreed to introduce reforms by forming an Executive Council, with Ali Imam at its head, though it seems pretty clear from the evidence that the Nizam and his administration did so only under pressure from the British.[36]

The open resistance shown by the members of the HSC to the Hyderabad administration and the Reform Committee's proposals was interpreted as threatening to the position of the Nizam. However, the attempt to retain monarchical rule was a losing battle for the Nizam and his administration, and we see the debates gradually turning to the question of the historical viability of the Hyderabad state. In other words, in the context of political reforms in British India and with respect to princely states, it was no longer possible to simply assert an unreformed monarchical state as the ultimate goal. Lines were drawn between democratic goals, as embodied in the idea of responsible or representative government and the political goal of retaining the territorial boundaries of the state. The activists in the HSC increasingly made representative government their primary goal, which undercut monarchical rule as a goal for both the administration as well as the Majlis. In September 1945, Vaidya returned to the issue of political reforms and calls for popular sovereignty in Hyderabad:

> This, in short, is the nature of Reforms intended to be introduced in 1946. The World War II is over and Fascism and Nazism are crushed and Democracy has gloriously come out victorious. Will the Hyderabad Govt. introduce the Functional Basis of election, a Fascist system? I would most sincerely request you to take into consideration the onward march of time and to introduce a scheme of Reforms, which would fit in with the principle accepted on all hands, that a Country should be governed according to the wishes of the people. I would remind you of the speeches made by yourself and the other Hon'ble Members of the Executive Council very recently. The Reforms, if introduced, as announced, will not justify the said speeches and they will badly reflect on the progressive views of the Hon'ble Members of the Executive Council. The Reforms should be shelved as they are out of date. A constitution at least, modelled (sic) on the lines of the constitution granted to the Provinces of British India under the Government of India Act 1935, be introduced in the State....
>
> In conclusion, I sincerely request you to reconsider and recast the Reforms by introducing:
> I) territorial representation,
> II) Franchise to at least fifty per cent of the adult population of the state,
> III) Responsibility of the Cabinet to the Legislature, and
> IV) Granting full powers to the legislature and assuring the people of their fundamental rights, namely, Freedom of Speech, Freedom of Association, Freedom of Press and freedom of Religion. The Reforms, remodeled on these lines, will be in conformity with the changed times and will be befitting the high prestige and dignity of a Premier State like Hyderabad.[37]

The reforms Vaidya proposed were devoid of historical and cultural claims for the integrity and unity of Hyderabad as an inclusive state. Activists such as Vaidya arguing for constitutional changes towards a representative government eschewed the rhetoric of nationalism in making the case for a new community. Instead, they centred their discussion exclusively on expanding representative institutions towards responsible government. One wonders whether this exclusion of culture, history, religion, and language from the discussions contributed to the narrow politics that eventually pitted Hindus and Muslims against one another.

From the 1920s, public associations in princely Hyderabad were unable to put forward an inclusive cultural movement (organized around a national culture) after the efforts of the NSL. In January 1946, a memorandum signed by Vaidya, Syed Siraj-ul-Hasan Tirmizi, and Narsing Rao was presented to the British parliamentary delegation. The memorandum again criticized the political reforms that were being considered in the Hyderabad state by recounting the series of steps the government took in the 1930s that led to the formation of the Reforms Committee. The memorandum pointed to the fact that the report released by the Reforms Committee proposed representation according to corporate interests: Samasthans, Jagirdars, Pattedars, labour interest. The memorandum deemed this functional basis of representation contradictory to the exercise of democracy.[38] The authors of the memorandum also argued that it was retrograde to return to this scheme of representation when British Indian proposals were far ahead on the path towards representative democracy. They wrote:

> India is one undivided whole and the people in Indian States cannot be differentiated from those in British India. They belong to the same race and they have inherited the same culture. They speak the same languages and they have their places of pilgrimage in every part of India. No political arbitrary divisions can separate them and if there appear some differences, they are merely artificial. The Indian States, therefore, should be integral parts of a free India. In such a Free India, there must be some common back-ground of free Institutions and standards of social and economic welfare. India cannot be free in British and unfree in Indian India.[39]

In short, the document made it clear that the culture and history of Hyderabad was not wholly separate from India; indeed, the two shared the same history and could not therefore be separated. Only in the last year of British rule were the INC intentions made starkly clear that princely Hyderabad needed to be part of the Indian Union because of shared culture, languages, and values. However, Vaidya, Tirmizi, and Narsing Rao did not give up on the idea of retaining the territorial boundaries of princely Hyderabad.

It is important to understand that those advocating for Hyderabad to formally join the Indian Union did not argue for the historical borders of the state to be dismantled. Jayaprakash Narayan in 1947 came to Hyderabad and gave a public speech on what political path princely Hyderabad should take. In the speech, Narayan declared that the 'world is marching towards democracy and socialism' and that the princes must accept this inevitability and abide by the will of the people. He went on to say that the HSC had in fact made a demand for responsible government while retaining the symbolic position of the Nizam. This, he also implied, was a great concession for holding on to the territorial integrity of the state. However, Narayan reminded the Nizam's supporters that the king was indeed a symbolic head of the state and that real political power must lie in the hands of the people.[40] There was no question that popular sovereignty was the goal for the Indian Union inclusive of the princely states. This is the radical democratic future envisioned by Narayan and other INC members after South Asia severed its ties with Britain and the colonial government.

Language and Self-Determination: The Nizam Andhra Mahasabha

The rhetoric around political reforms in the 1930s and into the 1940s was devoid of references to culture. There was an explicit absence of national symbols or culture for people's imaginations to hook on to; instead, the only form of cultural awakening that fuelled public life was linguistic nationalism, at least with respect to Telugu speakers. The idea of a Deccani nationalism or composite culture that defined the culture of princely Hyderabad remained an antiquated concern of the elites. As Leonard argues, and as discussed earlier, it was formulated in the 1930s by the NSL in an attempt to shape political opinion in Hyderabad towards its own diverse people and communities.[41] As the last chapter discussed, these civil societal organizations gave way to the formation of dynamic regional groups bringing together Telugu speakers, Kannada speakers, and Marathi speakers—all of whom expanded their linguistic affiliations with their British Indian counterparts. Urdu, on the other hand, did not have an equivalent organization. The movement to modernize Urdu and make it a suitable medium for education and public life was centred around the founding of Osmania University in 1918. The transformation of Urdu was taken up by scholars at the university and described by Kavita Datla in the opening lines of Maulvi Abdul Haq's *Bàbà-i Urdu* (Father of Urdu), published in 1919 for the ambitious purpose of regenerating the nation:

> In the life of every nation in the world, there comes a time when signs of deterioration begin to appear in its mental powers; material for discovery and creation, thought and consideration are nearly lost; the strength of imagination's flight and vision becomes narrow and limited; the agreement of scholarship rests upon a few customary facts and on mimicry. At that time, the nation either becomes defeated and lifeless, or to recover, it must accept the influence of other advanced countries. In every era of world history, there is evidence of this. Even now as we watch, this has happened to Japan, and this is the condition of India (Hindustan).[42]

The language debates and reforms that Urdu underwent at Osmania University resembled the modern Telugu movement spearheaded by reformers Gidigu Venkata Ramamurti and Gurzada Appa Rao in the northern coastal districts of the Madras Presidency. In Hyderabad, however, language reform was not the primary movement associated with Telugu. Rather, as I have tried to document, the formation of the Nizam Andhra Mahasabha in Hyderabad began its initial days as a library movement, promoting Telugu learning in schools through assertions of Telugu pride and then shifting to more overt political mobilization in the 1940s. Unlike the regionally based languages of Telugu, Kannada, and Marathi, Urdu was not territorial in its claims. When it replaced Persian as the official language of the Hyderabad administration in 1911, it was primarily the language of the ruling elite as well as the general population of Muslims in Hyderabad city. The census of 1871 showed that around 67 per cent of the population of Hyderabad were Urdu speakers.[43]

Tariq Rahman argues that the transition from Persian to Urdu was not a simple substitution of one language with another but rather a political shift. He argues that Urdu became important for the self-identification of Muslims in Hyderabad and broadly fit into the narrative of Muslim nationalism in north India.[44] Datla's research presents us with a complex history of Urdu in princely Hyderabad and its shaping of a literate class and culture centred in the city of Hyderabad. In other words, Urdu did not have the ability to connect up with bordering territorial languages in order to build and expand a people's movement. Rather, it relied on internal resources to broaden Muslim or Urdu nationalism within Hyderabad. Telugu, Marathi, and Kannada cultivated linguistic affiliations with bordering territories in British India and used those connections to organize their communities, as evidenced in the formation of public associations based on language. The Muslim community of princely Hyderabad was primarily organized by the Majlis. The Majlis as an organization began as a socio-religious reform movement that then transformed into a political organization attempting to represent the political interests of the Muslim community.[45] The Majlis organized the community by bringing together interests that cut across class divisions and claimed the Hyderabad state as a territory imbued with Muslim heritage and history. The Majlis' claim, in other words, was on the basis of history and heritage as opposed to the three linguistic communities that made claims on the basis of language and culture (as natural affinities). The latter also made territorial claims because their districts were contiguous with bordering territories and therefore also shared interests with the neighbouring British Indian provinces.

In effect, the Majlis took on the role of both the AMS and the HSC as an organization, trying to navigate both social and religious reforms alongside political reforms. In the Hyderabad state, the AMS was able to gather together liberal politicians like Narsing Rao and cultural revivalists such as Suravaram Pratapa Reddy to foster a forum for Telugu public life that would encourage political and social activism for Telugu speakers in princely Hyderabad. Pratapa Reddy began by trying to cultivate Telugu pride in Hyderabad, where Urdu was patronized by the state. Narsing Rao, on the other hand, focused on fostering a common political ground as a journalist (as the founder of the Urdu newspaper *Raiyat*) and building a broad coalition that cut across religious and linguistic lines. Narsing Rao eventually became immersed in Hyderabad political reforms and emerged as a spokesperson for the Telugu community, the guise under which he engaged in direct talks with the Majlis. The AMS also had within its group prominent communist leaders such as Ravi Narayana Reddy, who shifted from being a student activist immersed in INC politics and Gandhian activism to being a supporter of peasant insurgency in the Telangana countryside in the 1940s. What is distinct about the Andhra movement and its agitation for a separate province in the Madras Presidency dating to the 1910s was its ability to incorporate disparate political ideologies within its fold. As discussed in Chapters 1 and 2, the AMS in the Madras Presidency and princely Hyderabad encompassed conservatism, liberalism, socialism, and communism. Because it began as a public organization for the expansion of Telugu public life, it necessarily turned to political activity. We saw this with the early activists in the Madras Presidency who advocated for a separate province by arguing that self-rule and self-determination necessarily meant developing representative institutions at the regional level and the expansion of Telugu publics to enable vibrant political life. Because of its initial expansive set of goals, it was able to encompass and ultimately nurture divergent political ideologies towards the common anti-colonial goal of self-rule. The AMS thus became an organ that fostered both anti-colonial nationalist politics as well as regionalism.

In the Hyderabad state, however, the AMS had to initially downplay its affiliation with anti-colonial nationalist politics because of state censorship and the charge that becoming a political organization would disrupt the internal politics of the princely state. Instead, it was allowed to function as an organ for social reform and cultural revival. Because the language associations in princely Hyderabad had British India affiliations, they felt the impact of anti-colonial nationalism as embodied in the INC and as it shaped regional movements in British India. The other strands of the AMS in the Madras Presidency were felt as well in the Hyderabad state. The militant nationalist wing of the AMS in Madras

Presidency had stronger proposals regarding the relationship between Telangana and Andhra. For instance, as early as 29 October 1937, Gummudithala Venkata Subbarao (Secretary to the ASP, Bezwada) wrote an article in *The Mahratta* titled 'Andhra Province: A Programme. A Boycott Movement Foreshadowed', in which he declared:

> So far the Telangana area is concerned while it is true that there are no differences of opinion between the Telugus of British India and of the Nizam's dominion, since the suspension of the Andhra movement, there has been very little of fellow feeling between them, and to awaken a near relationship between the British Andhras and Nizam's Andhras it is essential to send a fraternal Delegation of British Andhras to the Telangana area, which should also meet and pay respects to H.E.H. the Nizam and his Premier, Sir Akbar Hydari. In this connection, it is not to be forgotten that H.E.H. the Nizam is not only the richest man of the world, but he is our first and most distinguished fellow Andhra kinsman.[46]

We saw earlier that the confidential files of the Nizam's political department kept abreast of public discourse on the Andhra movement in British India and its particular demands. In fact, as has been argued in Chapter 2, the Andhra activists had their designs on Telangana, the Telugu-speaking region in Hyderabad. They drew maps inclusive of the Hyderabad districts and made claims on that territory as it was linguistically and culturally contiguous. Within the Nizam AMS, the idea of forming a province with British Indian districts was never considered openly, but their Andhra counterparts did not hesitate to make such claims.

However, there was a shift in the 1940s, as the Nizam AMS anticipated the break-up of Hyderabad, given the growing strength of the HSC and the communists. By 1947, it became apparent to all parties that the leaders of the Andhra movement had set their sights on capturing Telangana from Hyderabad and incorporating it into a new Andhra state. The APCC was formed to encourage the 'freedom movement' in Hyderabad, with its headquarters in the British Indian city of Bezwada.[47] On 3 August 1947, J. Kesava Rao, the president of the APCC, and Dewan Bahadur M. Ramachandra Rao of the HSC sent a press statement that responded to a radio address delivered by the Nawab of Chhatari on 'Azad Hyderabad' charting a path for an independent and autonomous Hyderabad.[48] Kesava Rao and Ramachandra Rao decried what they saw as the Nawab's misleading address, which made a case for the Nizam but failed to represent the interests of the people. They wrote, 'His arguments in support of "Azad Hyderabad" are the same timeworn ones and ignore grievously the predominant people's fact and will.'⁴⁹ Furthermore, they noted, by going straight to the United Nations, the Nawab was undermining the efforts of the HSC to preserve the territorial integrity of Hyderabad:

> The President of the executive council of Hyderabad Government is treading on very dangerous and explosive ground when he is trying to pave the path for the entry of Azad Hyderabad into United Nations Organization justifying the same on the ground of population, extension, resources, etc. He is, we feel, encouraging rather instigating the Telangana of Hyderabad, with its population of 90 lakhs and an area of 41 thousand square miles and potential resources, and a dawning Andhra province as a neighbor, with two crores of population and all other potentialities to pave its own way into the Indian Union a nearer body a more sympathetic one to us than to what U.N.O. could never be to 'Azad Hyderabad.'⁵⁰

As Kesava Rao and Ramachandra Rao saw it, appealing to the United Nations for recognition of Hyderabad's autonomy risked encouraging Telangana, which shared a common language and culture with Hyderabad, to pursue its own path of aligning with their neighbouring region in the Indian Union. They also charged the Nawab with enabling the 'Balkanization' of India by insisting on autonomy from the Indian Union in reference to the Nawab's argument that a free Hyderabad would be similar to Switzerland—a country with multiple linguistic traditions and cultures: 'Nawab Chattari's histrionic part of the talk in shedding few tears for the division of India as a result of "communal frenzy" lost its dramatic tinge when he advocated in the same breath for the balkanization of India in the form of "Azad Hyderabad."' However, Kesava Rao and Ramachandra Rao took issue with that comparison and insisted that the Swiss government was based on the 'people's will' and elected representatives—both elements that the Hyderabad state had been suppressing, thus creating the current political impasse.

The 1940s as a decade and 1947 in particular were volatile times for Hyderabad. Following the death of Yar Jung in 1944, the Nizam's government became ever more disorganized in its political goals, even as it remained stubbornly fixed on the idea of an autonomous Hyderabad at any cost in the latter half of the 1940s. By 1947, the HSC no longer hesitated to declare their allegiance to the Indian Union while still holding on to the idea of Hyderabad remaining a state within the union. But the question of sovereignty was still earnestly pursued by the Hyderabad administration to the very end and beyond, as we saw with their attempts to take their case to the United Nations.⁵¹ The position of the

Hyderabad administration was that if the state chose to remain independent—which it had every indication of being able to do from the British—then the state and its people would choose their own path towards constitutional reforms. The administration saw the HSC and the Nizam AMS as doing the bidding for the INC and advocating full union with an independent India, in which case the political reforms would be imposed or inherited rather than organically emerging from within the state and the people's interests.

If, in fact, there was so much talk of unity of Hyderabad from the 1930s as we have seen and the various civil societal organizations' commitment to it, what led to the eventual break-up of Hyderabad in the aftermath of the police action in 1948? The NSL, the Society for Union and Progress, the Comrades Association, and even the early HSC all worked to gain mass followings that would shape the political future of Hyderabad. By comparing the emergence of civil societal activism in Hyderabad and in the Madras Presidency—and specifically the AMS—we can see very different histories and political trajectories in the two spaces. The AMS provided a meeting point for Telugu intellectuals and activists from coastal Andhra to congregate and explore their common cultural and historical roots as well as to examine the pros and cons of forming a separate province carved out on the basis of language. In the Madras Presidency, the organization successfully persuaded the INC that the Telugu-speaking districts should organize their own Congress unit, thereby advocating the linguistic reorganization of states after the departure of the British. The AMS in Hyderabad, meanwhile, shared with their counterpart in British India the goal of cultural and literary revival of Telugu but harboured very different political aspirations. While the AMS provided a cultural and political forum to imagine the future political shape of Hyderabad, its primary concern was to push for constitutional reforms similar to the other civil societal groups within Hyderabad.

In the 1940s, however, a radical faction within the AMS brought new politics to the fore—the political ascendance of the communist movement in Hyderabad. World War II divided political parties in princely Hyderabad just as it did in British India. The Hyderabad state, the AIML, and the communists supported the British war effort, albeit at different moments and for different reasons, while the INC withdrew support during the Quit India movement led by Gandhi. During these tumultuous years, communists gained ascendance in the Andhra Conference and were also viewed as threatening by the HSC.

Lucien Benichou suggests that the Comrades Association had significant influence in Hyderabad and shaped prominent AMS members who went on to lead the communist takeover that displaced the more centrist liberals such as Narsing Rao.⁵² In princely Hyderabad, while the AMS brought together disparate political ideologies, the communists rose to prominence in the 1940s. And while the Telugu activists were members in the HSC, they soon turned to the AMS to gather together to debate and discuss issues surrounding cultural revival of the Telugu language and literature. It is important to note that according to the census in 1941, Marathi speakers comprised approximately 24 per cent of the total population of the Hyderabad state, while Telugu speakers made up 46 per cent (for comparison, note that Urdu speakers were at 13 per cent).⁵³ The demographic divides are significant in order to understand the multiple identities mobilized by political movements that emerged in Hyderabad. Each linguistic group brought to the table distinct concerns that had to be negotiated by, first, the Hyderabad Conference and then the HSC in the 1940s. Each language group formed separate conferences: the Marathi Conference, the Kannada Conference, and the Telugu Conference, just as the INC established regional committees in British India to encourage political organization on the ground. However, the Marathi leaders in princely Hyderabad became outspoken supporters of the INC more so than the Telugu activists. And this could have been because the INC had some very prominent Marathi leaders in the organization from its very inception—ranging from Gopal Krishna Gokhale to Bal Gangadhar Tilak. They also had stronger ties to religion-based organizations such as the Arya Samaj and the Hindu Mahasabha.

Narayana Reddy, the prominent nationalist who was politicized through Gandhian activism in Hyderabad and the AMS, wrote a memoir of his childhood and his activism initially in Telangana and then afterwards in Andhra Pradesh after its formation in 1956. The memoir provides an important account of the times and charts his early years growing up in Telangana, his political awakening from his involvement in Gandhian activism, his involvement in the communist insurgency of the 1940s, and finally his participation in the 1952 elections in independent India. He was from Bollepalle village of Nalgonda district in Telangana. As a student in Hyderabad, he stayed at the Reddy Hostel, a place that housed prominent Telugu activists. It was at that time that he became politically active. He attributed his political awakening to his study of Gandhian literature in 1929—more specifically the autobiography. He singled out anti-imperialist ideas as what attracted him to Gandhi and the nationalist movement. He also was inspired by his reading of Nehru's *Glimpses of World History* and his socialist writings, as well as Jayaprakash Narayan's writings. He wrote in his memoir that he was moved to take part in Gandhi's call for civil disobedience in 1930, leaving his studies in order to participate in the all-India protest.⁵⁴ Because there was a lack of political activism in Hyderabad due to state censorship, he sought political engagement in the neighbouring Madras Presidency. He took part in civil disobedience activities and was soon appointed secretary of the Hyderabad branch of the All-India Harijan Sevak Sangh, where he worked to eradicate untouchability. He singles out Gandhi, Nehru, and Narayan as the nationalists who inspired his entry into politics in the 1930s: Gandhi for his agitational protest and his social reform agenda; Nehru and Narayan for their commitment to socialist ideas. Narayana Reddy joined the HSC in 1938 and before that participated in the formation of the AMS in Hyderabad.

Two incidents Narayana Reddy described in the first few meetings of the AMS serve to illustrate his politics. At the first meeting, when Bhagya Reddy Varma, a prominent Dalit leader, went up to speak at the meeting, many members walked out, and it seems no one defended Bhagya Reddy and his right to speak.[55] Although the AMS drew attention to some social reform issues, caste reform was not at the forefront of their agenda. Narayana Reddy noted that, at first, there was a concerted effort to use only Telugu in speeches and to not allow speakers to converse in other languages. The first meeting featured Marathi-speaking activist Vaman Naik. By the time of the fourth conference, however, there were very vocal 'language enthusiasts', or extremists, according to Narayana Reddy, who insisted on a Telugu-only policy at the meetings and complained that Telugu was not being given its fair share in the Hyderabad state. He spoke out against the tactics of these extremists and insisted that they must allow other languages at the meetings because the purpose of the AMS was not for Telugu advocacy alone.[56] He also argued that the AMS had always been political, despite claims by a faction of the organization that it was purely a cultural organization. By 1940, according to Narayana Reddy, the AMS was thoroughly political as members took part in the HSC-led *satyagraha* in 1938.[57] By this time it was clear Narayana Reddy was more taken by the revolutionary politics of communism globally, and he wrote in his memoir that he officially joined the CPI in 1939. He did not reveal this affiliation to his fellow AMS members until it was safe to do so in 1942, when the CPI was no longer banned. As the president of the AMS, he wrote about how the organization became a mass organization through two changes in focus: (*a*) reducing fees so that more people could join the group and (*b*) displacing the agenda of the 'language extremists'. On the other hand, the communists, Narayana Reddy insisted, shifted their focus to education and labour reform.[58]

Meanwhile, the HSC began to put pressure on the liberal members to push out the communists from the Andhra Conference. In 1946, when Narayana Reddy was the president of the Andhra Conference, he wrote to the president of the HSC, Swami Ramananda Tirtha, regarding the misguided policies of the

AISPC, which was at the time excluding members of the Andhra Conference and refused to view it as a representative body because it allowed communists to take part in the organization. Narayana Reddy wrote:

> This means that the major section of the Leadership and local members of the Andhra Conference who have made it what it is today will be excluded from the State Congress. Any person confersant [sic] with political situation in Hyderabad can understand the disastrous effects of such exclusion of the people's movement in the state.

He went on to write that it was not possible to have the members vote on the potential merger of the Andhra Conference with the HSC given the volatile political conditions of the Telugu-speaking districts:

> Regarding the other letters I have received concerning the merger of the Andhra Conference into State Congress, you have asked for a reply before 7 August. But the latest decision of AISPC has created an unprecedented situation for Andhra Conference, when it is asked to be merged minus the leaders who have built it up. Such a decision cannot easily be taken by the Working Committee. Also, in the conditions of repression in which we are working and the big battles we are fighting against Feudal Tyrants and police Zulum, it has not become possible to call a meeting of Delegates who alone can decide the issue.[59]

Just a year before, he had written to the AISPC's general secretary, Jai Narayanji Vyas, stating that in fact it was the HSC that was not representative. Rather, he argued, the three linguistically defined conferences—the Andhra, the Maharashtra and the Karnatak—were truly representative. In fact, the efforts made by the INC to make a single association the sole representative were, in Narayana Reddy's view, undemocratic. A report sent to the AISPC on repressive measures in Telangana stated:

> The struggle that Andhra Conference has lead in Jangaon Taluqa Nalgonda District, against the notorious Deshmukh, Vishnoor Ramachandra Reddy, and the famous watandar, Kathar Ramchander Rao; the fights Andhra Conference has conducted against the Jagirdars and other feudalism in Warangal District and other places; and the campaign it has carried against the corrupt officials, who hands in glove with the village tyrants, were actually fleecing the poor; have all made the Andhra Conference the most popular organization in Telingana.[60]

The struggles referred to here by Narayana Reddy were the people's revolts against landlords in the villages of Telangana—actions supported by the communist members of the AMS. However, with the existent dynamism of the regional and linguistic conferences, Narayana Reddy argued that the HSC could never achieve consensus amongst the people's groups in Hyderabad.

To take a step back, how did the three linguistically aligned conferences become truly representative, according to Narayana Reddy, in Hyderabad? The emergence of these civil societal associations organized by language were certainly strengthened by the increased use of vernaculars for public and political life, given their power to reach a broader public across the urban–rural divide. The use of regional languages in Hyderabad was an effective means of increasing politicization and ultimately cultivating political life and the democratic virtues of civic-mindedness. It was especially critical with the rise of mass politics in the 1920s and the 1930s when activists were expanding their support. By the 1940s, when political divisions were becoming clear in Hyderabad, Narayana Reddy alluded to conflict between the goals of the INC and those of the communists. With the communists at the helm of the Andhra Conference, Narayana Reddy and the leadership had diverging political goals for people's movements within the cities as well as the countryside, where there was a peasant uprising. The CPI's policies towards national determination, as outlined by Gangadhar Adhikari, made clear that they were supportive of the idea of nationalist determination and self-determination for different groups—hence their support of the AIML's demands and relative lack of support for the INC and its desire for a centralized Indian union. While the INC feared 'Balkanization', the communists supported regional and ethnic self-determination.

To take an important example from princely Hyderabad, the call for a united Andhra, or 'Visalandhra' ('Greater Andhra', which included the merging of Telangana districts), initially came from Telugu members of the CPI, who called for combining Telugu-speaking provinces from Madras with those that were part of Hyderabad. In 1945, P. Sundarayya, a prominent Andhra communist and leader of the Telangana peasant movement, published a pamphlet advocating the idea of a 'Greater Andhra'. The map in Figure 5.1, included in Sundarayya's pamphlet, shows Andhra, or the northern coastal districts in the Madras Presidency, and Hyderabad districts that have majority Telugu speakers. The southern border reaches all the way to the vicinity of the colonial city of Madras, while the northern border juts up against Bastar. Sundarayya shaded in areas where Andhras had been living in the border regions. While G. Venkatasubba Rao, an ardent activist and the founder of the ASP, made a case for an Andhra province or state that would comprise all Telugu-speaking regions inclusive of the Telangana regions of the Hyderabad state, Sundarayya's plea came from the growing communist movement in the 1940s, which connected peasant

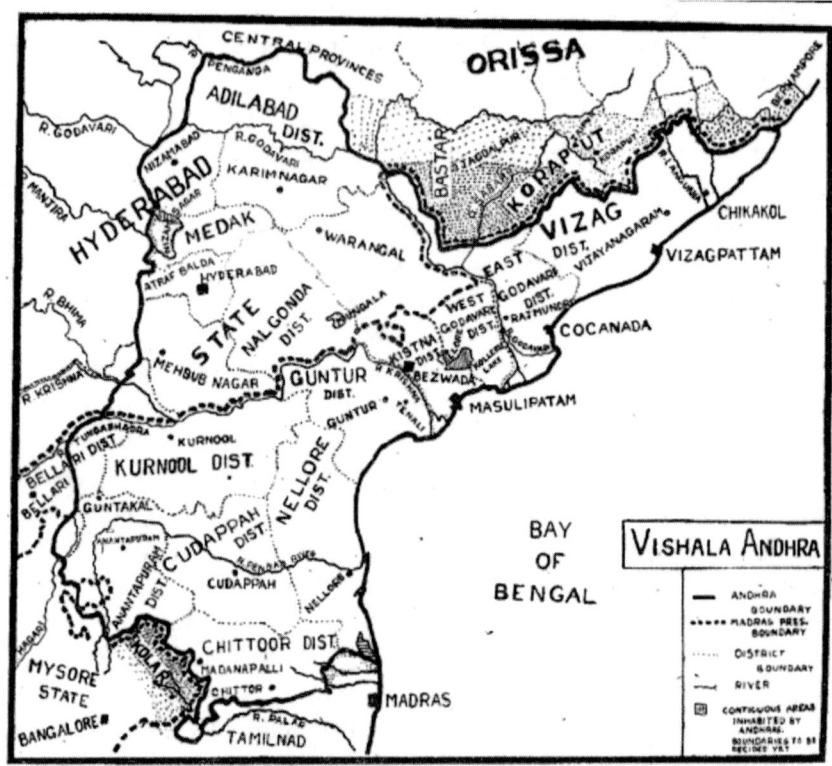

Figure 5.1 Map of 'Greater Andhra', 1945

Source: P. Sundarayya, *Vishala Andhra* (Bombay: People's Publishing House, 1945).

struggles across the border separating the northern coastal districts of the Madras Presidency from the boundaries of the Hyderabad state.

For the purpose of supporting the merging of Telugu districts in Hyderabad and those in the Indian Union, the Vishalandhra Mahasabha was formed in 1949, immediately after police action in Hyderabad that forced the state to integrate into the Indian Union. It is telling that the Vishalandhra Mahasabha was established in the midst of the Telangana people's movement. At that time than ever before, there were greater ties between Telangana and the Telugu districts in the Madras Presidency, where the Andhra movement had been at the forefront of politics for over three decades. The idea of Vishala Andhra came initially from the northern coastal districts of the Madras Presidency and was proposed by the ASP in the late 1930s. However, it was soon taken up by the communists as well. Sundarayya, with the support of the CPI, made a case for radicalizing the Andhra movement and connecting the peasant uprisings across the borders between the Hyderabad state and the Indian Union. As we saw earlier, Narayana Reddy used the platform of the AMS to politicize it by increasing its membership and transforming it into a mass organization. In Sundarayya's tract *Vishala Andhra*, which he published in 1945, prior to Indian independence, he identified both British imperialism and the 'feudal' autocracy of the Nizam of Hyderabad as targets of the movement. He argued that the Andhra people—those who speak Telugu—had been artificially split between British provinces and native princely states. He declared that the CPI

> stands for a unified Vishala Andhra in a free India, to frame its constitution through a sovereign constituent assembly elected by adult franchise, it wants the free constituent assembly of the Andhra people to join the comity of Indian peoples and form the free voluntary Indian Union of free peoples.[61]

He went on to write that the CPI would devote its energies to helping the people of Hyderabad decide their own future, thus exercising their 'sacred right of self-determination through a constituent assembly'.[62] Then, in the next paragraph, he declared that in an independent Indian state, the Andhra people would finally realize their dream of merging all the Telugu-speaking districts split between the Madras Presidency, Mysore, and the Hyderabad state—seemingly not recognizing the contradiction of allowing people to choose their political future and at the same time declaring that it was in the interest of all Andhras to unite all Telugu people into one province. What gave weight to the political imaginary of Vishala Andhra was a romanticized vision of peasant solidarity crossing what Sundarayya saw as artificial political boundaries. Rather than romanticizing timeless Telugu culture, Sundarayya elevated the Andhra peasant specifically and the people as a whole by connecting them through their labour and work to produce a shared political imaginary.

When the ban on the CPI was lifted in 1942, the party's central committee began to endorse the idea of the Indian Union, or federation, consisting of distinct nationalities:

> Every section of the Indian people which has a contiguous territory as its homeland, common historical tradition, common language, culture, psychological make up, and common economic life would be recognized as a distinct nationality with the right to exist as an autonomous state within the free Indian Union or federation and will have the right to secede from it if it may so desire.[63]

Taking their cue from the Soviet Union, the Indian communists endorsed the linguistic principle for the states' reorganization. The recognition of the self-determination of nations within India gave support to Andhra communists in their calls for the self-determination of the Andhra people. Sundarayya, in his pivotal pamphlet calling for a united Andhra, wrote, 'We believe that we must unequivocally concede to each of the seventeen growing nations in India the right to determine their destiny, their own sacred right of self-determination through their constituent assemblies, based on universal adult suffrage.'[64] He continued, 'We believe that a free Indian Union can come into existence only by the sovereign nationalities freely and voluntarily coming together and not by denying to them the just and sacred right of self-determination.'[65] Regionalism was endorsed by both the CPI and the INC leaders in Hyderabad, ultimately leading to calls for the break-up of the state along linguistic lines as the best political solution to a monarchical modernity that had reached its limits.

Beyond fostering linguistic regionalism, the CPI and the INC, along with other British Indian groups such as the Arya Samaj and the Hindu Mahasabha, anticipated the demise of the state of Hyderabad and hoped that political forces within would eventually compel princely Hyderabad to join the Indian Union. However, the most vocal political pressure came from the AISPC, an organization supported by the INC, to encourage the pursuit and attainment of representative government for the benefit of the people of the princely states. In its inaugural meeting of 1927, the organization declared its objective as 'the attainment of Responsible Government for the people in the Indian States through representative institutions under the aegis of their rulers'.[66] In reference to the 600 states and their standing in the way of a composite Indian identity, Bhogaraju Pattabhi Sitaramayya declared, 'They are the vestiges of an ancient civilization and must perforce disappear sooner or later like their betters of the past. At present they only constitute a wedge driven by the British between the people of India and their ideal of a composite nationality.'[67] The AISPC worked arduously from its inaugural year to encourage peoples' movements within the princely states to not only move towards representative government but also join the Indian Union. Combined with their policy of encouraging peoples' movements within the native states, the AISPC was equally committed to India achieving 'a composite nationality', to quote Sitaramayya. The composite nationality would be achieved with the merger of native states with the British Indian provinces and by encouraging regional identities along linguistic lines.

While the 1930s saw tension building between liberal HSC members with their reform proposals and the Majlis' proposals for giving equal weight to Muslim representation in any future constitutional arrangement, the 1940s saw increased political division among INC members. The HSC and its liberal members were prominent in organizing their regional Andhra, Karnatak, and Maratha conferences. It was the AMS that eventually became embroiled in a leadership struggle between the liberals and the communists that was characteristic of the politics of the 1940s. From Narayana Reddy's memoirs we learn that this struggle lasted throughout the decade, starting after Narayana Reddy gained leadership role in the AMS. The radicalizing of the Andhra movement in Hyderabad and the cultivation of movement ties across the borders between princely Hyderabad and British India contributed to the strength of the Vishala Andhra movement. These cross-border linguistic nationalisms and regionalisms displaced the older arguments for the integrity and autonomy of princely Hyderabad—an autonomy that had united the political imaginaries of associations such as the NSL, the Anjuman, and the Comrades Association. However, in the volatile politics of the 1940s, lines were drawn not only between liberals and communists but also between the language enthusiasts (of the AMS), making alliances with their counterparts across the border in British India more appealing than working together to preserve the unity and integrity of the Hyderabad state.

Notes

1. See Sunil Purushotham, 'Internal Violence: The "Police Action" in Hyderabad', *Comparative Studies in Society and History* 57, no. 2 (2015): 435–466 and Taylor C. Sherman, 'The Integration of the Princely state of Hyderabad and the Making of the Postcolonial State in India, 1948-56', *Indian Economic Social History Review* 44 (2007): 489–516.
2. For a nuanced discussion of the Nizam's position on sovereignty, see Kavita S. Datla, 'Sovereignty and the End of Empire', *Ab Imperio* 3 (2018): 63–88.
3. See Purushotham, 'Internal Violence' and Sherman, 'The Integration of the Princely State of Hyderabad'.
4. Nehru Museum and Memorial Library (NMML), AISPC File Nos. 71, 72, 73, 74, Letter dated 11 November 1948 from members of the All-Hyderabad Congress Committee. The letter details the activities of the Congress members between August 1947 and September 1948.
5. Razakars (Volunteers) were the paramilitary wing of the Majlis.
6. See A. G. Noorani, *The Destruction of Hyderabad* (London: Hurst, 2014); Purushotham, 'Internal Violence'; Sherman, 'The Integration of the Princely State of Hyderabad'; Eric Lewis Beverley, *Hyderabad, British India, and the World: Muslim Networks and Minor Sovereignty, c. 1850–1950* (New York: Cambridge University Press, 2015); and Kavita S. Datla, *The Language of*

Secular Islam: Urdu Nationalism and Colonial India (Honolulu: University of Hawaii Press, 2013).

7. Michael Witmer, 'The 1947–1948 India–Hyderabad Conflict: Realpolitik and The Formation of The Modern Indian State', PhD dissertation, Temple University, Philadelphia, 1996, 112.
8. Syed Abid Hasan, *Whither Hyderabad? A Brief Study of Some of the Outstanding Problems of the Premier Indian State* (Madras: BN Press, 1935).
9. Hasan, *Whither Hyderabad?*, 2.
10. Hasan, *Whither Hyderabad?*, 16.
11. Hasan, *Whither Hyderabad?*, 16.
12. *Mulki*, or native to the country. It was a movement or identification of those who considered themselves home-born. In this context of the NSL, the discussion of the *mulki*s was in relation to north Indian Muslims who found prominent positions in the Hyderabad administration, many of whom were also involved in the establishment of Osmania University. The Mulki movement emerged again in the 1950s in the discussions of whether Hyderabad should be broken up and split between the bordering states of Andhra, Bombay, and Mysore.
13. Hasan, *Whither Hyderabad?*, 62.
14. See Chapters 3 and 4 on political reforms advocated by the Reforms Committee of 1938.
15. See Karen Leonard, 'The Deccani Synthesis in Old Hyderabad', *Journal of the Pakistan Historical Society* 21, no. 4 (October 1973): 205–218. Also see Margrit Pernau's *The Passing of Patrimonialism: Politics and Political Culture in Hyderabad 1911–1948* (New Delhi: Manohar, 2000).
16. Leonard, 'The Deccani Synthesis', 213, fn. 1.
17. John Roosa, 'The Quandary in the Qaum: Indian Nationalism in a Muslim State, Hyderabad, 1850–1948', PhD dissertation, University of Wisconsin–Madison, 1998, 21.
18. See Carolyn Elliot, 'Decline of a Patrinomial Regime: The Telangana Rebellion in India 1946–1951', *Journal of Asian Studies* 34, no. 4 (November 1974): 27–47. Elliot argues that with the lack of political parties within the Nizam's territories, Hyderabad witnessed more communal and divisive politics rather than an encouragement of coalitions across religious and language affiliations or lines. In other words, Elliot attempts to understand why Hyderabad appears politically backward and resistant to political modernization. If we take Elliot's assessment of the underdevelopment of political conditions in Hyderabad, then it seems likely that a lack of institutional development to garner political sentiment led to the crisis of the integration of the Hyderabad state into the Indian Union. While I am not entirely sympathetic with Elliot's developmental

model of political modernization in her analysis of Hyderabad politics, there clearly was a failure of consensus within Hyderabad on becoming part of the Indian Union.
19. John Roosa, 'The Quandary in the Qaum', 21.
20. To get a sense of the political and social conditions of Hyderabad in this period, Roosa provides figures for the proportion of Muslims and Hindus in the administration. Discerning from the list of civil officials between 1894 and 1931, Roosa writes that the ratio of Hindus and Muslims ranged from about 1:4 to 1:5. In the mid part of the 1880s, Muslims held five out of six posts at the ministerial level, ten out of eighteen posts at the secretarial level, 152 out of 207 in the revenue administration, and finally fifty-two out of fifty-four posts in the courts. See Roosa, 'The Quandary in the Qaum', 134.
21. Roosa, 'The Quandary in the Qaum', 147.
22. Roosa, 'The Quandary in the Qaum', 147.
23. Roosa, 'The Quandary in the Qaum', 410.
24. *Raiyat*, 22 April 1935, quoted in Roosa, 'The Quandary in the Qaum', 411.
25. *Raiyat*, 30 November 1928, quoted in Roosa, 'The Quandary in the Qaum', 411.
26. Janaki Nair, *Mysore Modern: Rethinking the Region under Princely Rule* (Hyderabad: Orient Blackswan, 2011).
27. V. P. Menon, *The Integration of the Indian States* (Madras: Orient Longman, 1995 [1956]), 317.
28. See Srinath Raghavan, *War and Peace in Modern India* (London: Palgrave Macmillan, 2009) and Noorani, *The Destruction of Hyderabad*.
29. Mohamad Siddeek, 'A Letter to Mahatma Gandhi on the Communal Problem in Hyderabad State', Delhi, 23 September 1938, NMML, All India States People Conference (AISPC), File No. 65.
30. Siddeek, 'A Letter to Mahatma Gandhi on the Communal Problem in Hyderabad State'.
31. M. A. Moid and A. Suneetha, 'Rethinking Majlis' Politics: Pre-1948 Muslim Concerns in Hyderabad State', *Indian Economic and Social History Review* 55, no. 1 (2018): 29–52, 40.
32. Aamir Mufti, 'Secularism and Minority: Elements of a Critique', *Social Text*, no. 45 (Winter 1995): 75–96, 84.
33. Mufti, 'Secularism and Minority', 85.
34. Moid and Suneetha, 'Rethinking Majlis' Politics', 45.
35. NMML, AISPC File no. 65, 29 May 1939, 'Letter from Azhar Hassan (Home Secretary to the Nizam) to Kashinathrao Vaidya'.
36. Pernau, *The Passing of Patrimonialism*; Roosa, 'The Quandary in the Qaum'.

37. NMML, AISPC File No. 66, part 1, 'Letter from K. S. Vaidya to Nawab Saeed-ul-Mulk Bahadur, President of the Executive Council of the Hyderabad Government', 21 September 1945. Vaidya criticized the reforms scheme arguing that it was based along communal lines and not democratic.
38. NMML, AISPC File No. 66, part 1, 'Memorandum Presented to the British Parliamentary Delegation at Hyderabad Deccan', 25 January 1946, signed by Kashinathrao Vaidya, Syed Siraj-ul-Hasan Tirmizi, M. Narsing Rao, and G. Ramachar.
39. NMML, AISPC File No. 66, part 1, 'Memorandum Presented to the British Parliamentary Delegation at Hyderabad Deccan', 27.
40. N. Ramesan (ed.), *The Freedom Struggle in Hyderabad*, vol. 4 (Hyderabad: Andhra Pradesh State Archives and Research Institute, 1997), 271.
41. Karen Leonard, 'Hyderabad: The Mulki–Non-Mulki Conflict', *People, Princes and Paramount Power: Society and Politics in the Indian Princely States* (Delhi: Oxford University Press, 1978), 88–89.
42. Kavita S. Datla, 'A Worldly Vernacular: Urdu at Osmania University', *Modern Asian Studies* 43, no. 5 (September 2009): 1117–1148, 1117.
43. Tariq Rahman, 'Urdu in Hyderabad State', *Annual of Urdu Studies* 23, nos. 36–54 (2008): 36–54, 39.
44. Rahman, 'Urdu in Hyderabad State', 41.
45. The Majlis' move to represent the political interests of the Muslims in the Hyderabad state was similar to how Muhammad Ali Jinnah took up the mantle of leading the AIML as the representative of Muslims to seek protections from Hindu majoritarianism.
46. Gummudithala Venkata Subbarao, 'Andhra Province: A Programme. A Boycott Movement Foreshadowed', *Mahratta*, 29 October 1937.
47. 'Support for Hyderabad Freedom Movement', *Indian Express*, 8 August 1947.
48. Hyderabad Andhra Provincial Congress Committee, August 1947.
49. G. V. Subba Rao collection, newspaper clippings, 1947, press statement published on 3 August 1947, Telangana State Archives (TSA), Hyderabad.
50. G. V. Subba Rao collection, newspaper clippings, 1947, press statement published on 3 August 1947, TSA, Hyderabad.
51. See Sunil Purushotham, 'Federating the Raj: Hyderabad, Sovereign Kingship, and Partition', *Modern Asian Studies* 54, no. 1 (2020): 157–198 and Datla, 'Sovereignty and the End of Empire'.
52. Lucien Benichou, *From Autocracy to Integration: Political Developments in Hyderabad State (1938–1948)* (Chennai: Orient Longman, 2000), 137, 147.
53. Mazhar Husain, 'Part II Tables', in *Census of India 1941*, vol. 21: *H.E.H. The Nizam's Dominions (Hyderabad State)* (Hyderabad: Government Press of Hyderabad, 1941), 696.

54. See Ravi Narayana Reddy, *Heroic Telangana: Reminiscences & Experiences* (New Delhi: Communist Party Publications, 1973), 5–6; Narendra Luther, *Hyderabad: A Biography* (New Delhi: Oxford University Press, 2006), 318.
55. Reddy, *Heroic Telangana*, 12.
56. Reddy, *Heroic Telangana*, 14–15.
57. Reddy, *Heroic Telangana*, 16.
58. Reddy, *Heroic Telangana*, 19.
59. Letter from Ravi Narayana Reddy, President of Andhra Conference, to Swami Ramananda Tirtha, 30 July 1946, NMML, AISPC, File No. 66, part 1.
60. Ravi Narayana Reddy, 'Repression in Hyderabad State: Andhra Conference Leaders Interned', NMML, AISPC, File No. 66, part 1.
61. P. Sundarayya, *Vishala Andhra* (Bombay: People's Publishing House, 1945), 3.
62. Sundarayya, *Vishala Andhra*, 3.
63. N. K. Krishnan (ed.), *National Unity for the Defense of the Motherland: Resolutions of the Plenums of the Central Committee of the CPI Held in 1942* (Bombay: People's Publishing House, 1943), 24–25.
64. Sundarayya, *Vishala Andhra*, 72.
65. Sundarayya, *Vishala Andhra*, 73.
66. Bhogaraju Pattabhi Sitaramayya, *The Indian States' People's Conference*, presidential address of Dr B. Pattabhi Sitaramayya, fifth session, 18–19 July 1936, Karachi, 2.
67. Sitaramayya, *The Indian States' People's Conference*, 21.

Conclusion

After Empire

Language and Regionalism

From debates over federation to the place of civil liberties in discourses of democratic reforms in colonial south India, the different chapters in this book have brought into conversation social and political histories of princely Hyderabad with those of the British Indian province of the Madras Presidency—histories that have previously been examined separately. The aim of the book has been to illustrate a dynamic and interconnected history of anti-colonial politics in twentieth-century south India that shaped not only the directly ruled provinces of British India but also the indirectly ruled territories. By using the example of princely Hyderabad to investigate parallel political and cultural developments, the chapters aimed to unravel the Hyderabad state's cross-border connections with neighbouring British Indian provinces—in particular the Telugu-speaking districts that a large part of Hyderabad's people shared linguistic and cultural ties with. In other words, what I have argued is that the rise of liberal politics and the subsequent social and political movements not only shaped British Indian political imaginaries but also those of princely Hyderabad. The dynamism of civil societal institutions in the Telugu-speaking districts across this differentiated political landscape gave rise to two important trends: (*a*) politics based on language and community and (*b*) the proliferation of political ideologies stemming from liberalism to radicalism that complicated independence from colonial rule in 1947–1948 and the making of the modern Indian nation state. With these two processes of political diversification and the rise of language politics, earlier discourses of self-determination from the interwar period (that dominated both princely India and British India) culminated in linguistic regionalism in the late 1940s and into the 1950s, when the Indian Union took up the task of the reorganization of states based on language.

Each chapter of the book shifted between an analysis of the political conditions of the Hyderabad state and the Telugu-speaking districts of the Madras Presidency to reveal how the political and cultural movements that shaped the region's

Conclusion

political imaginaries ultimately culminated in the break-up of the Hyderabad state, making way for the consolidation of the newly independent Indian nation state. While the Nizam's administration took part in federation debates in the 1930s to argue for greater autonomy and the regaining of sovereignty after empire, the discourse of self-determination in British India gave impetus for regional groups to demand provincial autonomy all the while supporting a strong federal centre for the emerging nation state. The break-up of Hyderabad in 1948 was a direct result of the strength of provincial movements encouraged by the INC throughout British India and the princely states—in this case, it was the Andhra movement that shaped Hyderabad's political future. As the previous chapters have shown, the rise of the nation state in South Asia after imperial withdrawal was not a foregone conclusion. Rather, as I have argued throughout the book, the political imaginary of a centralized nation state was forcefully put forward by the INC and its provincial representatives. The most vociferous of INC members on the problem of provincial nationalism and strategies to negotiate a workable Indian union was Bhogaraju Pattabhi Sitaramayya. Sitaramayya, who was himself a Telugu speaker from the northern districts of the Madras Presidency, advocated for a separate APCC in 1916–1917 all the while cautioning the Andhra activists to tread slowly on the issue of a separate province because of the various borders one had to negotiate for any provincial reorganization structure.[1] From granting separate provincial (linguistically based) units to nurturing affiliates in princely states, the INC intervened and shaped debates over what kind of nation would result by knitting together the political futures of the princely states along with those of the regions in British India. These efforts led to the reorganization of provinces into linguistically defined regional states after independence, which ultimately called for the disintegration of the princely states. In 1947, the *Indian Express* reported that independence and the creation of the two nation states of India and Pakistan had 'whetted the people's desire to become free' in princely Hyderabad, Mysore, and Travancore.[2] In August 1947, all of these important princely states in the south were caught up in similar circumstances. Yet it was Hyderabad that remained most recalcitrant in the eyes of outside observers as the Nizam and his administration were trying to negotiate with Louis Mountbatten and the two new nation states. While Muhammad Ali Jinnah wanted the princely states to have the power to decide to remain autonomous or to join either of the two states, Jawaharlal Nehru believed Hyderabad had to be persuaded to join the Indian Union, respecting the wishes of the majority of its people.[3]

The 1940s brought greater division between liberals, conservatives, and radicals, with all of them projecting their competing visions of Hyderabad's political future as well as the future of a Telugu province in independent India.

Historians of Hyderabad have written on the unprecedented violence that erupted at the end of the decade in 1947–1948, when colonial India achieved independence from British imperial rule. Civil unrest from partition violence cascaded throughout the subcontinent—from the borders of East and West Pakistan to the princely states of Hyderabad and Kashmir.[4] Historians have documented the unrest in the princely states as isolated incidences, especially so with respect to princely Hyderabad. However, when delving into why there was heightened communal conflict in the last decade before British withdrawal from the subcontinent, it becomes clear that the violence unleashed was the direct result of a lack of consensus (and community) amongst the rivalling political parties—the Majlis, the HSC, the CPI, and the linguistically defined groups such as the AMS. When the Nizam and his administration reached a standstill agreement with newly independent India, these groups took their grievances to the streets and the countryside. The HSC (in conjunction with the INC) and the Majlis deliberately directed their movement to public protest while the communists organized in the Telangana countryside spilling over into Telugu districts in the Madras Presidency. What ensued was a battle fought by rivalling people's movements who took Hyderabad's future into their own hands. While the Hyderabad administration was firmly positioned centre stage in the decades leading up to the standstill agreement, after British withdrawal from the Indian subcontinent, it no longer had control over popular upsurge unfolding throughout the state.

The *Andhra Herald* on 20 July 1947 published an article titled 'Hyderabad Buzzing with Activity', in which we get a sense of the tension in the air just before the announcement of independence and its impact on Hyderabad's future.[5] The author mocks the Nizam and his intentions of declaring independence from the Indian Union and suggests that all parties seem uncertain as to what the negotiations for a standstill agreement would bring about. While the Majlis was preparing 'Defence Committees', the HSC was trying to organize a future programme as rumours were circulating that their leaders such as Swami Ramanand Tirtha would be rounded up and put in jail. The HSC held its meeting in Sholapur expecting arrests from the state's administration. Meanwhile, the Andhra activists gathered in Bezwada in the neighbouring Madras Presidency. The article also reported that the uncertainty and fear of violent unrest led businesses to move out across state lines. This cross-border movement of INC workers led to a solidarity of Andhras (or Telugu speakers)—what the AMS and the Vishala Andhra movement were both working towards. Meanwhile, an 'Azad Hyderabad Association' was organized to consolidate support for Hyderabad's independence.[6] The president of the Hyderabad Andhra Provincial State Congress (HAPSC) along with the

HSC's president condemned the attempt by the Hyderabad administration to seek entry into the United Nations. Rather, J. Kesava Rao, the president of the HAPSC, argued that this move could push the people of Telangana—the most numerous region in the Hyderabad state—to seek its own path to the Indian Union by merging with the Andhra districts in the Madras Presidency and work towards forming a separate province.[7] The *Indian Express* reported on 27 August 1947 that the HSC condemned the Hyderabad state government and its desire for independence and declared that nothing short of a responsible government (by joining the Indian Union) would be acceptable.[8] The president of the Majlis, Syed Kasim Razvi, lent his support to the Hyderabad administration's move to seek independence—a move that was supported by Jinnah. Ravzi was quoted in an article in *The Hindu* pointing out that Vallabhbhai Patel threatened Hyderabad with an ultimatum that 'if Hyderabad did not join the Union, dire consequences would follow. These threats clearly implied the imposition of economic sanctions and cutting off Hyderabad's communications and transport with the rest of India'.[9] Razvi, however, believed that Hyderabad was powerful enough to defend itself against any 'kingdom' in the world and that it would resist the fate of other princely states in India that were in effect occupied by the Indian Union army. Ravzi was convinced that the Nizam was wrongly advised to join the Indian Union and that only the path of independence would truly take 'the interests of the State at heart'.

Newspapers in August 1947 routinely mentioned communal tension as being high and violence breaking out in the urban and rural areas as the future of Hyderabad was left hanging in limbo. Some sample headlines include the *Times of India*'s 'Causes of Riots in Secunderabad: Alleged Shouting of Slogans' (30 August 1947) and *The Hindu*'s 'More Arrests in Hyderabad' (25 August 1947). Military exercises by any private institution were banned in Hyderabad by the administration seeking to curtail the heightening of communal tension.[10] The *Deccan Chronicle* reported that British Indian publications were being seized within Hyderabad such as the *Janatha*, a socialist publication from Delhi, and the *New Life*, a weekly from Bombay.[11] Hyderabad had long-standing policies of restricting the circulation of British Indian print media as well as regulating those that were printed within the Hyderabad state during the height of anti-colonial nationalism. All of these efforts undertaken by the Hyderabad state were to contain the disparate movements and the increased possibility of violence unleashed onto the streets. As the Chapter 5 documented, by the time India achieved independence in 1947, Hyderabad was in turmoil because of the uncertainty of its political future. An all-encompassing political identity did not emerge that could bind together rivalling political factions in Hyderabad.

Even those alliances that worked together for decades began to fall apart as we witnessed with the AMS in the late 1940s when the liberals parted ways with the radicals. The disarray that the AMS found itself in was also commented on in the confidential fortnightly report of the Hyderabad Residency in July 1944:

> The Nationalist section of the Andhra Conference seem to have realized the mistake they have made in giving place to Communists, and now feel that their policy may result in losing their hold on the public. They are reported to be discussing plans for retiring altogether from the present organization, and for setting up a rival organization. They have not yet handed over office records and certain funds to the Communist section.[12]

When tensions were rising within the AMS in the late 1940s, Mandumula Narsing Rao wrote an editorial in the *Raiyat* against the communist takeover of the association. He retorted that the AMS was 'neither a students' association nor a textile mill workers' union; it is not even a peasant's association (kisan sabha)'. Rather, it was 'a public gathering for representatives of all parties and schools of thought among all social classes and all Andhra people involved in public life'.[13] Narsing Rao attempted to return the AMS to its inclusive days as a public cultural organization representing a multitude of political viewpoints without it becoming a political organ. This is a clear statement of the dynamics of public life and political aspiration that characterized the early decades of the twentieth century and formed the undercurrents of anti-colonial solidarity.

However, the picture that emerges of Hyderabad in the mid- and late 1940s is one of division and communal tension with no single political imaginary that would appeal to the broad swath of the population. As Ian Copland argues, princely Hyderabad was relatively free of communal conflict (as were other princely states) as opposed to in British India in the early decades of the twentieth century where communal tension increased as negotiations over what kind of state would result after British withdrawal.[14] Rather, it was only in the mid-1930s that we see a rise in communal tension between Hindus and Muslims in the Hyderabad state. It would not be wrong then to conclude that the rise of communalism was intimately connected to the success of British Indian organizations such as the Arya Samaj and the Hindu Mahasabha. Alongside these organizations, the INC had been, through its representatives within the state, organizing successfully in Hyderabad to demand civil liberties and political reforms in order to put the state on a path towards representative government. When princely Hyderabad found itself in a precarious position in August 1947, one cannot help but think about alternative trajectories that Hyderabad could have taken if the administration's efforts to build consensus amongst the rivalling groups proved fruitful. The consequences of a princely state such as Hyderabad not coming to an agreement on its political future after empire were dire. Hyderabad in effect was left vulnerable to an eventual break-up or disintegration of the state as I discussed in Chapter 5. The volatility of the political conditions at the time led to the emergence of more powerful forces that were consequential in determining the shape of an Indian union and regional reorganization. Mainly it gave rise to a newly independent India that would be preoccupied with taking up the lingering questions of how to redraw regional boundaries on the basis of language.

Linguistic Reorganization of Regions in Post-Independence India

The INC's organizing proved to be exceptionally successful in striking contrast to the Hyderabad administration's bid for independence, which at the time was nevertheless supported by Jinnah and the AIML. This was a consequence of the INC beginning its plan to not only organize within the princely states starting in the 1920s and make demands for greater civil liberties and responsible government but also accept the idea that language was critical in reorganizing provincial boundaries (which they believed were haphazardly drawn by imperial expediency). This continued discussion and support on the part of the INC sustained linguistic regionalism from the 1920s onwards. In other words, alongside forces compelling the princes to join the Indian Union, the INC began discussions with regards to the linguistic reorganization of states.

In 1946, INC stalwart Sitaramayya published a plea for linguistic reorganization of states addressed to the Constituent Assembly to take up the issue of redrawing of provinces. He quoted John Simon on this particular issue from 1929 to support his plea:

> When we come to consider the constituent elements out of which the federation of British India is to be built we are met with an initial difficulty. Federation schemes usually start with a number of clearly defined States each already possessed individuality and consciousness, whereas in India there are only a number of administrative areas which have grown up almost haphazard as the result of conquest, suppression of former rules or administrative convenience. No one of them has been deliberately formed with a view to its suitability as a self-governing unit within a federated whole. Most of them are populous and extensive, having regard to the cultural level and economic conditions of their inhabitants, to allow of the easy working of the machinery of representative Government on a reasonably extensive franchise.[15]

Sitaramayya's views illustrate for us that the INC did recognize the need for the reorganization of states as far back as 1920, after the Nagpur Congress session in December 1920. It was in 1938 that three new provinces were created by the colonial government taking into account regional and language criteria: Sindh, the North-West Frontier Province, and Orissa.[16] At the time, in 1938, if we recall, V. Ramadas Pantulu argued in his *Memorandum on Andhra Province*:

> The moment we visualize each of the fifteen or sixteen provinces constituted on linguistic basis, functioning each in its own as, fostering its own language, promoting its own culture, imparting its own instruction and administering its justice through its vernacular language and dealing with its villages and their rural problems through the vernaculars of the heart, the very moment we visualize India as a nation whose nationalism is not the steam-road-rolled product exhibiting a dull uniformity, but as a harmonious combination of diverse cultures exhibiting a fundamental unity.[17]

However, since the INC resigned from ministries before World War II, it led to the deferral of the question of Andhra becoming a separate province. Though, as Chapters 1 and 2 illustrated, the question of Andhra forming a new province had many more challenges coming from within the Madras Presidency. Then in 1945–1946, in the election manifestos of the INC, the idea of linguistic provinces was again mentioned:

> It [the INC] has stood for full opportunities for the people as a whole to grow and develop according to their own wishes and genius: It has also stood for the freedom of each group and territorial area within the nation to develop its own culture within the larger frame work and it has stated that for this purpose such territorial area or provinces should be reconstituted, as far as possible, on a linguistic and cultural basis.[18]

The 1948 report of the Linguistic Provinces Commission, or the Dar Commission, suggested that linguistic reorganization should not be conducted hastily. The commission was appointed by the Constituent Assembly on 17 June 1948 to report on the question of formation of the provinces of Andhra, Kerala, Karnataka, and Maharashtra. The commission toured for twenty-six days examining witnesses at Vizagapatam, Madras, Madura, Mangalore, Calicut, and Coimbatore. Another tour took place in October of that year in Hubli, Nagpur, Poona, and Bombay. One anxiety the commission expressed was that the new Indian government was in a critical, volatile state with the recent partitioning of British India, the ongoing war with Pakistan, and the continuing refugee crisis.

Furthermore, complicating the plan to reorganize states on the basis of language was the novel and precarious experiment the new government was embarking on under a new constitution with autonomous states and adult franchise without a national language. While there was a sense that the urgency came from the INC, it stemmed from their promise of forming linguistic provinces which was a concession to the demand emerging from the regional units of the INC. However, this potentially volatile period of transition made it a difficult moment to initiate the process of carving up new states. Finally, the commission also pointed out the necessary time and work involved in building consensus for the reorganization plans.

While the INC clearly supported the idea of a link between language and territory and signalled that they would support linguistic reorganization from the 1920s onwards, they began to hesitate in the immediate post-independence period in the aftermath of partition and communal violence. With newly independent India's forcible takeover of the Hyderabad state from the Nizam's administration in September 1948, Nehru remained hesitant on the issue of the break-up of Hyderabad. Because of the communal violence that erupted in Hyderabad between 1947–1948, Nehru was careful to move gradually on the issue of the future of Hyderabad in relation to the question of linguistic provinces. The communist uprising in Telangana also presented a clear challenge to the newly independent Indian state. At this time, the question of unity and the economic and political integration of India became the primary concern.

ల ల ల

The States Reorganization Commission formed on 29 December 1953 with S. Fazal Ali, H. N. Kunzru, and K. M. Panikkar. It submitted a report in 1955:

> The Commission, after consultations and interactions with various groups of people, is reported to have found the public will in favour of linguistic reorganization. The rationale was that language being the most faithful reflection of the culture of an ethnic group, ethno-lingual boundaries would be considered the most stable and suitable arrangement for the effective working of democratic entities and institutions. It was also perceived that the same would also have the advantage of ease for people's interaction with the government.[19]

These are the opening lines of the States Reorganization Commission's report of 1955, which assessed the territories that were part of the Indian Union:

> The existing structure of the States of the Indian Union is partly the result of accident and the circumstances attending the growth of the British power in India and partly a by-product of the historic process of the integration of former Indian States. The division of India during the British period into British provinces and Indian States was itself fortuitous and had no basis in Indian history. It was a mere accident that, as a result of the abandonment, after the upheaval of 1857, of the objective of extending the British dominion by absorbing princely territories, the surviving States escaped annexation.[20]

Nehru, after the election of 1952, appointed the commission to 'objectively' investigate how best to promote the welfare of the people with each 'constituent unit' of the union.[21] In its assessment of the problem of states, the commission pointed to the accident of empire and conquest that led to the constitution of the provinces and the native states and that these territorial boundaries had no natural or cultural affinities that bound the communities together. The new nation state, it was deemed, should take on the task of reassessing borders or boundaries between the provinces and the native states in order to produce states that aligned with the cultural, political, and economic needs of the peoples and communities. It was a grand task for a young nation state to take on while recovering from violence that erupted from the partition of British India and the integration of the princely or native states into the union (Kashmir and Hyderabad in particular). The commission put out a press release inviting documents from peoples and public organizations on their views and suggestions. As a result, it received around 152, 250 documents ranging from telegrams to memoranda. As part of the framework to objectively assess the needs of the people, the commission embarked on interviewing people and interested public organizations, starting in New Delhi in March 1954 and ending in July 1955. It toured all around India, visiting 104 places and interviewing around 9,000 people.[22] It was an ambitious project for a newly formed nation state and an ambitious task in the history of decolonization to align political boundaries with cultural and economic criteria (attuned to the welfare of the people) and to undo boundary-making that was part and parcel of the exercise of imperial control.

Even before the commission was formed, Andhra was awarded a separate state following the death of Potti Sriramulu (resulting from a hunger strike) in 1952 during protests demanding a separate Andhra state. Andhra became a state in October 1953 after a series of unexpected events. While it seemed clear that the INC was bent on delaying the process of reorganization of states in the immediate post-independence period, the latest generation of Andhra activists stepped up their pressure on the Nehru government. Swami Sitaram, a Gandhian, began a series of fasts for the creation of an Andhra province on 16 August 1951 (until 20 September) and again on 25 May 1952 (until 15 June). Then in December 1952, Sriramulu, another Gandhian, took to a fast that ended with his death. Afterwards, a violent upsurge from the Telugu-speaking population in Madras forced Nehru's government to concede to the creation of an Andhra state. However, the city of Madras was not to be included in the new state—a demand made by Sriramulu and other Andhra activists. This was always the sticking point for the Andhra activists from the 1930s onwards. Most recently, both the Dar Commission and the internal INC report on linguistic reorganization did not see how the city of Madras would ever become part of a new state of Andhra. Meanwhile, in 1952, there was student agitation in Telangana, specifically in Warangal, protesting a potential merger with Andhra.[23] As the break-up of Hyderabad seemed inevitable, there had been a steady movement within Hyderabad towards the formation of Telangana as a separate state. Clearly, there were strong reservations in Telangana against joining Andhra towards a common statehood. In Telangana, a *mulki* agitation erupted between 1948 and 1952 in response to the incoming coastal Telugu speakers who began to take up posts in the administration of Hyderabad in the aftermath of the police action of 1948. Meanwhile, in 1955, the Andhra assembly passed a resolution to form a single state merging with Telangana.[24] However, the majority of members of the parliament in Telangana supported a separate state for Telangana in late 1955. Even the *Golkonda Patrika* switched its support of a united Andhra in 1954 and began to support a separate state of Telangana in 1955.[25] This necessarily raises doubts with regards to the connections between vernacular publics and linguistic nationalism. Telugu publics, as they emerged simultaneously in Telangana (in Hyderabad) and in Andhra (in the Madras Presidency), intersected on many issues ranging from cultural revival to social reform issues and were often in dialogue with one another. However, the shared language did not necessarily lead to the articulation of a singular cultural or regional identity. The Telangana movement was broader than language as it often asserted the idea of *mulki* (native to Hyderabad) rights. Nor did the AMS in Hyderabad necessarily work towards a united Andhra (or Vishala Andhra); rather, it often worked towards a democratic future within the boundaries of a historical Hyderabad. This was the position that Narsing Rao continued to hold. The re-emergence of the Mulki movement after Indian independence and police action in Hyderabad clearly points to the persistence and strength of cross-linguistic solidarities in Hyderabad—a legacy of popular movements that organized to push for political reforms within princely Hyderabad.

The States Reorganization Commission recognized the administrative convenience of language but it, too, hesitated to force Telangana to merge with Andhra. While making statements and acknowledging how there were real differences in Andhra and Telangana, the committee initially rejected that Hyderabad should be retained as a unit. With that premise, it stated the argument for linguistic reorganization for the explicit purpose of the ease of communication within a given state. As such, language became primary in the commission's analysis of how to redraw provinces. With the inevitability of the break-up of Hyderabad, there seemed to be no way of arguing against the linguistic principle to merge Telangana with Andhra even with the growing opposition to the proposal. In order to satisfy the critics of the merger, regional committees were to be formed to deal with the economic inequities between Telangana and Andhra. The lead-up to 1953 when Andhra was formed and to 1956 when Andhra Pradesh was established by including Telangana, a region formerly part of the Hyderabad state, showed fissures between the Telugu-speaking regions of Rayalseema, Telangana, and Coastal Andhra.

From the assurances of responsible government made by the Government of India in the first decade of the twentieth century to its Indian subjects to the post-World War I impact of the language of self-determination, political ideologies erupted into public life and shaped the political aspirations of Indians throughout the subcontinent. Public life, as expressed through civil societal activism in the Madras Presidency and in princely Hyderabad, led to not only cultural revivalism of language and literature but also possibilities for political community and citizenship. The language of self-determination impacted the anti-colonial tenor of Indian nationalism as it seeped into regional discourses of governance and the path towards popular sovereignty. The invocation of P. Sundarayya, a leading figure in the Telangana people's movement, for the language of self-determination in outlining the logic for linguistic provinces in a free Indian Union illustrates the elasticity of these concepts and their mobility in multiple political discourses. Ultimately, popular forces instigated and nurtured by the different political parties anticipated the dissolution of British India into what they considered to be a more rationally ordered group of linguistically organized provinces. Moreover, political aspirations, as they erupted in the AMS in Hyderabad, anticipated the dissolution of the Nizam's monarchical authority as part of the global movement towards representative democracy and popular sovereignty. The Telangana demand, as it was articulated at the time, was a product of this dynamic historical conjuncture between the end of an old monarchical order, the political turmoil in the aftermath, and the inauguration of a new nation state. While protests against Telangana's merger with Andhra were launched between 1948 and 1956, the logic of the linguistic argument made in the States Reorganization Commission took on its own momentum to silence the opposition on the path towards the reorganization of states along language. The confluence of two historical processes— (*a*) the Andhra movement culminating in the creation of a separate state in 1952 and (*b*) the forced integration of princely Hyderabad with the Indian Union in 1948—enabled the language enthusiasts to take advantage of the precarious position of the Hyderabad state and to push through the break-up of the old borders of Hyderabad. And with the concession of the creation of regional committees to assure the equitable distribution of resources in the newly formed Andhra Pradesh, Telangana's merger with Andhra began on an unsure footing.

Congress (INC) Liberalism and Competing Political Ideologies

The last three decades in the twenty-first century have brought forth a resurgence of Hindutva populism in redefining the political legacies of anti-colonial nationalism in India.[26] Hindutva, an extreme version of Hindu nationalism that emerged at the same time as other political ideologies discussed in this book, such as liberalism and communism, had limited influence in princely Hyderabad and in south India.[27] The current Bharatiya Janata Party (BJP) government in power, with the aid of Hindutva ideology, has become increasingly uncomfortable with the country's nationalist past. Hindutva's particular interest in rewriting the nationalist past, rather than the imperial or colonial past, is critical in shaping its political vision. Curiously, the Hindutva movement is not interested in engaging with India's colonial past and legacy. The fact that it places more emphasis on rewriting the nationalist past demonstrates the centrality of nationalist discourse and thought for the broader Hindu right—and as such it is equally important for historians at this current political moment. Our current moment indeed calls on historians to revisit and rethink the different strands of political imaginaries that emerged at the end of the era of European empires. These histories are important because they will help us to understand the competing forces shaping nationalist thought in India—and, by extension, in other post-colonial countries. It would be apt for us to begin by unsettling the assumption of an INC consensus at the moment of independence.

The BJP projects a form of *ressentiment* with the nationalist past, increasingly articulating an ambivalent view of Mohandas K. Gandhi and his politics, combined with an all-out war against Nehru's legacy in the independence movement. Because Nehru, as the first prime minister of India, and Gandhi, as the symbol of the nationalist struggle against the British Empire, are central to the nationalist past, they have become the targets of Hindutva revisionism.

Gandhi is depoliticized as representing the revival of Hindu thought with his reconceptualization and universalizing of *ahimsa* and the philosophy of non-violence for the modern world. The Hindu right pays scant attention to the fact that Gandhi relied deeply on the interpretation of ideas from Leo Tolstoy, John Ruskin, and Henry David Thoreau to develop his concept of *satyagraha*, or the strategy of non-violent resistance. Nehru and his supporters, on the other hand, are perceived as deracinated mimic men who viewed Hindu institutions through Western eyes. The resentment on the part of the Hindu right stems from being left out of the dominant INC nationalist narrative and, they argue, not being given their proper due. Yet, at the turn of the twentieth century, the leaders of the Hindu right's political and cultural movements (the Hindu Mahasabha) were not at the forefront in shaping anti-colonial politics and constitutional discussions at the end of empire. Rather, it was their chauvinistic nationalism that appears in the history, fomenting communal conflict during the height of nationalist agitation—increasing tension between Hindus and Muslims as Hindutva nationalism sought to define the impending nation as Hindu with a great past, enlightened religious thought, and brave monarchs—a past that needed no revision. The Hindu right, in other words, fought not only to defend Hinduism from colonial critique but also, and more importantly, to uphold Hindu institutions against the liberal critique of compatriots who joined the movement in order to disrupt the existing social order and build a new democratic one.

Critique of the INC and Hindu nationalism came from different quarters, especially so from Dalit leaders—the most influential of which was B. R. Ambedkar, who focused on the conservatism of the INC party leaders and their adherence to maintaining Hindu caste order and upper-caste dominance in cultural, social, and political institutions. In south India, the Justice movement and the Self-Respect movement sought to draw attention to caste inequality and the dominance of the Brahman caste in colonial administration and educational institutions. In Hyderabad, Dalit leader Bhagya Reddy Varma joined forces with Hindu religious reformers with the Brahmo Samaj and the Arya Samaj to further caste reform and brahminical conservatism.[28] Ambedkar's ultimate fear as he participated and shaped the political outcome of the nationalist movement was that change in the social order would not come soon enough—that the upper castes, once ensconced in positions of political power in an independent India, would perpetuate Hindu caste hierarchy. Gandhi, too, opposed the transfer of power from English masters to Indian ones without disrupting traditional social hierarchies and working towards a radically new society. Ambedkar's challenge was monumental. It laid bare the tenuousness of INC consensus, revealing rifts between liberals, socialists, and religious nationalists. In *The Hindu*, G. Sampath penned a provocative editorial, titled 'The Missing Conservative Intellectuals', reflecting on the lack of a conservative movement in India. He writes, 'It would be no exaggeration to say that most of India's left-liberal intellectuals (mostly drawn from the upper castes) are socially conservative—and conservative in the classical sense of not considering their society's determining antagonism (caste) as the ultimate problem.'[29] Sampath argues that the left intelligentsia actually remained socially conservative throughout the period of anti-colonial nationalism since they never confronted caste as the real basis of social inequality. One might conclude that INC's pursuit of political liberty dominated nationalist discourse to such an extent that social liberty was indeed deferred.

With these rifts in place between the progressives and the conservatives within the INC, and despite the fact that the Hindu right itself was constituted through a coming together of disparate social and religious reform agendas, Hindu nationalism has found a way back to the nationalist limelight in recent years as majoritarianism or populist insurgents responding to the grievances of the majority. When we attend to these rifts in political and social ideologies in the early twentieth century, it is clear that the clash of nationalisms was never resolved. While those raising calls for regional autonomy were aware of the dangers of majoritarianism, they tried to address those dangers with proposals for federal arrangements. Our current moment urges us to re-examine the nationalist era in order to unravel competing political ideologies and proposals for a democratic future.

Notes

1. Konda Venkatappayya, *The Andhra Movement* (The Andhra Maya Sabha Publication, series no. 1) (Madras: Andhra Maha Sabha Publication, 1938), 26.
2. 'States in South India', *Indian Express*, 25 August 1947.
3. Srinath Raghavan, 'Hyderabad 1947–48', in *War and Peace in Modern India*, 65–100 (London: Palgrave Macmillan, 2010).
4. See Sunil Purushotham, 'Destroying Hyderabad and Making the Nation', *Economic and Political Weekly* 49, no 22 (31 May 2014):29–33; Sunil Purushotham, 'Democratic Origins III: Violence and/in the Making of Indian Democracy', in *Indian Democracy: Origins, Trajectories, Contestations*, edited by Alf Gunvald Nilsen, Kenneth Bo Nielsen, and Anand Vaidya, 39–50 (London: Pluto Press, 2019); and Taylor C. Sherman, *State Violence and Punishment in India* (London: Routledge, 2009).
5. 'Hyderabad Buzzing with Activity', *Andhra Herald*, 20 July 1947.
6. 'Hyderabad Buzzing with Activity'.

7. '"Azad Hyderabad" Cry, A Voice in the Wilderness', 3 August 1947, G. V. Subba Rao Papers, Telangana States Archives (TSA), Hyderabad.
8. 'Hyderabad Congress Rejects Nizam's Reforms: Nothing Short of Responsible Government Is Acceptable', *Indian Express*, 27 August 1947.
9. 'Hyderabad and the Indian Dominion: Majlis Leader Commends Nizam's Attitude', *The Hindu*, 14 September 1947.
10. 'Military Exercises by Private Institutions: Strict Ban to be Imposed', *Deccan Chronicle*, 8 August 1947.
11. 'Surprise Raid by Police on Book Stalls', *Deccan Chronicle*, 23 August 1947.
12. IOR/R/1/1/4179 Hyderabad affairs, appointment of Abdul Hassan Syed Ali as President, Anjuman Ittehadul Muselman, Hyderabad, press articles about post-war position of Hyderabad, fortnightly report of the Hyderabad Residency for the fortnight ending 15 July 1944.
13. John Roosa, 'Passive Revolution Meets Peasant Revolution: Indian Nationalism and the Telangana Revolt', *Journal of Peasant Studies* 28, no, 4 (2001): 57–94, 64.
14. Ian Copland, '"Communalism" in Princely India: The Case of Hyderabad, 1930–1940', *Modern Asian Studies* 22, no. 4 (1988): 783–814.
15. Bhogaraju Pattabhi Sitaramayya, *Convention on Linguistic and Cultural Provinces in India. Delhi, 8th December, 1946: Presidential Address Delivered by B. Pattabhi Sitaramayya* (Delhi: Delhi Printing Works, 1946).
16. *Report of the Linguistic Provinces Commission* (New Delhi: Government of India Press, 1948), 1.
17. *Memorandum on Andhra Province*, part 1: *A General View of the Problems Arising from the Formation of the Andhra Districts of the Madras Presidency into a Separate Province*, with foreword by B. Pattabhi Sitaramayya and published by the Andhra Provincial Congress Committee (Madras: GS Press, 1939), 33.
18. Sitaramayya, *Convention on Linguistic and Cultural Provinces*, 10.
19. *Sri Krishna Committee Report* (Report of Second Commission on Centre–State Relations), vol. 1 (New Delhi: Ministry of Home Affairs, Government of India), 64.
20. *Report of the States Reorganisation Commission* (New Delhi: Government of India Press, 1955), 1.
21. *Report of the States Reorganisation Commission*, i.
22. *Report of the States Reorganisation Commission*, ii.
23. Marshall Windmiller, 'Linguistic Regionalism in India', *Pacific Affairs* 27, no. 4 (December 1954): 291–308, 306.
24. Gautam Pingle, 'The Historical Context of Andhra and Telangana, 1949–1956', *Economic and Political Weekly* 45, no. 8 (20 February 2010): 57–65, 63.
25. Pingle, 'The Historical Context of Andhra and Telangana', 63.

26. Vinayak D. Savarkar came up with the concept of Hindutva as 'Hinduness', a nationalist identity not necessarily tied to the religious identity of being Hindu. This nationalist discourse was a departure from Hindu social reform that focused on religious reform. The Hindu Mahasabha was founded precisely to forge a political identity. There is a vast literature on Hindu nationalism, the Hindu right, and the rise of the BJP in the 1990s. See Christophe Jaffrelot, *The Hindu Nationalist Movement and Indian Politics: 1925 to the 1990s: Strategies of Identity-Building, Implantation and Mobilisation (with Special Reference to Central India)* (London: Hurst, 1996); Thomas Blom Hansen, *The Saffron Wave: Democracy and Hindu Nationalism in Modern India* (Princeton, NJ: Princeton University Press, 1999); John Zavos, *The Emergence of Hindu Nationalism in India* (New Delhi: Oxford University Press, 2000).
27. The Hindu Mahasabha chapter was established in 1923 in Hyderabad after a group led by prominent Hyderabad leaders such as Waman Naik, Vinayak Rao, Bhagya Reddy Varma, and M. Hanumantha Rao in an effort to consolidate Hindu organizations in Hyderabad. See John Roosa, 'The Quandary in the Qaum: Indian Nationalism in a Muslim State, Hyderabad, 1850–1948', PhD dissertation, University of Wisconsin–Madison, 1998, 353–358.
28. See Chinnaiah Jangam, *Dalits and the Making of Modern India* (New Delhi: Oxford University Press, 2017).
29. G. Sampath, *The Hindu*, 25 July 2015.

Bibliography

Archives and Libraries

British Library, London
Acharya, M. K. *India's Self-Determination: An Open Letter to His Excellency Lord Reading.* Madras: Vavilla Press, 1921.
Addresses Delivered at the 7th Session of the Deccan States Subjects' Conference, Bombay, 1927; the Indian States' Peoples' Conference, Bombay, 1927; the Indian States' Subjects' Conference, Madras, 1927; and the Southern States' People's Conference, Trivandrum, 1929. Bombay, 1929.
All-India States Peoples' Conference. *Mr. Bhulabhai J. Desai and The Peoples of the States.* Bombay: All-India States Peoples' Conference, 1947.
Andhra Conferences Committee. *The Andhra Movement.* Guntur: Radha Press, 1913.
Chandramouli, Kalluri. *Nanadesa Rajyanga Niranyanamulu* (An Account of Constitutions of Various Countries). Nidubrolu: Tatamudraksharasalayandu, 1933.
Constitutional Reforms Scheme in Hyderabad State. A memorandum submitted by the Hyderabad State Praja (People's) Party. 19 August 1946.
Digavalli, Venkatasivaravu. *Adinivesya Swarajyamu.* Bezwada: Andhra Grandhalayam Mudraksharasalayam, 1933.
Digavalli, Venkatasivaravu. *Vyavaharakosamu: English–Telugu Dictionary of Technical Terms; Telugu Synonyms, Meanings, Explanations and Definitions of English Words and Phrases Relating to Politics, Economics and Law; Public Finance, Stock Exchange, Business and Cooperation; with a Glossary of Hindustani Words.* Bezwada, 1934.
Gurunatham, J. *Viresalingam: The Founder of Telugu Public Life.* Rajahmundry: Chintamani Printing Works, 1911.
Hasan, Syed Abid. *Whither Hyderabad? A Brief Study of Some of the Outstanding Problems of the Premier Indian State.* Madras: BN Press, 1935.
Hyderabad State Congress. *The Struggle for Freedom in Hyderabad State.* Bombay: Ramkishan Dhoot for the Hyderabad State Congress, 1938.

Bibliography

Pantulu, V. Ramdas. *Memorandum on Andhra Province*, part 1: *A General View of the Problems Arising from the Formation of the Andhra Districts of the Madras Presidency into a Separate Province*, with foreword by B. Pattabhi Sitaramayya and published by the Andhra Provincial Congress Committee. Madras: GS Press, 1939.

Ramadas Pantulu, V. *A General View of the Problems Arising from the Formation of the Andhra Districts of the Madras Presidency into a Separate Province*. Foreword by B. Pattabhi Sitaramayya. Masulipatam: Andhra Provincial Congress Committee, 1939.

Report of the Linguistic Provinces Commission. New Delhi: Government of India Press, 1948.

Report of the Reforms Committee 1938. Hyderabad-Deccan: Government Central Press, 1938.

Report of the Second Godavery District Conference Held at Rajahmundry, on the 8th 9th and 10th June 1896. Rajahmundry: Vivekavardhani Press, 1897.

Report of the Sixth Kistna District Conference held at Bapatla, June 1897. Masulipatam: Bhyrava Press, 1898.

Report of the States Reorganisation Commission. New Delhi: Government of India Press, 1955.

Sitaramayya, Bhogaraju Pattabhi. *Convention on Linguistic and Cultural Provinces in India. Delhi, 8th December, 1946: Presidential Address delivered by B. Pattabhi Sitaramayya*. Delhi: Delhi Printing Works, 1946.

———. *History of the Indian National Congress*, vol. 1: *1885–1935*. New Delhi: S. Chand Publishing, 1969.

———. *Some Fundamentals of the Indian Problem*. Bombay: Vora, 1946.

———. *The Indian States' People's Conference*. Presidential address of Dr B. Pattabhi Sitaramayya, fifth session, 18–19 July 1936, Karachi.

Venkatappayya, Konda. *The Andhra Movement* (The Andhra Maha Sabha Publication, series no. 1). Madras: Andhra Maha Sabha Publication, 1938.

Voice of Progress. A monthly journal (in English, Tamil, and Telugu) conducted by a Committee of the Madras Hindu Social Reform Association 1, nos. 1–8 (October 1901–May 1902).

Center for Research Libraries, Chicago, IL

Federated India, 1932–1939.

Madras Legislative Council Debates.

Madras Legislative Debates.

Work in England of the Deputation of the Indian States People's Conference. Poona: Aryabhushan Press, 1929.

Nehru Memorial Museum and Library, New Delhi
All-India States Peoples' Conference, 1933–1949.
Oral history transcripts.

Telangana State Archives (TSA), Hyderabad
Constitutional Affairs Secretariat.
G. V. Subba Rao collection.
Nizam Political Department.

Other Primary Sources
Adhikari, G. *Pakistan and National Unity: The Communist Solution*. Bombay: People's Publishing House, 1944.

Andhra Mahasabha Proceedings. Hyderabad: Golkonda Press, 1936.

Andhraratna D. Gopalakrishnayya. *Life and Message*. Goshti Book House, 1928.

Das, Chittaranjan. *Freedom through Disobedience*. Madras: Arka Publishing House, 1922.

Gandhi, Mohandas K. *'Hind Swaraj' and Other Writings* (Cambridge Texts in Modern Politics), edited by Anthony Parel. Cambridge, UK: Cambridge University Press, 1997.

Hanumantha Rao, Madapati. *Telangana Andhrodyamamu* (Telangana Andhra Movement). Hyderabad: Telugu Viswavidyalayam, 2000 (1949).

Harisarvottamaravu, Gadicherla. *Votu*. Bezwada: Andhra Parishad, 1923.

Haskar, K. N., and K. M. Panikkar. *Federal India*. London: Martin Hopkinson, 1930.

H. E. H. The Nizam's Educational Department. *Curriculum for Primary and Middle Schools*. Hyderabad: Government Central Press, 1931.

Husain, Mazhar. 'Part II Tables'. In *Census of India 1941*, vol. 21: *H.E.H. The Nizam's Dominions (Hyderabad State)*. Hyderabad: Government Press of Hyderabad, 1941.

Krishnan, N. K. (ed.). *National Unity for the Defense of the Motherland: Resolutions of the Plenums of the Central Committee of the CPI Held in 1942*. Bombay: People's Publishing House, 1943.

Lohia, Ram Manohar. *The Struggle for Civil Liberties* (All India Congress Committee, 1936), with a foreword by Jawaharlal Nehru. Allahabad: Foreign Department, All India Congress Committee, 1936.

Nehru, Jawaharlal. 'The Unity of India'. *Foreign Affairs*, January 1938.

Nizam Rashtra Andhra Mahasabha, vols. 1–2. Hyderabad: Golkonda Mudraksharasaala, 1936.

Ramesan, N. (ed.). *The Freedom Struggle in Hyderabad*, vol. 4. Hyderabad: Andhra Pradesh State Archives and Research Institute, 1997.

Ranade, Mahadev. *Miscellaneous Writings of the late Hon'ble Mr Justice M.G. Ranade.* New Delhi: Sahitya Akademi, 1992.
Rao, Mandumula Narsing. *Yabhai Samvatsaramula Hyderabad.* Hyderabad: Mandumula Narasingaravu Smaraka Samiti, 1977.
Razvi, S. M. Jawad. *Political Awakening in Hyderabad.* Hyderabad: Visalandhra Publishing House, 1980.
Reddy, Ravi Narayana. *Heroic Telangana: Reminiscences and Experiences.* New Delhi: Communist Party Publications, 1973.
Reddy, Suravaram Pratapa. *Prajaadhikaaramulu* (People's Rights). 1953 (1938).
Report on India's Constitutional Reforms. Calcutta: Superintendent of Government Printing, India, 1918.
Sri Krishna Committee Report (Report of Second Commission on Centre–State Relations), vol. 1 New Delhi: Ministry of Home Affairs, Government of India.
Sundarayya, P. *Telangana People's Struggle and Its Lessons.* New Delhi: Foundation Books, 2006 (1972).
———. *Vishala Andhra.* Bombay: People's Publishing House, 1945.
Vadivelu, A. *The Aristocracy of Southern India.* Madras: Vest and Co., 1903.
Venkatappayya, Konda. *Adhunika Rajyanga Samasthalu.* 1932.
Work in England of the Deputation of the Indian States People's Conference. Poona: Aryabhushan Press, 1929.

Secondary Sources

Anghie, Anthony. *Imperialism, Sovereignty, and the Making of International Law.* Cambridge, UK: Cambridge University Press, 2005.
Ansari, Sarah, and William Gould. *Boundaries of Belonging: Localities, Citizenship and Rights in India and Pakistan.* Cambridge, UK: Cambridge University Press, 2019.
Austin, Granville. *The Indian Constitution: Cornerstone of a Nation.* New Delhi: Oxford University Press, 2002 [1966].
Aydin, Cemil. *The Politics of Anti-Westernism in Asia: Visions of World Order in Pan-Islamic and Pan-Asian Thought.* New York: Columbia University Press, 2007.
Baker, Christopher John. *The Politics of South India 1920–1937.* Cambridge, UK: Cambridge University Press, 1976.
Barnett, Marguerite Ross. *The Politics of Cultural Nationalism in South India.* Princeton, NJ: Princeton University Press, 1976.
Baruah, Sanjib. *India against Itself: Assam and the Politics of Nationality.* New Delhi: Oxford University Press, 1999.
Basu, Srimati. *The Trouble with Marriage: Feminists Confront Law and Violence in India.* Berkeley: University of California Press, 2015.

Bate, Bernard. *Tamil Oratory and the Dravidian Aesthetic: Democratic Practice in South India*. New York: Columbia University Press, 2009.

———. 'The Ethics of Textuality: The Protestant Sermon and the Tamil Public Sphere'. In *Ethical Life in South Asia*, edited by Anand Pandian and Daud Ali, 101–115. Bloomington: Indiana University Press, 2010.

———. '"To Persuade Them into Speech and Action": Oratory and the Tamil Political, Madras, 1905–1919'. *Comparative Studies in Society and History* 55, no. 1 (2013): 142–166.

Bayly, C. A. *Empire and Information: Intelligence Gathering and Social Communication in India, 1780–1870*. Cambridge, UK: Cambridge University Press, 2000.

———. *Recovering Liberties: Indian Thought in the Age of Liberalism and Empire*. Cambridge, UK: Cambridge University Press, 2012.

Benichou, Lucien. *From Autocracy to Integration: Political Developments in Hyderabad State (1938–1948)*. Chennai: Orient Longman, 2000.

Benton, Lauren. *The Search for Sovereignty and Law and Colonial Cultures* (Studies in Comparative World History). Cambridge, UK: Cambridge University Press, 2001.

Beverley, Eric Lewis. *Hyderabad, British India, and the World: Muslim Networks and Minor Sovereignty, c. 1850–1950*. New York: Cambridge University Press, 2015.

Bhagavan, Manu. 'Princely States and the Making of Modern India: Internationalism, Constitutionalism and the Postcolonial Moment'. *Indian Economic and Social History Review* 46, no. 3 (2009): 427–456.

———. 'Reflections on Indian Internationalism and a Postnational Global Order: A Response to Partha Chatterjee'. *Comparative Studies of South Asia, Africa and the Middle East* 37, no. 2 (August 2017): 220–225.

Bhukya, Bhangya. *Subjugated Nomads: The Lambadas under the Rule of the Nizams*. Hyderabad: Orient Blackswan, 2010.

Bose, Neilesh. *Recasting the Region: Language, Culture, and Islam in Colonial Bengal*. New Delhi: Oxford University Press, 2014.

Casolari, Marzia. 'Hindutva's Foreign Tie-Up in the 1930s: Archival Evidence'. *Economic and Political Weekly* 35, no. 4 (22 January 2000): 218–228.

Chatterjee, Partha. 'A Religion of Urban Domesticity: Sri Ramakrishna and the Calcutta Middle Class'. *Subaltern Studies* 7, no. 7 (1992): 40–68.

———. 'Nationalism, Internationalism and Cosmopolitanism'. *Comparative Study of South Asia, Africa and the Middle East* 36, no. 2 (2016): 320–334.

———. 'The Curious Career of Liberalism in India'. *Modern Intellectual History* 8, no. 3 (2011): 687–696.

———. *The Nation and Its Fragments*. Princeton, NJ: Princeton University Press, 1993.

Cohen, Benjamin B. *Kingship and Colonialism in India's Deccan: 1850–1948*. New York: Palgrave Macmillan, 2007.

Cohn, Bernard. *Colonialism and Its Forms of Knowledge: The British in India*. Princeton, NJ: Princeton University Press, 1996.

Collins, Michael. 'Decolonisation and the "Federal Moment"'. *Diplomacy & Statecraft* 24, no. 1 (2013): 21–40.

Cooper, Frederick. *Citizenship between Empire and Nation: Remaking France and French Africa, 1945–1960*. Princeton, NJ: Princeton University Press. Kindle edition.

Copland, Ian. '"Communalism" in Princely India: The Case of Hyderabad, 1930–1940'. *Modern Asian Studies* 22, no. 4 (1988): 783–814.

———. 'The Princely States, the Muslim League, and the Partition of India in 1947'. *International History Review* 13, no. 1 (February 1991): 38–69.

———. *The Princes of India in the Endgame of Empire, 1917–1947*. Cambridge, UK: Cambridge University Press, 1997.

Dasgupta, Sandipto. '"A Language Which Is Foreign to Us": Continuities and Anxieties in the Making of the Indian Constitution'. *Comparative Studies of South Asia, Africa and the Middle East* 34, no. 2 (2014): 228–242.

Datla, Kavita S. 'A Worldly Vernacular: Urdu at Osmania University'. *Modern Asian Studies* 43, no. 5 (September 2009): 1117–1148.

———. 'Sovereignty and the End of Empire: The Transition to Independence in Colonial Hyderabad'. *Ab Imperio* 3 (2018): 63–88.

———. *The Language of Secular Islam: Urdu Nationalism and Colonial India*. Honolulu: University of Hawaii Press, 2013.

———. 'The Origins of Indirect Rule in India: Hyderabad and the British Imperial Order'. *Law and History Review* 33, no. 2 (May 2015): 321–350.

De, Rohit. 'Rebellion, Dacoity, and Equality: The Emergence of the Constitutional Field in Postcolonial India'. *Comparative Studies of South Asia, Africa and the Middle East* 34, no. 2 (2014): 260–278.

Devji, Faisal. *Muslim Zion: Pakistan as a Political Idea*. Cambridge, MA: Harvard University Press, 2013.

Dirks, Nicholas. *Castes of Mind: Colonialism and the Making of Modern India*. Princeton, NJ: Princeton University Press, 2001.

Elliot, Carolyn. 'Decline of a Patrimonial Regime: The Telangana Rebellion in India 1946–1951'. *Journal of Asian Studies* 34, mo. 4 (November 1974): 27–47.

Erdman, Howard. *The Swatantra Party and Indian Conservatism*. Cambridge, UK: Cambridge University Press, 1967.

Frykenberg, Robert Eric. *Guntur District, 1788–1848: A History of Local Influence and Central Authority in South India*. New York: Oxford University Press, 1965.

Getachew, Adom. 'Securing Postcolonial Independence: Kwame Nkrumah and the Federal Idea in the Age of Decolonization'. *Ab Imperio* 3 (2018): 89–113.

———. *Worldmaking after Empire: The Rise and Fall of Self-Determination*. Princeton, NJ: Princeton University Press, 2019.

Gilmartin, David. 'Nationalism, Internationalism, Cosmopolitanism—and Empire'. *Comparative Studies of South Asia, Africa and the Middle East* 37, no. 2 (August 2017): 185–189.

———. 'Towards a Global History of Voting: Sovereignty, the Diffusion of Ideas, and the Enchanted Individual'. *Religions* 3 (2012): 407–423.

Goswami, Manu. 'Autonomy and Comparability: Notes on the Anticolonial and the Postcolonial'. *boundary 2* 32, no. 2 (2005): 201–225.

———. 'Colonial Internationalisms and Imaginary Futures'. *American Historical Review* 117, no. 5 (2012): 1461–1485.

———. 'Swadeshi to Swaraj: Nation, Economy, Territory in Colonial South Asia, 1870 to 1907'. *Comparative Studies in Society and History* 40, no. 4 (October 1998): 609–636.

Gundimeda, Sambaiah, 'Mapping Dalit Politics in Contemporary India: A Study of UP and AP from an Ambedkarite Perspective'. PhD thesis, Department of Politics, SOAS, University of London, 2013.

Hansen, Thomas Blom. *The Saffron Wave: Democracy and Hindu Nationalism in Modern India*. Princeton, NJ: Princeton University Press, 1999.

Hatcher, Brian. 'Bourgeois Vedānta: The Colonial Roots of Middle-Class Hinduism'. *Journal of the American Academy of Religion* 75, no. 2 (June 2007): 1–26.

———. *Idioms of Improvement: Vidyasagar and Cultural Encounter in Bengal*. New Delhi: Oxford University Press, 2001.

Ingram, Brannon, and J. Barton Scott, 'What Is a Public? Notes from South Asia'. *South Asia: The Journal of South Asian Studies* 38, no 3 (2015): 357–370.

Irschick, Eugene F. *Politics and Social Conflict in South India: The Non-Brahman Movement and Tamil Separatism, 1916–1929*. Berkeley: University of California Press, 1969.

Jaffrelot, Christophe. *The Hindu Nationalist Movement and Indian Politics: 1925 to the 1990s: Strategies of Identity-Building, Implantation and Mobilisation (with Special Reference to Central India)*. London: Hurst, 1996.

Jangam, Chinnaiah. *Dalits and the Making of Modern India*. New Delhi: Oxford University Press, 2017.

Jeffries, Robin. 'Telugu: Ingredients of Growth and Failure'. *Economic and Political Weekly* (1 February 1997): 192–195.

Jha, Munmun. 'Nehru and Civil Liberties in India'. *International Journal of Human Rights* 7, no. 3 (2003): 103–115.

Jha, Shefali. 'Democracy on a Minor Note: The All-India Majlis-e-ittehad'ul Muslimin and Its Hyderabadi Muslim Publics'. PhD dissertation, University of Chicago, 2017.

Jones, Kenneth. *Socio-Religious Reform Movements in British India*. Cambridge, UK: Cambridge University Press, 1989.

Kapila, Shruti. 'Self, Spencer and Swaraj: Nationalist Thought and Critiques of Liberalism, 1890–1920'. *Modern Intellectual History* 4, no. 1 (2007): 109–127.

Kamat, Sangeeta. 'Neoliberalism, Urbanism and the Education Economy: Producing Hyderabad as a "Global City"'. *Discourse Studies in the Cultural Politics of Education* 32, no. 2 (May 2011): 187–202.

Kopf, David. *British Orientalism and the Bengal Renaissance*. Calcutta: Firma K. L. Mukhopadhyay, 1969.

Lee, Christopher. *Making a World after Empire: The Bandung Moment and Its Political Afterlives*. Athens, OH: Ohio University Press, 2010.

Legg, Stephen. 'Political Lives at Sea: Working and Socialising to and from the India Round Table Conference in London, 1930–1932'. *Journal of Historical Geography* 68 (April 2020): 21–32.

Leonard, John Greenfield. 'Kandukuri Viresalingam, 1848–1919: A Biography of an Indian Social Reformer'. PhD dissertation, University of Wisconsin–Madison, 1970.

Leonard, Karen. 'The Deccani Synthesis in Old Hyderabad'. *Journal of the Pakistan Historical Society* 21, no. 4 (October 1973): 205–218.

———. 'Hyderabad: The Mulki–Non-Mulki Conflict', *People, Princes and Paramount Power: Society and Politics in the Indian Princely States.* Delhi: Oxford University Press, 1978.

Louro, Michele L. *Comrades against Imperialism: Nehru, India, and Interwar Internationalism*. Cambridge, UK: Cambridge University Press, 2018.

Luther, Narendra. *Hyderabad: A Biography*. New Delhi: Oxford University Press, 2006.

Manela, Erez. 'Imagining Woodrow Wilson in Asia: Dreams of East–West Harmony and the Revolt against Empire in 1919'. *American Historical Review* 111, no. 5 (December 2006): 1327–1351.

———. *The Wilsonian Moment Self-Determination and the Origins of Anticolonial Nationalism*. New York: Oxford University Press, 2007.

Manjapra, Kris. *M. N. Roy: Marxism and Colonial Cosmopolitanism*. New Delhi: Routledge, 2010.

Mantena, Karuna. *Alibis of Empire: Henry Maine and the Ends of Liberal Imperialism*. Princeton, NJ: Princeton University Press, 2010.

Mantena, Rama Sundari. 'The Andhra Movement, Hyderabad State and the Historical Origins of the Telangana Demand'. *India Review* 13, no. 4 (2014): 337–357.

———. *The Origins of Modern Historiography in India: Antiquarianism and Philology, 1780–1880*. New York: Palgrave Macmillan, 2012.

———. 'Vernacular Futures: Colonial Philology and the Idea of History in Nineteenth-Century South India'. *Indian Economic and Social History Review* 42, no. 4 (2005): 513–534.

———. 'Vernacular Publics and Political Modernity: Language and Progress in Colonial South India'. *Modern Asian Studies* 47, no. 5 (2013): 1678–1705.

Mehta, Uday. *Liberalism and Empire: A Study in Nineteenth-Century British Liberal Thought*. Chicago: University of Chicago Press, 1999.

Menon, V. P. *The Integration of the Indian States*. Madras: Orient Longman, 1995 [1956].

———. *The Transfer of Power in India*. Calcutta: Orient Longman, 1957.

Mishra, Pritipuspa Amarnath. 'Beyond Powerlessness: Institutional Life of the Vernacular in the Making of Modern Orissa (1866–1931)'. *The Indian Economic and Social History Review* 48, no. 4 (2011): 531–570.

———. 'Divided Loyalties: Citizenship, Regional Identity and Nationalism in Eastern India (1866–1931)'. PhD dissertation, University of Minnesota, 2008.

Mitchell, Lisa. *Language, Emotion, and Politics in South India: The Making of a Mother Tongue*. Bloomington: Indiana University Press, 2009.

Moid, M. A., and A. Suneetha. 'Rethinking Majlis' Politics: Pre-1948 Muslim Concerns in Hyderabad State'. *Indian Economic and Social History Review* 55, no. 1 (2018): 29–52.

Moyn, Samuel. *The Last Utopia: Human Rights in History*. Cambridge, MA: Harvard University Press, 2010.

Mufti, Aamir. 'Secularism and Minority: Elements of a Critique'. *Social Text*, no. 45 (Winter 1995): 75–96.

Mukherjee, Mithi. 'The British Empire in India: A Liberal Empire?' *Comparative Studies of South Asia, Africa and the Middle East* 34, no. 3 (2014): 625–630.

Murthy, N. Chandra Bhanu. 'Identity, Autonomy and Emancipation: The Agendas of the Adi-Andhra Movement in South India, 1917–30'. *Indian Economic and Social History Review* 53, no. 2 (2016): 225–248.

Nair, Janaki. *Mysore Modern: Rethinking the Region under Princely Rule*. Hyderabad: Orient Blackswan, 2011.

Naregal, Veena. *Language Politics, Elites, and the Public Sphere: Western India under Colonialism*. New Delhi: Permanent Black, 2001.

Noorani, A. G. *The Destruction of Hyderabad*. London: Hurst, 2014.

Orsini, Francesca. *The Hindi Public Sphere, 1920–1940: Language and Literature in the Age of Nationalism*. New York: Oxford University Press, 2002.

Overstreet, Gene D., and Marshall Windmiller. *Communism in India*. Bombay: Perennial Press, 1960.

Pandian, M. S. S. 'Beyond Colonial Crumbs: Cambridge School, Identity Politics and Dravidian Movement(s)'. *Economic and Political Weekly* 30, nos. 7–8 (February 1995): 385–391.

———. *Brahmin and Non-Brahmin: Genealogies of the Tamil Present*. New Delhi: Permanent Black, 2007.

———. 'From Culture to Politics: The Justice Party'. In *Brahmin and Non-Brahmin: Genealogies of the Tamil Present*, 144–186. New Delhi: Permanent Black, 2007.

———. 'One Step outside Modernity: Caste, Identity Politics and Public Sphere'. *Economic and Political Weekly* 37, no. 18 (4 May 2002): 1735–1741.

———. 'The Brahmin as a Trope: The Self-Respect Movement'. In *Brahmin and Non-Brahmin: Genealogies of the Tamil Present* (New Delhi: Permanent Black, 2007): 187–232.

Parasher, Tejas. 'Federalism, Representation, and Direct Democracy in 1920s India'. *Modern Intellectual History* 19, no. 2 (June 2022): 444–472.

Pernau, Margrit. *The Passing of Patrimonialism: Politics and Political Culture in Hyderabad 1911–1948*. New Delhi: Manohar, 2000.

Pederson, Susan. *The Guardians: The League of Nations and the Crisis of Empire*. New York: Oxford University Press, 2015.

Pillai, Sarath. 'Fragmenting the Nation: Divisible Sovereignty and Travancore's Quest for Federal Independence'. *Law and History Review* 34, no. 3 (August 2016): 743–782.

Pingle, Gautam. 'The Historical Context of Andhra and Telangana, 1949–1956'. *Economic and Political Weekly* 45, no. 8 (20 February 2010): 57–65.

Pitts, Jennifer. *A Turn to Empire: The Rise of Imperial Liberalism in Britain and France*. Princeton, NJ: Princeton University Press, 2009.

P. Sundarayya. *Telangana People's Struggle and Its Lessons*. New Delhi: Foundation Books, 2006 (1972).

Purushotham, Sunil. 'Democratic Origins III: Violence and/in the Making of Indian Democracy'. In *Indian Democracy: Origins, Trajectories, Contestations*, edited by Alf Gunvald Nilsen, Kenneth Bo Nielsen, and Anand Vaidya, 39–50. London: Pluto Press, 2019.

———. 'Destroying Hyderabad and Making the Nation'. *Economic and Political Weekly* 29, no 22 (31 May 2014): 29–33.

———. 'Federating the Raj'. *Modern Asian Studies* 54, no. 1 (2020): 157–198.

———. *From Raj to Republic: Sovereignty, Violence, and Democracy in India*. Stanford, CA: Stanford University Press, 2021.

———. 'Internal Violence: The "Police Action" in Hyderabad'. *Comparative Studies in Society and History* 57, no. 2 (2015): 435–466.

Raghavan, Srinath. *War and Peace in Modern India*. London: Palgrave Macmillan, 2009.
Rahman, Tariq. 'Urdu in Hyderabad State'. *Annual of Urdu Studies* 23 (2008): 36–54.
Ramakrishna, Vakulabharanam. *Social Reform in Andhra (1848–1919)*. New Delhi: Vikas Publishing, 1983.
Ramaswamy, Sumathi. *Passions of the Tongue: Language Devotion in Tamil India, 1891–1970*. Berkeley: University of California Press, 1997.
Ramusack, Barbara. *The Indian Princes and Their States* (The New Cambridge History of India). Cambridge, UK: Cambridge University Press, 2007.
Rao, K. V. Narayana. *The Emergence of Andhra Pradesh*. Bombay: Popular Prakashan, 1976.
Rao, Velcheru Narayana. 'Print and Prose: Pundits, Karanams, and the East India Company in the Making of Modern Telugu'. In *India's Literary History: Essays on the Nineteenth Century*, edited by Stuart Blackburn and Vasudha Dalmia, 146–166. New Delhi: Permanent Black, 2004.
Rao, G. Venkatasubba. 'From 1947–1954'. *Goshti* 10, no. 1 (October 1954): 3–4.
Ray, Bharati. *Hyderabad and British Paramountcy, 1858–1883*. New York: Oxford University Press, 1988.
Raychaudhuri, T. *Europe Reconsidered: Perceptions of the West in Nineteenth-Century Bengal*. Delhi: Oxford University Press, 1988.
Reddy, C. R. 'Dyarchy and After'. *Indian Review* 23, no. 5 (May 1922): 294–304.
Reddy, Gautham. 'The Andhra Sahitya Parishat: Language, Nation and Empire in Colonial South India (1911–15)'. *Indian Economic and Social History Review* 56, no, 3 (2019): 283–310.
Reddy, G. Sudarshan. 'Caste Reform in Andhra 1900–1930'. *Proceedings of the Indian History Congress* 63 (2002): 855–863.
Roosa, John. 'Passive Revolution Meets Peasant Revolution: Indian Nationalism and the Telangana Revolt'. *Journal of Peasant Studies* 28, no, 4 (2001): 57–94.
———. 'The Quandary in the Qaum: Indian Nationalism in a Muslim State, Hyderabad, 1850–1948', PhD dissertation, University of Wisconsin–Madison, 1998.
Rudolph, Lloyd I., and Susanne Hoeber Rudolph. 'Federalism as State Formation in India: A Theory of Shared and Negotiated Sovereignty'. *International Political Science Review (Revue Internationale de Science Politique)* 31, no. 5 (2010): 553–572.
Sarkar, Tanika. 'A Prehistory of Rights: The Age of Consent Debate in Colonial Bengal'. *Feminist Studies* 26, no. 3 (Autumn 2000): 601–622.
Sartori, Andrew. 'The British Empire and Its Liberal Mission'. *Journal of Modern History* 78, no. 3 (September 2006): 623–642.

Bibliography

Scott, J. Barton. *Spiritual Despots: Hinduism and the Genealogies of Self-Rule*. Chicago: University of Chicago Press, 2016.

Schmithenner, Peter. *Telugu Resurgence: C.P. Brown and Cultural Consolidation in Nineteenth-Century South India*. New Delhi: Manohar, 2001.

Sen, Sudipta. 'Liberalism and the British Empire in India'. *Journal of Asian Studies* 74 (2015): 711–722.

Sever, Adrian (ed.). *Documents and Speeches on the Indian Princely States*, vol. 2. New Delhi: B. R. Publishing Corporation, 1985.

Sherman, Taylor C. *Muslim Belonging in Secular India: Negotiating Citizenship in Postcolonial Hyderabad*. Cambridge, UK: Cambridge University Press, 2015.

———. *State Violence and Punishment in India*. London: Routledge, 2009.

———. 'The Integration of the Princely State of Hyderabad and the Making of the Postcolonial State in India, 1948-56'. *Indian Economic Social History Review* 44 (2007): 489–516.

Sherman, Taylor, William Gould, and Sarah Ansari. 'From Subjects to Citizens: Society and the Everyday State in India and Pakistan, 1947–1970'. *Modern Asian Studies,* 45, no. 1 (January 2011): 1–6.

Sinha, Mrinalini. 'Is "Region" Still Good to Think?' *Comparative Studies of South Asia, Africa and the Middle East* 33, no. 3 (2013): 264–267.

———. 'Premonitions of the Past'. *Journal of Asian Studies* 74, no. 4 (2015): 821–884.

———. *Specters of Mother India: The Global Structuring of an Empire*. Durham, NC: Duke University Press, 2006.

Srinivas, S. V. 'Maoism to Mass Culture: Notes on Telangana's Cultural Turn'. *South Asian Screen Studies* 6, no. 2 (1 July 2015): 187–205.

Srinivasan, Vasanthi. *Gandhi's Conscience Keeper: C. Rajagopalachari and Indian Politics*. New Delhi: Permanent Black, 2009.

Stokes, Eric. *The English Utilitarians and India*. Delhi: Oxford University Press, 1982.

Sultan, Nazmul S. 'Between the Many and the One: Anticolonial Federalism and Popular Sovereignty'. *Political Theory* 50, no. 2 (2021): 247–274. DOI: 10.1177/00905917211018534.

———. 'Self-Rule and the Problem of Peoplehood in Colonial India'. *American Political Science Review* 114, no. 1 (2020): 81–94.

Suntharalingam, R. *Politics and Nationalist Awakening in South India, 1852–1891*. Tucson, AZ: University of Arizona Press, 1974.

Tareen, Sherali. 'Narratives of Emancipation in Modern Islam: Temporality, Hermeneutics, and Sovereignty'. *Islamic Studies* 52, no. 1 (Spring 2013): 5–28.

Tillin, Louise. 'India's Democracy at 70: The Federalist Compromise'. *Journal of Democracy* 28, no. 3 (July 2017): 64–75.

Vakulabharanam, Rajagopal. 'Anti-Reform Discourse in Andhra: Instance of Failed Cultural Nationalism?'. In *Ritual, Caste, and Religion in Colonial South India*, edited by Heiko Free, Michael Bergunder, and Ulrike Schroder, 310–329. Delhi: Primus Books, 2011.

———. 'Fashioning Modernity in Telugu: Viresalingam and His Interventionist Strategy'. *Studies in History* 21, no. 1 (2005): 45–77.

———. 'Left Cultural Movement in Andhra Pradesh: 1930s to 1950s'. *Social Scientist* 40, nos. 1–2 (January–February 2012): 21–30.

———. 'Self and Society in Transition: A Study of Autobiographical Practice in Telugu'. PhD dissertation, University of Wisconsin–Madison, 2004.

Venkatarangaiya, M. (ed.). *The Freedom Struggle in Andhra Pradesh (Andhra)*, vol. 1: *1800–1905 A.D.* Hyderabad: AP State Archives and Research Institute, 1965.

———. (ed.). *The Freedom Struggle in Andhra Pradesh (Andhra)*, vol. 2: *1906–1920 A.D.* Hyderabad: AP State Archives and Research Institute, 1969.

Vora, Rajendra, and Anne Feldhaus. *Region, Culture, and Politics in India*. New Delhi: Manohar, 2006.

Washbrook, David. *The Emergence of Provincial Politics: The Madras Presidency 1870–1920*. Cambridge, UK: Cambridge University Press, 1976.

Wilder, Gary. *Freedom Time: Negritude, Decolonization, and the Future of the World*. Durham, NC: Duke University Press, 2015.

Windmiller, Marshall. 'Linguistic Regionalism in India'. *Pacific Affairs* 27, no. 4 (December 1954): 291–308.

Witmer, Michael. 'The 1947–1948 India–Hyderabad Conflict: Realpolitik and The Formation of The Modern Indian State'. PhD dissertation, Temple University, Philadelphia, 1996.

Zavos, John. *The Emergence of Hindu Nationalism in India*. New Delhi: Oxford University Press, 2000.

Index

Abbas, Sayed Mohamad, 149
Abhyankar, G. R., 112
Adhikari, Gangadhar, 68, 96–97, 195
Adi Andhra Maha Sabha, 16, 79
administrative convenience, idea of, 82
adult franchise, 211
African Union, 110
agitational politics, 69
ahimsa, reconceptualization and universalizing of, 216
Aiyangar Committee, 160
Aiyangar, Dewan Bahadur Aravamudu, 157
'alien' culture and society, 123
Ali, S. Fazal, 211
All India Congress Committee
  Jubbulpore session (24–25 April 1935), 7
All-India Federation, 119–120, 123
All-India Harijan Sevak Sangh, 193
All-India Muslim League (AIML), 5–7, 9, 33, 68, 96–97, 107, 119, 156, 168–169, 191, 195, 202, 209
All-India States Peoples' Conference (AISPC), 98, 111–112, 120, 123–125, 129, 139, 142–143, 151, 153–154, 156, 159, 168n46, 168n53, 171, 194, 198
  aim to create a forum for all states' peoples' organizations, 129
  Bombay conference of, 123
  Trivandrum conference of, 124
All-India States' Workers' Convention, 159
Ambedkar, B. R., 122, 216
  criticism of INC politics and Gandhian tactics, 107
  representation of Dalits, 119
American Civil Liberties Union (ACLU), 140
Amrutha Bazaar Patrika, 145
ancient Indian aristocracy, 57
'ancient regime' cosmopolitanism, 4
Andhra (English weekly), 50, 56
Andhrabhashabhivarthini Sangham, 49
Andhra Conference, 149, 150, 193, 194, 195
  in Bezwada (1914), 49, 51–52
  Direct Action, 87
  Nationalist section of, 208
Andhra Congress Circle (ACC), 46, 48, 50, 77, 79, 99n5
Andhra Defence League (ADL), 85–86, 90
Andhradesa, Telugu-speaking people of, 86
Andhra Herald (newspaper), 206
Andhra Janasangham, 54
Andhra Jatheeya Kalasala, 53

Andhra Mahasabha (AMS), 15, 35, 46, 50, 55–56, 58, 155, 165*n*3, 188
  founding of, 79, 84, 95
  meeting, 81
  militant nationalist wing of, 188
  role in promoting Telugu language and literature in public life, 56
  Standing Committee of, 82
  on Vetti, 151
Andhra movement, 15, 35–36, 46, 51, 56, 74, 84, 92, 149, 188
  beginnings of, 75
  in British India, 189
  demand for redrawing of provinces according to linguistic criteria, 78
  and ethnic nationalism, 85–91
  radicalizing of, 199
  self-determination and, 78–85
  suspension of, 189
  Vishala Andhra movement, 199
Andhra Parishad, 76
Andhra Patrika (newspaper), 50, 53
Andhra Pracharini Grandha Nilayam, 49
Andhra Pradesh
  'ancient regime' cosmopolitanism, 4
  creation of, 84, 213
  demand for a separate province, 90
  domination of the INC in, 18
  formation of, 52
  map of, 88
  merging with Telangana, 213, 215
  national flag, 89
  political and economic foundations of, 43
  statehood of, 82
  swadeshi politics, 69–72
Andhra Provincial Congress Committee (APCC), 15, 95, 189, 205
Andhra Sahitya Parishad, 49, 53
Andhra Swarajya Party (ASP), 16, 56, 85–86, 90, 189, 195–196
Andhra University, 84
Anghie, Anthony, 108

Anjaneyulu, P., 95
Anjuman-i Taraqqi-i Hyderabad, 165*n*3, 177–178
anti-colonial agitation, in southern India, 52
anti-colonialism, in South Asia, 1–2
anticolonial mass subject, 81
anti-colonial movements, 6, 109
  goal of, 110
anti-colonial nationalism, 2–4, 11, 12, 20, 31, 108, 123, 140, 176
  goal of, 91
  in India, 46, 215
anti-colonial nationalist politics, 188
anti-monarchical political movements, 106
Appa Rao, Gurzada, 187
Ardha Shastra (Cautilya), 56
Aryan League, 56
Arya Samaj, 40, 44, 139, 142, 145, 154–155, 164, 192, 198, 208, 216
Asadullah, Sayyad, 145
Asaf Jahi Dynasty, 128
Asiatic Federation, 67
Attlee, Clement, 172
autonomy of Hyderabad, 178, 190
Azad Hyderabad, 189–190
  entry into United Nations Organization, 190, 207
Azad Hyderabad Association, 206

Bàbà-i Urdu (Father of Urdu, 1919), 186
Bahadur, Kishen Persad, 125
Baker, Christopher, 10–11, 12–14, 26*n*39, 69, 70, 79
'Balkanization' of India, 190, 195
'Balkanization' of South Asia, 95
Bate, Bernard, 13, 146
Bayly, C. A., 30, 32, 34, 57, 64*n*70, 166*n*13
Bengal, partition of (1905), 49, 67
  agitation against, 80
  Swadeshi movement in response to, 70

Index   235

Benichou, Lucien, 24*n*30, 165*n*6, 191
Besant, Annie, 46, 69, 73
Beverley, Eric, 6–7
Bezwada (modern-day Vijayawada), 76, 189
Bharatiya Janata Party (BJP), 215
Bhavanacharlu, V., 50
Bhimavaram Taluq People's Association, Bondada, 45
Bombay Chronicle (newspaper), 104, 156, 161
Bombay Presidency, 7
Borayya, Kavali, 85
border incidents, 171
boundaries redrawing, linguistic criteria for, 78, 92
Brahmo movement, 42
Brahmo Samaj, 40, 216
Bright, John, 80
British administrators, 138
British Andhras, 87, 189
British colonial government, 1
British colonial rule
  agitational politics against, 71
  INC-led agitation against, 121
  in India, 1
  legitimacy of, 70, 76
British creations in India, 105
British Crown, 114, 118, 124, 159
  granting of independence to India under international law, 175
British Empire, 2, 105–106, 111, 113, 121, 137–141, 173, 215
  anti-colonial struggle against, 140
  civil liberties and, 139–144
  departure from India, 174
  South Asian colonial territories, 5
  withdrawal of, 2
    from South Asia, 6
British government, 25, 67, 78, 98, 111, 113, 118, 124, 137–139, 171, 179
British imperialism, 197
British imperial order, 106
British imperial rule, 4, 34, 206
British India, 3, 17–18, 84, 123, 127–128, 172, 191, 192
  administrative units, 94
  anti-colonial nationalist movement, 104, 130
  colonial publics in, 57
  colonized territories of, 118
  communal conflicts in, 154
  communist movement in, 56
  creation of provincial borders of, 105
  cultural nationalism in, 70
  demands for provincial autonomy in, 2
  devolution of power, 138
  Hyderabad's borders with, 145
  INC activism in, 139
  Indians residing in, 124
  liberal political discourse in, 76
  motivations of the ICLU within, 140
  nationalist movement in, 106
  partitioning of, 210
  political goals of, 113
  political imaginaries in, 97
  political reforms within, 107, 111
  proliferation of political imaginaries in, 57
  provinces and presidencies of, 1
  provincial autonomy, idea of, 80
  relation with princely states, 5
  rise of democratic politics in, 11
  Round Table Conferences in, 110
  self-rule in, 1
  social reform issues, 55
  socio-economic conditions of, 104
  strength of the INC in, 112
  Telugu-speaking districts of, 81
  Urdu nationalism in, 6
British Indian politics, 110, 118, 204
British Parliament, 114, 141
British Parliamentary Delegation at Hyderabad Deccan (1946), 129, 185
British power, growth of, 94

Brown, Charles P., 14
Butler Committee (1929), 111–113, 124, 154
Butler, Harcourt, 111

Cabinet Mission, 172
Cambridge School, 10–13
caste discrimination, issue of, 148
caste organizations, proliferation of, 16
caste politics, in India, 13
Cesaire, Aime, 109
Chamber of Princes, 111, 113
Chandramouli, Kalluri
  Nanadesa Rajyanga Nirmanamulu (An Account of Constitutions of Various Countries, 1933), 77
  participation in Mohandas K. Gandhi's Salt Satyagraha, 77
Chatterjee, Partha, 3, 21n4, 59n6, 107–108
Chattopadhyay, Aghornath, 147
Chattopadhyay, Virendranath, 147
Chetty, G. Lakshmanarasu, 1
child marriage, problem of, 55, 146–148
Chintamani, C.Y., 72
Christianity, 42
Christian missionaries, influence on British colonial policy, 1
Chudgar, Paputlal, 112
citizenship, rights of, 8, 120
Civil Disobedience movement, 77, 90, 160, 171
civilization defence, idea of, 83
civil liberties, 2, 123
  and the British Empire, 139–144
  discourse of, 139
  in Europe, 140
  Hindu, 155
  Hyderabad state's policy of placing restrictions on, 155
  Muslim, 155
  and publicity in Hyderabad, 144–156
civil service system, 38

civil societal activism, 15, 58, 79, 191, 214
civil societal organizations, 21, 55, 155, 170, 172, 178, 183, 186, 191, 195
civil unrest, from partition violence, 206
Coconada Literary Association, 81
Collins, Michael, 108
colonial administration, 7, 11, 35, 45, 69, 216
colonial governmentality, strategies of, 60n14, 79
common singular language, idea of, 18
Commonwealth of India, 126, 173
communal conflicts, in British India, 154
communal violence, 155, 211
Communist Party of India (CPI), 16, 56, 68, 96–98, 193, 195–198, 206
communists, emergence of, 170
composite culture, idea of, 173
Comrades Association, 165n3, 191, 199
Congress-Khilafat unity, 96
Congress Socialist Party (CSP), 56
conservatism, definition of, 117
Constituent Assembly of India, 77, 119, 122–123, 197, 209–210
  plea for linguistic reorganization of states, 209
constitutional future, of Hyderabad, 161
constitutional monarchy, 6, 182
Cooper, Frederick, 3, 109–110
Copland, Ian, 5, 137, 208
Crescent (newspaper), 1
crisis of representation, for Indian Muslims, 181
culturally autonomous regions, 118
cultural pride, notion of, 83
Curzon, George, 70

Dalits, 107, 119, 175
Dar Commission (1948), 210, 213
Dar ul Ulum High School, 144

Das, Chittaranjan, 67–68
Datla, Kavita, 6, 8, 105–106, 114, 186
Deccan Chronicle (newspaper), 207
Deccani nationalism, 174–176, 186
Deccan sultanates, 17, 173
decolonization, 2, 109–110, 212
democratic consolidation, 119
democratic governments, rise of, 77
democratic participation, concept of, 76
Desai, Bhulabhai J., 7
Deshabhimani (newspaper), 74
devolution of power, 67, 73, 138
devolution schemes, 144
Dhar, Bishan Narayan, 1
Dravida Munnetra Kazhagam (DMK), 14
Dravidar Kazhagam (DK), 14
Dravidian nationalism, 12
  rise of, 10, 12
dynastic succession, rights of, 122

economic and political integration, of India, 211
Elliot, Carolyn, 24n29, 176, 200n18,
English East India Company, 105–106
English education, 23n21, 39, 51
equality, principle of, 77
Erdman, Howard, 33, 117
Erksine, John, 87
ethnic nationalism, 58
  Andhra movement and, 85–91
ethno-lingual boundaries, 211

farqavarana tahrikat, 177
federal citizenship
  rights of, 159
  structure of, 153
Federal Republic of the United States of India, 68
Federal Structure Committee (FSC), 114
Federated India (journal), 153
federation, idea of, 3

Federation of all Asiatic people, 67
feudal Indian State system, 105
'Fifty Years of Reform in Southern India' essay, 44
First Godavery District Conference (1895), Coconada, 44
Foreign Affairs (magazine), 104
forest laws, breaking of, 171
free cooperation of the state, 128
'freedom movement' in Hyderabad, 189
freedom of expression of opinion, 128
freedom of speech, 122
'free' nation states, 1, 73
free press, 1, 120, 122, 146
French League of the Rights of Man, 141
French West Africans, 109
Frykenberg, Robert, 11

Gandhian activism, 188, 192
Gandhi, Mohandas K., 20, 26n39, 27n50, 33, 77, 84, 86, 90, 107, 115, 119, 121–122, 150, 156, 161, 179, 181, 191–193, 215–216
  anti-colonial nationalist movement led by, 107
  anti-tax *satyagraha*, 90
  Civil Disobedience movement, 77, 192
  concept of *satyagraha*, 216
  goal of an independent nation state, 119
  Hind Swaraj (Indian Home Rule), 121
  idea of self-rule, 121
  political philosophy of, 121
  Quit India movement, 191
  Salt Satyagraha, 77
  social reform agenda, 193
Gasthi 53 Committee, 55, 139–140, 151–152, 164
Getachew, Adom, 3, 110
Ghosh, Aurobindo, 70
Gokhale, Gopal Krishna, 49, 121, 192

Golkonda Patrika (newspaper), 16, 54–55, 77, 145, 147–149, 151, 155, 213
Gopalakrishnayya, Duggirala, 90
Goshti (journal), 85–86, 90
Government of India, 74, 82, 95, 104, 111, 114, 118, 159, 163, 173, 175, 179
  commitment to federalism, 119
  impasse with Nizam's administration, 137
  quasi-federalism adopted by, 119
  relations with princely states, 114
Government of India Act, 87
  of 1919, 10, 30, 111
  of 1935, 7, 92, 95–96, 120, 124, 126, 159, 184
Governor-General in Council, 73
Governor in Council, 10
Greater Andhra
  idea of, 195
  map of, 196
Gundimeda, Sambaiah, 27n52
Gurunatham, J., 15, 31, 35, 38–39, 42, 46, 57
  doubt over Viresalingam's knowledge of Hindu texts, 42
  intellectual biography of Viresalingam, 44
  views on
    politicization of religion, 42
    Viresalingam's brand of social reformism, 43, 90

Haitian revolution, 110
Hanumantha Rao, M., 54–55, 149, 151
Haq, Abdul, 146, 186
Hardinge, Charles, 72, 78
Harijan (newspaper), 121
*harijan*s, 150–151
Harijan School for Children, 151
Harisarvottamarao, Gadicharla, 75–76
Hasan, Syed Abid
  strategy of framing a new Deccani nationalism, 174
  Whither Hyderabad? (1935), 173
Hassan, Azhar, 127, 183
heritage and tradition, idea of, 117–118, 122
Hind Swaraj (Indian Home Rule, 1909), 121
Hindu caste hierarchy, 216
Hindu-caste society, 41
Hindu customs and practices, 36
Hindu Mahasabha, 139, 142, 154–155, 192, 198, 208, 216, 219n26
Hindu majoritarian politics, 182
Hindu–Muhammadan union, 70
Hindu–Muslim Unity, 128
Hindu nationalism, 215
  rise of, 57
Hindu religious practice, 40, 43
Hindustan Republican Association (HRA), 68
Hindutva, politics of, 57
Hindutva populism, resurgence of, 215
His Exalted Highness (HEH), 162, 189
His Majesty's government, 114–115, 172
Hobbes, Thomas, 77
Holderness, Thomas, 94
home, idea of, 59n6
Home Rule movement, 46, 72
House of Commons, 74, 111
Hume Club of Kopalli, 45
Hydari, Akbar, 6, 57, 87, 113, 116, 125, 146
Hyderabad administration, 7–8, 17, 125
Hyderabad Andhra Provincial State Congress (HAPSC), 206–207
Hyderabad Bar Association, 175
Hyderabad Bulletin (newspaper), 145, 151
Hyderabad Conference, 192
Hyderabadi Muslims, 147
Hyderabad nationalism, 175

Hyderabad People's Convention, 160–162, 164
Hyderabad Political Conference (HPC), 125–128, 134
Hyderabad Political Reform Association of 1919, 176
Hyderabad Reforms (1939), 56
Hyderabad state, 5–6, 86
  administration, 113, 213
  Aiyangar report on constitutional reforms in, 157
  'anti-government' sentiment, 151
  borders with British India, 145
  break-up of, 175, 189, 191, 205, 211
  civil liberties and publicity in, 144–156
  civil society organizations, 9, 138, 140
  communist movement in, 171
  connection with British India, 6
  consensus for an acceptable All-India Federation, 116
  constitutional reforms within, 182
  cross-border connections with neighbouring British Indian provinces, 204
  culture of, 186
  demand for civil liberties, 137
  emergence of Muslim politics in, 8
  forced political merger in 1948 with Indian Union, 116, 144, 171, 175
  freedom movement in, 189
  Gandhian activism in, 192
  Gasthi 53 Committee, 55, 139, 151–152
  Hindus as second-class citizens in, 179
  historical borders and the unity of, 172–186
  HSC political struggle against, 171
  as inheritor of Mughal legacy, 6
  integrity of the political boundaries of, 126
  Legislative Council of, 154
  migration of the Muslim intelligentsia from north India to, 6
  municipality of, 175
  Muslim internationalism of, 8
  Nizam's administration (*see* Nizam's administration)
  non-*mulki*s, 147
  Osmania University, 6
  policy of placing restrictions on the civil liberties, 155
  political history of, 4
  political impasses of 1947–1948, 172
  preservation of, 170
  problem of political representation, 150
  proliferation of political imaginaries in, 57
  Reforms Committee (*see* Reforms Committee of 1938)
  as representative democracy, 173
  restriction on civil liberties of the states' subjects, 154
  sovereignty as an autonomous state, 114
  Telugu-speaking districts of, 48, 189, 204
  'unity talks' of July 1937, 127
  Urdu nationalism in, 6
  work towards an 'All-India Federation', 114
Hyderabad State Congress (HSC), 17, 56, 127, 128, 147, 165*n*3, 170
  goals of, 171
  opposition to the proposals made by the Reforms Committee, 183
  political struggle against the Hyderabad state, 171
  stand-off with the Majlis, 170
  working committee of, 171
Hyderabad State Reform Association (HSRA), 125

Imam, Ali, 156–157, 183
imperial citizenship, 109
imperialism, policies of, 181
imperialist federation, 97
Imperial Legislative Council, 84
imperial politics, complexity of, 30
Indian Civil Liberties Union (ICLU), 140, 153
Indian Express, 205, 207
Indian Independence Bill, 179
Indian Industrial Conference, 72
Indian Legislature, 8
Indian liberalism, 57
rise of, 34
Indian National Congress (INC), 1, 5, 16, 45, 51, 69, 86, 95, 104, 117
activism in British India, 139
agitation against colonial rule in India, 121
aid to people's movements within the princely states, 121
anti-colonial nationalism and agitational politics, 138
Bardoli Resolution, 91
Calcutta session (1928), 120
domination in Andhra Pradesh, 18
liberalism and competing political ideologies, 215–217
linguistic regionalism, 209
nationalism of, 3, 110
pursuit of political liberty, 217
Rao's criticism of, 86, 90
report on linguistic reorganization, 213
support to Hindu interests in Hyderabad, 176
victory in 1937 elections, 120
Working Committee of, 91, 122
Indian nationalism, 78, 121, 171, 181
anti-colonial tenor of, 214
Indian 'native' states, autonomy for, 2
Indian Review, 11
Indian Social system, 56

Indian states, internal administration in, 123
Indian subcontinent, political future of, 124
individual freedom, right of, 76
Information Bureau of Hyderabad, 125, 128, 148, 149, 151
institutionalization of language, processes of, 80
insular nationalism, idea of, 2
International Congress against Colonial Oppression and Imperialism (1927), 147
Irschick, Eugene, 12, 14, 79
Iyengar, Srinivas, 123

Jagirdar's Association, 175
Jamadiul Awwal 1338 Hijri, 126
Janatha, 207
Jayanti Ramayya Pantulu, 49
Jinnah, Muhammad Ali, 169n69, 207
Fourteen Points, 68
rise of the AIML under the leadership of, 107
Jung, Salar, 125, 174–175, 177
Jung, Yavar, 148
Justice Party movement, 12–14, 28n54, 69, 78–79, 96, 216

Kanchi Krishnaswamy Rao Pantulu Garu, Dewan Bahadur, 45
Kannada Conference, 192
Kannadigas, 78–79
Karnataka Parishad, 148, 176
Kesava Rao, J., 189–190, 207
Khaddar, 128
Khan, Akbar Ali, 126
Khan, Liaquat Hyat, 117
Khilafat movement, 8–9, 156
kotwal (police commissioner), 145
Krishna Patrika (newspaper), 49–50
On the Duty of Candidates (1920), 70
Kunzru, H. N., 211

Index

Lakshminarayana, U., 46
Landholders' Association of Alamur, 45
landlord system, 105
land tenure systems, 17
language debates and reforms, 187
language extremists, 193
language politics
  as a politics of self-determination, 13–17, 186–199
  rise of, 204
League of Nations, 3, 35, 77, 156
  formation of, 108
  political goals, 108
  recognition of national sovereignty, 108
Legislative Council of Hyderabad, 35, 70, 81, 84, 95, 152, 154, 160
Lenin, Vladimir, 1
Leonard, Karen, 175–176, 186
liberalism and anti-colonialism, in South India, 45
liberal–political institutions, 69
liberal selfhood and individuality, notion of, 60*n*14
linguistic nationalism, 15, 186
  cross-border, 199
  rise of, 2
Linguistic Provinces Commission. *see* Dar Commission (1948)
linguistic regionalism, 198, 204, 209
linguistic reorganization of states, 2, 21, 198
  Andhra movement demand for, 78
  criteria for, 78
  Dar Commission (1948) report on, 210
  INC report on, 213
  in post-independence India, 126, 209–211
  problem of pitting one linguistic group against another, 91
  schemes during the Nehruvian period, 4
local and regional literary societies, 81
Lohia, Ram Manohar, 140–141

Mackenzie, Colin, 85
Madras Hindu Social Reform Association, 43
Madras legislative assembly (MLA), 15, 77
Madras Legislative Council, 95
Madras Mail, 71, 73, 87, 89, 91, 94, 115
  'India on a Federal Basis' article, 98
Madras Native Association, 43
Madras Presidency, 2, 4, 15, 18, 31, 36, 77–78, 96, 144, 146, 172, 176, 187–188, 191, 193, 210
  anti-colonial nationalism, 68
  Baker's dismissal of politics as 'faction' politics, 13
  civil societal activism in, 214
  creation of, 81
  dominance of the INC in, 69
  establishment of George Norton's literary circle, 43
  expansion and success of non-Brahmanism in, 79
  INC Home Rulers in, 12
  political activism in, 11
  rise of
    Dravidian nationalism, 10
    non-Brahmanism, 13, 78
    provincial politics, 9–13
  Self-Respect movement, 79
  Swadeshi agitation, 13, 71
  Telugu-speaking districts in, 46, 69, 79, 204
Maharashtra Parishad, 176
Mahratta Parishad, 148
Mahratta, The, 86, 145, 189
Majlis, 155, 164, 170, 182, 184
  Defence Committees, 206
  proposals for giving equal weight to Muslim representation, 198–199
  standoff with the Hyderabad State Congress (HSC), 170
Majlis-e-Ittehadul Muslimeen (Majlis), 20, 126, 165*n*3
Mallikarjunudu, K. P., 92–94

Manchester Guardian, 111
Mandate System, 108
Manela, Erez, 1, 3, 108
Maratha Parishad, 176
Marathi Conference, 192
mass boycotts, 69
mass political mobilization, 139
mass politics, 118
Masulipatam, 71
Memorandum on Andhra Province (1938), 82, 91, 210
militant nationalism, 107
'minoritization' of the community, 180–181
Mirza, Baqar Ali, 146–147
Mitchell, Lisa, 15
Moid, M. A., 8, 181
'monarchical modern' form of power, 23n16
Montagu–Chelmsford reforms (1918), 10, 69, 73, 92
  impact on provincial autonomy in south India, 78
Montagu, Edwin, 5, 74, 111
Montford reforms. *see* Montagu–Chelmsford reforms (1918)
Mookherji, Radhakumud, 90
Morley–Minto reforms (1909), 69, 159
Mountbatten, Louis, 172, 205
Mudaliar, Rao Bahadur C. Jumbulingam, 44–45
Mufti, Aamir, 180
Mughal Empire, 17
mulki cultural nationalism, 175–176, 213
Mulki movement, 174
*mulki*s, politics of, 147
'Muslim' Hyderabad, 155
Muslim minority
  in British India, 119
  political interests of, 119
  'trans-regional' idea of, 25n35
Muslim modernism, 180–181

Muslim population of Hyderabad, 180
Muslim sovereignty
  idea of, 9
  movement for, 175
Muslim *ulema*, 175
Mysore, princely state of, 23n16, 46

Naidu, Padmaja, 173
Naidu, Sarojini, 147, 152
Naik, Vaman, 193
Nair, Janaki, 178
Naoroji, Dadabhai, 121
Narayan, Jayaprakash, 56, 185, 192
Narsing Rao, Mandumula, 16, 56, 144–147, 155, 161–162, 170, 177, 179, 185, 188, 192, 208
National Council for Civil Liberties (NCCL) of Britain, 140
national identity, 2, 33, 69, 91
nationality
  growth of, 68
  principle of, 96–98
national self-determination, 2, 132n21
native states
  as conservative islands, 116–120
  emergence of, 2
  global normalization of, 108
  idea of, 120
  policy of non-interference in states matters, 139
  representative government, 119
  in South Asia, 205
Nawab of Chhatari, 189–190
Nehru, Jawaharlal, 7, 20, 68, 104, 179
  anti-colonial nationalist movement led by, 107
  assessment of British rule in India, 105
  establishment of ICLU, 140
  as first prime minister of India, 215
  Glimpses of World History, 192
  goal of an independent nation state, 119
  on issue of the break-up of Hyderabad, 211

Index 243

letter to Swami Ramananda Tirtha, 160
report of 1928, 113, 159
vision of fundamental rights, 23*n*16
New Era (English daily), 145
New Life, 207
Nilgiri (newspaper), 54, 145
Nizam Andhra Mahasabha, 186–199
Nizam College, 147
Nizam of Hyderabad, 8, 37, 48, 87, 173
  'feudal' autocracy of, 197
  monarchical power of, 177–178
  as symbol of Muslim heritage, 181
Nizam's administration, 6, 8, 126, 128, 145, 148, 172, 178, 182
  attempt to prevent Hyderabad from merging with the Indian Union, 171
  constitutional, educational, and administrative reforms, 152
  debates over greater autonomy and the regaining of sovereignty, 205
  discussions on political reforms, 156–164
  Executive Council, 125, 143, 152, 175, 179, 183
  federation debates carried on by, 137
  handling of the railway strikers in 1928, 150
  impasse with the Government of India, 137
  India's forcible takeover of the Hyderabad state from, 211
  Information Bureau, 128
  issue of lifting the ban on political processions, 152
  Political Department (Constitutional Affairs Secretariat), 150–151
  presence of non-*mulki*s in, 147
  proposals for constitutional reforms, 170
  recruitment of Hyderabadi Muslims into, 147
  scrutiny of the AMS, 155

Nizam's Andhras, 87, 189
Nizam's Dominions, 46, 75, 189
Nizam's Subjects League (NSL), 147, 165*n*3, 173, 175–176, 178, 185, 191
non-Brahman movement, 12, 26*n*38, 69, 75, 78
non-*mulki* modernization schemes, 175
non-payment of levy and taxes, 171
non-violent resistance, strategy of, 216
Northern Circars, 17, 40, 61*n*22, 75, 78
North-West Frontier Province, 210
Norton, George, 43

Oriya language movement, 78
Osmania Graduates Association, 176
Osmania University, 6, 55, 145–146, 161
  founding of, 186, 200*n*12
  pan-Islamism, 8
  Senate, 175
  'Vande Mataram' controversy, 161
Ottoman Empire, 5, 130
  fall and dissolution of, 8–9, 108

Pakistan, 9, 96, 205–206, 210
Pakistan and National Unity (1944), 68
Pal, Bipin Chandra, 71, 72
Pan-Asianism, 67
Pandian, M. S. S., 12
  'Beyond Colonial Crumbs' article, 13
  critique of Baker's work, 13
Panikkar, K. M., 211
Pan-Islamism, 67
Paramount News, 113
parliamentary democracy, 119
passive intellectuals, 38
Patel, Vallabhbhai, 207
Patiala, princely state of, 154
peasant insurgency, in Telangana, 188, 196
peoplehood, problem of, 99*n*16

People's Association
  of Akeed, 45
  at Pittapore, 45
  Sivadevamchikkala, 45
  of Tanuku, 45
Periyar's Self-Respect movement, 13, 27n50
Pittapur, rajah of, 49
pluralist federalism, theory of, 132n21
police *chouki*s, 171
political activism, in Hyderabad, 5, 11, 30–31, 40, 43, 157, 188, 192
political and social activism, for Telugu speakers, 188
political consciousness, of the masses, 93
political conservatism, rise of, 34
political education, 152
political federalism, 19
political freedom (*rajakiya svatantryam*), 11, 76
political future, of Hyderabad, 178
political imaginaries, 2
political modernity, 21, 82–83
politicization of the people, 46, 75
politicized youth of Hyderabad, 176
Politics of South India 1920–1937, The, 69
popular sovereignty
  in Hyderabad, 184
  principle of, 8, 76–77, 106, 110
  radical politics based on, 121
  states' people and, 120–130
Prajaadhikaaranamulu (People's Rights), 77
praja prabhutvam (people's government), 76
Prarthana Samaj, 44
princely states, in colonial India
  British protection of, 122
  civil unrest in, 206
  debate on sovereignty and democracy, 5–9
  historiography on, 5
  INC aid to people's movements within, 121
  Indian nationalism and, 5
  interpretations of self-government, 138
  merging with Indian Union, 121
  political future of, 109
  political power of the Muslim minority in, 162
  power of, 121
  relationship with British India, 5
  relations with the Government of India, 114
  sovereignty of, 5–9, 114
provincial autonomy, idea of, 80
provincial individuality, 85
provincial nationalism, 4, 91, 205
provincial politics and federation, 91–96
public associations, in princely Hyderabad, 184
public organizations, proliferation of, 139
public secular morality, 42

Quit India movement, 191

racial divide, 123–124
Radhakrishnan, Sarvepalli, 84
radicalized political movements, 118
Rahman, Fazlur, 146, 165n3
Rahman, Tariq, 187
Raiyat (newspaper), 16, 56, 144–145, 177, 188, 208
  anti-sectarian identity, 177
Rajagopalachari, C., 85
Rajahmundry, 16, 36, 53, 71–72, 76
  Municipal Council, 87
  Social Reform Association, 40
Rajan, T. S. S., 95
Rajasekharacaritramu (1880), 41
Ramachandra Rao, M., 112, 123, 153–154, 189–190
Ramakrishna Rao, Burgula, 144

Ramamurti, Gidugu Venkata, 14
Ramamurti, Venkata, 187
Rama Rao, N.T., 18
Ramkishen Rao, B., 173
Ramusack, Barbara, 139
Ranade, Mahadev, 41
Rao, C. Veerabhadra, 72
Rao, Gurzada Appa, 14
Rao, Harisarvottama, 71, 72
Rao, Kasinadhuni Nageswara, 50
Rao, K. Krishnaswamy, 71
Razakars, 171
Razvi, Syed Kasim, 207
real national union, 75
Recovering Liberties, 30
Reddy, C. R., 11
Reddy, Ravi Narayana, 16, 56, 148, 188, 192, 194, 197
   joining of HSC, 193
   Telugu-only policy, 193
Reddy, Suravaram Pratapa, 16, 54, 77, 144, 145, 149–150, 188
Reddy, Venkata Rama, 145, 146
Reforms Committee of 1938, 57, 158–159, 160, 171, 175, 183
   constitutional reforms proposed by, 163
   HSC opposition to, 183
   proposal for representation according to corporate interests, 185
refugee crisis, 210
regional 'cultural' organizations, 126, 176
regional-cultural politics, 14
regional identity, 18, 82, 213
regional territorial consciousness, 91
religion-based organizations, 192
religious morality, 39
Report on India's Constitutional Reforms (*see* Montagu–Chelmsford reforms [1918])
representative democracy, 173
responsible government, idea of, 162, 183

Roosa, John, 24n30, 176–177, 201n20
Round Table Conferences (1930–1932), 67, 77, 92, 106, 113–114, 116, 119, 122, 124–125, 127, 129, 137, 146–147, 153
Rowlatt Act, 34
Royal Proclamation (8 February 1921), 111
Roy, Rammohun, 1
Rudolph, Lloyd, 119
Rudolph, Susanne, 119
Ruling Princes of the Indian States, 120

Salt Satyagraha, 77
Sampath, G., 216–217
*satyagraha*s of 1938–1939, 153, 161, 163–164, 171, 193
Savarkar, Vinayak D., 90, 219n26
Scott, J. Barton, 60n14
self-determination, 19, 30
   Adhikari's radical interpretation of, 97
   and the Andhra Movement, 78–85
   of the Andhra people, 198
   demands for, 2
   discourses of, 10, 68, 96
   language and, 186–199
   and language politics, 13–17
   principle of, 74, 94, 96–98, 108, 154
   and provincial politics, 72–77
   right to, 68, 96–97, 197
Self-Determination for the States People, 112
self-governing institutions, development of, 111
self-government
   discourses of, 58, 68
   goals of, 107, 114, 124
   idea of, 138
   'people' entitled to, 68
self-identification, of Muslims in Hyderabad, 187
Self-Respect movement, 79, 96, 216

self-rule
  anti-colonial goal of, 188
  Gandhi's idea of, 121
  principle of, 1, 5, 17, 19, 30
Senghor, Leopold, 109
Sharma, S. B., 173
shastris, 175
Sherman, Taylor, 25*n*35
shuddhi movement, 164
Siddeek, Mohamad, 179–180
Simon Commission, 159
  protest against, 68
  review of the Government of India Act of 1919, 111
Simon, John, 209
Singh, Ganga, 137
Sinha, Mrinalini, 81
Sitaramayya, Bhogaraju Pattabhi, 46, 77, 105, 116, 142, 143, 205
Sitaram, Swami, 212
slavery history of, 110
small nations, right of, 73
social and religious customs, 39
social contract theory, 77
social customs
  of Hindus, 42
  and practices, 41
social improvement, idea of, 40
social inequality, 217
social reform conferences, 43
social reformism, 40, 42, 57
  in Telugu culture and society, 14
social transformation, 41
Society for Union and Progress of 1926, 176, 191
Sri Krishnadevaraya Andhrabhasa Nilayamu. *see* Sri Krishnadevaraya Andhra Language Association
Sri Krishnadevaraya Andhra Language Association, 54
Sriramulu, Potti, 212–213
Standstill Agreement, 26*n*36
state censorship, 188

States Reorganization Commission (1953), 211, 214–215
  report of 1955, 211
Stokes, Eric, 30
Subaltern Studies Collective, 10, 12
Subbarao, Gummudithala Venkata, 189
Subba Rao, Nyapathi, 16, 40, 49, 51, 72
  presiding over the second Andhra Conference, 51
  views on national system of education, 52
Sujata (newspaper), 54
Sultan, Tipu, 26*n*37
Sundarayya, P., 195, 214
Suneetha, A., 8, 181
Suntharalingam, R., 43
Supreme Legislative Council, 35
Suryanarayana, M., 52
Swadeshi League (1930), 72, 147, 165*n*3
Swadeshi movement, 67, 70, 72
  during 1906–1907 in the cities of Madras and Rajahmundry, 76
  agitation in the Madras Presidency, 13, 71
  Gandhian phase of, 34
  ideals of self-reliance and self-rule, 78
  launching of, 71
  meetings, 71
  politics in Andhra Pradesh, 69–72
  use of the vernacular language, 76
Swaraj Party, 67
swaraj (self-rule), politics of, 31, 72
Swarajya Party, 90
Swatantra Party, rise of, 117
Syed Ali, Abdul Hassan, 173

tabligh movement, 164, 165*n*3
Tagore, Rabindranath, 152
Taheer, Basheer Ahmad, 145
Tamil Nadu Congress, Working Committee of, 84
Tamil nationalism, 12–13
Telangana, 18, 75

communist revolution in, 21, 211
merging with Andhra, 213, 215
peasant insurgency in, 188, 196
relationship with Andhra, 189
Telangana Revolt, 148
Telugu Academy, 49
Telugu Conference, 192
Telugu Desam Party (TDP), 18
Telugu language and literature, 18
  cultural revival of, 192
  delimitation of regional province on the basis of, 48
  as language of education, 78
  patronage of, 48, 53
  revitalization of, 40
  revival of, 52
  standardization of, 18
Telugu library movement, 52
Telugu nationalism, 2, 12, 15–16
Telugu Patrika, 145
Telugu prose works, publication and circulation of, 49
Telugu society, reformation of, 39
Telugu-speaking community, 76
  political mobilization of, 51
Telugu-speaking districts
  of Hyderabad state, 48, 189, 204
  of Madras Presidency, 46, 69, 79, 204
Tenugu Patrika (newspaper), 54
territorial linguistic community, 83
The Hindu, 16, 36, 40, 50, 51, 53, 56, 145, 207, 216
  editorial commenting on the Swadeshi movement, 71
  letter from V. Subrahmanyam, 78
  report on Vande Mataram processions, 72
Thompson, Edward J., 104–106, 110–111, 130n2
Tilak, Bal Gangadhar, 143, 192
Tillin, Louise, 119
Time and Tide (newspaper), 105
Times of India (newspaper), 85, 207

Tirmizi, Syed Sirajul Hassan, 152, 185
Tirtha, Swami Ramananda, 193, 206
transfer of power, 172, 216
two nation states, creation of, 205
Tyabji, Badruddin, 6

united federation, idea of, 68
United Nations Organization, 190, 207
unity of Hyderabad, 191
unity talks, 171
  of August 1938, 161, 163
  between Bahadur Yar Jung and Narsing Rao, 179–180
  of July 1937, 127
universal suffrage, 68
untouchability, eradication of, 90, 150
Upanishads, 42
Urdu language, 186
  for self-identification of Muslims in Hyderabad, 187
Urdu literary societies, proliferation of, 176
Urdu nationalism, in Hyderabad and in colonial India, 6
Uriyas of Ganjam, 49

Vaidya, Kashinathrao, 126, 128, 183, 184
Vakulabharanam, Rajagopal, 40
'Vande Mataram' song, 81
  controversy of 1938, 161
  student movement, 171
Varma, Bhagya Reddy, 193, 216
Vavilla, Venkateswara Sastrulu, 84
Venkatagiri, maharajah of, 49
Venkatappayya, Konda, 15, 46, 50, 53, 77, 79, 80–81, 83–84
Venkatarangaiya, M., 74
Venkatasivaravu, Digavalli, 77
Venkatasubba Rao, G., 16, 56–57, 85, 87, 195
  criticism of the INC and Gandhian politics, 86, 90

defence of the aristocracy and the monarchy, 57
formation of ASP, 90
political organization and activism, 86
vernacularization of education, 152
vernacular languages, 93, 149
  adoption of, 93
  newspapers, proliferation of, 34
  use in public speaking, 81
vernacular orator (politician), rise of, 13
vernacular public spheres, 1
vernacular schools, use of Oriya in, 78
vernacular university, in colonial India, 6
vetti, 150
Vignanachendrika series, 49
Village and Taluq Associations, 45
village *panchayat* system, 57
Viresalingam, Kandukuri, 14, 16, 32, 90
  social reform work, 43
Viresalingam Pantulu, 51
Vishala Andhra, idea of, 196–197, 199, 206, 213
V. Ramadas Pantulu, 82, 210
Vishalandhra Mahasabha, 196
Visveswaraya, M., 124
Vivekavardhani (journal), 40
Vizianagaram Literary Association, 81

Voice of Progress (journal), 43
Votu (Vote, 1923), 75–76
Vyas, Jai Narayanji, 194

Washbrook, David, 14, 26*n*39, 70
weaving industry, revival of, 71
'White List', 149
White Paper, 123
widowhood, Hindu practices of, 31
Widows Marriage Association, 40
Wilder, Gary, 3, 109–110,
Williams, Rushbrook, 154
Wilson, Woodrow, 1, 108
  Fourteen Points, 77
women in Indian society
  uplift of, 44

Yar Jung, Nawab Bahadur, 126, 128, 155, 161, 179
  death of, 190
Young Men's Literary Association (1903–1904), 35
Young Men's Literary Association of Guntur, 81

*zamindar*s (landlords), 38, 61*n*22
zamindari system, 37, 57